Peter Brandl

Office Of Tomorrow

Peter Brandl

Office Of Tomorrow

The Design, Implementation and Evaluation of an Interactive Meeting Room

Südwestdeutscher Verlag für Hochschulschriften

Imprint

Any brand names and product names mentioned in this book are subject to trademark, brand or patent protection and are trademarks or registered trademarks of their respective holders. The use of brand names, product names, common names, trade names, product descriptions etc. even without a particular marking in this work is in no way to be construed to mean that such names may be regarded as unrestricted in respect of trademark and brand protection legislation and could thus be used by anyone.

Publisher:
Südwestdeutscher Verlag für Hochschulschriften
is a trademark of
Dodo Books Indian Ocean Ltd., member of the OmniScriptum S.R.L Publishing group
str. A.Russo 15, of. 61, Chisinau-2068, Republic of Moldova Europe
Printed at: see last page
ISBN: 978-3-8381-1989-2

Zugl. / Approved by: Linz, JKU, Diss., 2010

Copyright © Peter Brandl
Copyright © 2010 Dodo Books Indian Ocean Ltd., member of the OmniScriptum S.R.L Publishing group

Acknowledgements

This work would not have been possible without the support and guidance of many people who either directly or indirectly contributed to the outcome of this thesis.

First of all I would like to thank Prof. Michael Haller for his unlimited support, advice and interest in my work. I would like to thank him for introducing me to HCI and along with that to a really inspiring community. He connected me with leading researchers in this field and opened the opportunity to collaborate with them. I feel lucky to have worked under his guidance and I am thankful for all the confidence he had in me, and for freedom and responsibilities I received in my work. I really appreciate his competent feedback that finally helped me to publish my research in this thesis.

I would also like to extend special thanks to Prof. Gabriele Kotsis, who provided valuable feedback throughout my work on the thesis. She came up with many additional perspectives that helped to improve the quality of this work. Her insightful critical remarks really helped shaping this thesis.

I want to especially thank my colleagues Jakob, Thomas and Adam from the Media Interaction Lab. Through our frequent discussions, I learned to better reflect upon my own work and always received great new input. They are a source of inspiration and I really think about our time in the lab with a smile.

During my research, I had the opportunity to spend an internship at Mitsubishi Electric Research Laboratories (MERL) in Boston. I had a great time with the team and learned a lot about scientific work practices from them. Therefore, I want to thank Chia Shen, Daniel Wigdor and Clifton Forlines for inviting me and helping to improve my skills.

Clifton Forlines helped me again when he agreed to proof-read my thesis. Erin Hvizdak was the second person who invested a lot of time correcting my writing mistakes. I want to thank both of them for their patience and invaluable help.

Acknowledgements

I would like to express my deepest gratitude to my wife Birgit who supported me during the time when I was busy working on my thesis and sacrificed one or the other weekend for reaching my goal. Without her appreciation, friendship and love this thesis would not have been completed.

Finally, I want to thank two very special persons that changed my life during the last year of finishing my thesis. While one of them, my father, unforeseeable left this world, the other one, my daughter Mona was born. My father inspired me to choose a scientific career and always supported me on my way. I want to thank him for everything he did for me. Mona gave me the encouragement I needed during that time. She was, without knowing it, helping me to finish my work.

Contents

Acknowledgements   i

1 Introduction   1
- 1.1 Research Context 4
- 1.2 Problem Statement and Hypothesis 5
- 1.3 Research Objectives 7
- 1.4 Methodological Approach 9
- 1.5 Organizational Overview 10

2 Related Work   12
- 2.1 Digital Surface Technologies 13
  - 2.1.1 Interactive Tables 13
  - 2.1.2 Digital Wall Displays 24
  - 2.1.3 Interactive Rooms 30
  - 2.1.4 Mobile Paper Interfaces 33
- 2.2 Interaction with Digital Surfaces 44
  - 2.2.1 Pen Based Interaction 44
  - 2.2.2 Direct Touch Interaction 51
  - 2.2.3 Bimanual Interaction 57
- 2.3 Digital Workspace Design 60
  - 2.3.1 Digital Tabletop Interfaces 60
  - 2.3.2 Comparing Horizontal and Vertical Surfaces 63
- 2.4 Summary and Open Research Issues 65
  - 2.4.1 Digital Surface Technologies 65
  - 2.4.2 Interaction with Digital Surfaces 66
  - 2.4.3 Integration of Paper 67

3 Conceptual Framework   69
- 3.1 Collaborative Space Design Parameters 70
  - 3.1.1 Multiplicity and Heterogeneity of Tasks 70
  - 3.1.2 Fostering the Creation of Shared Documents 71
  - 3.1.3 Integration of Individual and Shared Spaces 72

Contents

       3.1.4   Multiple and Interrelated Documents 73
       3.1.5   Multi-Modal Input and Task Assignment 73
       3.1.6   Consistency of Input Devices 74
       3.1.7   Visibility and Transparency of Actions 74
       3.1.8   Integration into Overarching Activities 75
  3.2 Considerations for Horizontal and Vertical Displays 75
       3.2.1   Surface Size and Group Size 75
       3.2.2   Offering Custom Functionality 76
       3.2.3   Arranging Content within Reach 77
       3.2.4   Accounting for Different Orientations 77

4 Interactive Meeting Room Prototype   78
  4.1 Meeting Activity Survey 79
  4.2 Hardware 84
       4.2.1   Interactive Surfaces 84
       4.2.2   Anoto Digital Pen Technology 88
       4.2.3   Anoto Tracking for Large Surfaces 89
       4.2.4   Anoto Tracking for Mobile Controls 92
  4.3 Interaction with the Room 94
       4.3.1   Interaction with Digital Pens and Palettes 94
       4.3.2   Interaction with Digital Content 96
  4.4 Workspace and Menu Design 96
       4.4.1   Personal Workspace Concept 97
       4.4.2   Physical and Digital Menus for Personal Workspaces . 99
  4.5 Meeting Activities in the Interactive Room 100
       4.5.1   Presentations 101
       4.5.2   Data Import 102
       4.5.3   Data Manipulation 103
       4.5.4   Document Sharing 104
  4.6 Evaluation 105
  4.7 Conclusion 111

Contents

5 Interactive Meeting Room Redesign — 113
- 5.1 Redesign Project Goals — 114
- 5.2 Hardware — 117
  - 5.2.1 Rear-projected Anoto surfaces — 117
  - 5.2.2 Combined Pen and Touch Input — 120
- 5.3 Interaction with the Room — 136
  - 5.3.1 Pen and Touch Interaction — 136
  - 5.3.2 Interaction with Digital and Real Documents — 148
- 5.4 Workspace and Menu Design — 163
  - 5.4.1 Shared Workspace Concept — 163
  - 5.4.2 Menu Design for Large Shared Workspaces — 165
- 5.5 Meeting Activities in the Interactive Room — 174
  - 5.5.1 Presentations — 175
  - 5.5.2 Data Import — 177
  - 5.5.3 Data Manipulation — 179
  - 5.5.4 Data Export — 180
- 5.6 Implementation — 181
  - 5.6.1 Input Device Framework — 182
  - 5.6.2 Application Development — 191

6 Discussion — 193

7 Conclusions — 197
- 7.1 Research Contributions — 198
  - 7.1.1 Identifying design parameters for a collaborative interactive space — 198
  - 7.1.2 Developing an interactive room prototype — 199
  - 7.1.3 Evaluating in a real world environment — 200
  - 7.1.4 Refining the first prototype and development of particular interaction solutions — 200
  - 7.1.5 Combining and developing emerging technologies — 201
- 7.2 Future Work — 202
  - 7.2.1 Extended use of paper for overarching activities — 202

Contents

	7.2.2	Remote connection of multiple meeting rooms 203
	7.2.3	Alternative room setups 203
	7.2.4	Pen and touch combinations 203
	7.2.5	Evaluation methods 204
	7.2.6	Meeting supporting applications 204
7.3	Closing Remarks 205

Bibliography **206**

Introduction

Meetings and collaborative group activities are an integral part of todays work environments. Traditionally, groups meet in spaces that are equipped with tables, flipcharts and whiteboards. The information that is used in these collaborations is nowadays available in different types of digital and physical media. Therefore, current collaborative work uses a mixture of traditional paper documents and digital information that have to be managed across physical and digital resources. For that reason, most meeting rooms additionally support the presentation of digital content. However, the access to digital information from different sources during meetings is becoming increasingly important, thus only presenting information is not sufficient anymore. As depicted in Figure 1.1, groups need to modify, extend and share documents in collaboration.

On the other hand, traditional desktop computing shifted towards the ubiquitous computing vision described by Mark Weiser [171]. The emergence of interactive surfaces like digital tabletops and whiteboards has pointed to new possibilities of using display technology for interaction and collaboration [155] [65] [144] [69] [55]. The display technology is constantly improving in quality and new ways to interact with large surfaces are explored. In future, displays will increasingly be embedded in everyday furniture, such as the tables in a meeting room [155] [65]. Moreover, surfaces will have the ability to communicate amongst each-other. The range of emerging technologies and applications could enable more natural and human centered interfaces

1. Introduction

Figure 1.1: Typical meeting situation with four participants.

so that interacting with digital surfaces and content becomes more fluent and intuitive.

Therefore, the right choice of technologies that should realize this vision is increasingly important. There might be multiple technology candidates available that could enable a certain activity. However, is is not sufficient to select any one of these technologies; the context of the activity must be considered. For example, it is technically possible to write with digital ink using one's finger or with a digital pen. Nevertheless, writing with a finger may be suitable for a children's application but not for a business meeting. Designing a space for collaboration is challenging because the different contexts of meetings result in an increasing diversity of capabilities that should be supported. Within this room concept, the multiplicity and heterogeneity of tasks and data have to be managed. Moreover, collaborative environments that should benefit from emerging technologies must consider communication principles such as verbal and non-verbal cues that are necessary to communicate clearly.

In order to develop an interactive room in which the devices indeed seamlessly work together to support fluent collaboration, we need to explore its

1. Introduction

Figure 1.2: Prototype of the interactive meeting room.

design space. On the one hand, we have the group of people who will finally use the room with certain expectations. It is a key factor for a successful design to understand the activities that they want to perform. This involves the nature of the activity (what they want to do) and the way they want to perform it (how they want to do it). To define these design parameters, we can draw on the experience from observing traditional meetings and the related activities. On the other hand, we have emerging technologies that offer new possibilities for interacting with computer systems. This enables us to bridge the gap between the traditional work practices and the capabilities that an interactive digital space offers. However, a careful design of the components and applications is necessary to create a system that supports more natural interaction. The extended possibilities that these emerging technologies offer must be complemented with according interfaces to create a new experience for the user. The overall goal is to provide an environment that supports users to accomplish tasks more easily and intuitively.

1. Introduction

This dissertation explores the design and technical development of technologies that can be used to create a collaborative interactive space for meetings. Through observation and experiments we identify the design parameters and verify our decisions for this concept. In this work, we show how these design parameters can be applied to develop a prototype of the interactive room as depicted in Figure 1.2. Furthermore, we present the lessons-learned during this process and provide details about the redesign of our interactive room implementation. This discussion about the development process and the refinement of particular components of the room should help other developers to understand how technologies that will emerge in the future can be applied to create such a room. The aim of this work is to investigate how existing practices could benefit from the introduction of emerging technologies. However, it is not our goal to replace current workspaces but rather to complement them with enabling technologies. For instance, we develop solutions that allow to connect traditional paper to digital systems. Based on this development, we show interaction mechanisms that allow for a fluid transfer between these two worlds. We demonstrate the benefit of this approach in combination with an application that is designed for co-located collaboration in our interactive room. The main motivation behind this work to explore if an interactive space that is based on these solutions has the potential to actually increase the fluidity of workflows and positively affect collaboration.

The remainder of this chapter discusses the research context of this dissertation, describes the problems that are addressed by our research, presents the research objectives and the methodological approach, and provides an overview of the remaining chapters in the dissertation.

1.1 Research Context

This dissertation explores the design space and development issues of emerging technologies in the context of meeting activities. Figure 1.3 illustrates the research context of this work.

The general research field of this dissertation is the broad context of

1. Introduction

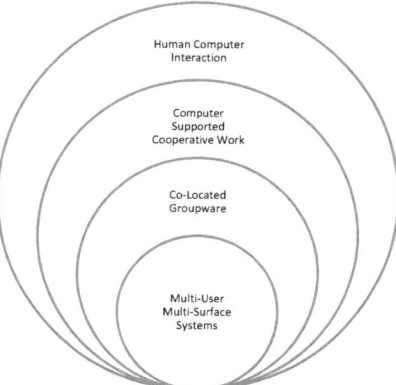

Figure 1.3: Research context.

human-computer interaction (HCI). Within HCI, the work pertains to computer supported cooperative work (CSCW), technologies designed to support collaborative activities. More precisely, the work is dealing with technologies that are used by co-located groups. The dissertation focuses on their interaction with multiple interactive surfaces in a novel meeting room.

1.2 Problem Statement and Hypothesis

This thesis addresses several key design challenges of interactive multi-display environments for collaboration. In current meetings, a multiplicity of different media such as paper documents, plans, presentation handouts and digital documents are used. Because of the heterogeneity of these artifacts, different tools are required to support collaborative interaction with them. However, technology is often abandoned for traditional media such as notepads, whiteboards, flipcharts or paper printouts of the digital documents. As a consequence, fluid transition between different kinds of media (especially paper and digital media) is distracted which makes the consistent tracking of changes and annotations cumbersome. For that reason, workarounds like translating results into a digital format after a meeting have been established. But these practices are not ideal since they introduce additional costs and often lead to the loss of information as the workflow is too complex. Moreover, the continuity between several meetings over a period of time is not guaranteed. With current practices, it is time expensive to reconstruct the state of the last meeting in order to continue with the actual session.

To address these problems, a range of emerging technologies and applications could enable more natural and human centered interfaces so that interacting with computers and content becomes more intuitive. This would help to decrease the barrier of using technology during meetings that supports collaboration and fosters the interaction with different heterogeneous data. The goal of this dissertation is to explore the scientific questions that are related to this approach.

Problem One. It is not clear yet which design parameters influence the development of a collaborative interactive room for meetings and brainstormings. The first step towards the development of a room that addresses shortcomings of current meeting practices is to explore the underlying design parameters. In order to discover solutions that actually overcome existing problems, an understanding of activities and related problems has to be created first. Based on that insights, according design parameters that should guide the development of appropriate solutions can be formulated.

Problem Two. The essential features that such a space should provide in order to enhance workflows are not yet identified. The goal of the development of an interactive room for meetings is to better support the collaborative activities and interaction with data within this space. Although the design parameters mentioned in Problem 1 define the conceptual framework for this work, it is still an open question which specific features are appropriate to implement the guidelines. Therefore, we need to explore the benefit of specific solutions for the current workflows during meetings.

Problem Three. It has to be explored how the combination of

1. Introduction

multiple digital surfaces can support the concept of a collaborative interactive space. The aim to support current meeting activities through emerging technologies requires to select the right components. However, the challenge is to combine technical solutions in order to facilitate activities. Today, workspaces are commonly equipped with computers that simplify a lot of processes. Similarly, the resulting combination of different components in the interactive room should enhance collaborative processes during and around meetings.

Problem Four. It is not clear how different input mechanisms can be combined to improve the human-computer interface as well as foster collaboration among users. A key design criterion for the successful interaction with the components of the room that were mentioned in Problem 3 are the appropriate input mechanisms. Since there exist a variety of possibilities to interact with digital surfaces, the right choice is challenging. If the introduction of technology in the context of meetings should enhance workflows and address specific problems, the input mechanisms must ensure that the barrier to use this technology is decreased. Again, the design parameters mentioned in Problem 1 can be a guideline.

Summarizing the research questions, it cannot be the goal to replace existing workspaces but rather to observe the current processes and draw from that experience to formulate design parameters for a new kind of collaborative interactive space. Based on this supposition, the research hypothesis of this dissertation is that *considering the appropriate design principles for multi-user multi-surface systems enhances workflows in meetings and enables the exploration of new communication paradigms.* The aim of the dissertation is to identify these design guidelines that are strongly coupled with input technologies, the characteristics of interactive surfaces like digital tables and walls as well as the interaction between users.

1. Introduction

1.3 Research Objectives

The overarching goal of the research objectives is to address the hypothesis through the following activities: an observation of current meeting processes in the real world environment of a company; the articulation of design parameters for a collaborative interactive room based on this observation; the development and evaluation of a prototype that follows these design criteria; the redesign of the prototype based on the evaluation's results; the adaption and development of hardware to support the concept.

Objective 1. Identify the design parameters that influence the development of an interactive room for collaboration. In order to identify the design parameters that should finally lead to the concept of the interactive space for collaboration, we carried out an exploratory field study about current meeting practices in our research partner's company Voestalpine[1]. The study focused on the interaction between the participants and the mediating activities based on the documents and tools that were used during the meetings. We applied the results of the observations to derive design parameters for a new collaborative interactive space concept.

Objective 2. Develop the concept and show a practical implementation of the interactive room prototype. To achieve this goal, we applied the design parameters that resulted from the exploratory field study to develop the concept for the interactive room. Based on this concept, we developed a prototype that included a digital tabletop, a digital whiteboard and additional presentation displays. Furthermore, we explored the feasibility of digital pens as input devices for these interactive surfaces and for the interaction with tangible tools.

Objective 3. Deploy the prototype setup in a real world environment and evaluate the design assumptions. To be able to evaluate the implemented prototype setup, we observed meetings that were arranged in the new interactive room. The observation focused on the interaction with the novel interfaces and the effect on the collaboration among the group. Through personal interviews after the meetings, we investigated the ability

---
[1] http://www.voestalpine.com

1. Introduction

of particular components to support the activities during the meetings.

Objective 4. Refine the first prototype implementation and further develop particular solutions that explore specific parts of the interactive room concept. Motivated by the results of the exploratory evaluation, we redesigned parts of the interactive room and extended some of the concepts to better suit the overall vision. In the course of this redesign, we developed novel hardware solutions, interaction techniques and applications. For instance, we explored the benefits of combined pen and touch input and the integration of traditional paper within this room. In two areas, we conducted formal laboratory experiments to support our assumptions.

Objective 5. Apply existing hardware to realize the interactive room concept and develop new hardware solutions if necessary. In oder realize the interactive space concept, we investigated the usability of multiple hardware solutions. The final choice of technologies is influenced by Objective 1, which suggests essential features that should be supported. We applied existing hardware solutions if feasible and developed new approaches otherwise.

1.4 Methodological Approach

After describing the scope of the concept, we present our approach to realize this vision of an interactive room. Since the whole project was planned together with the furniture company Team7[2], we agreed to set up a prototype room that could be used to investigate the ideas in detail. Through studying the concepts in smaller sub-projects, we could further redesign the components that should finally lead to the full interactive room goal. We were especially interested in setting up a digital tabletop and a digital whiteboard and explore the combined possibilities of using both devices. To complement this setup, we would include tangible objects and real paper as interfaces to the table and the whiteboard.

As a starting point, we gathered the requirements for the application and the according input devices together with our company partner. We

---
[2]http://team7.at

1. Introduction

observed the procedure of meetings in their company and conducted interviews to learn about the shortcomings of the current situation. The results of this exploratory field study were distilled to a selection of design parameters that provided a conceptual framework for the development of the interactive room. Based on these design parameters and the related work in this field, we implemented the application and constructed the hardware setup that should address the issues raised by the field study. The developed prototypes could then be evaluated with the company again and undergo an iterative refinement process. Moreover, we conducted two laboratory experiments to evaluate specific designs in an experimental setup.

For selecting the primary input devices, we gathered feedback from our partners and defined the hardware for the meeting room on these results. This led to the decision to use digital pens because note taking, sketching and precise pointing were essentially required.

1.5 Organizational Overview

The remainder of this dissertation develops the concept of a collaborative interactive space by first formulating design parameters on which the development of two prototypes is based. Furthermore, specific solutions within the broader context are designed, implemented and evaluated.

In Chapter 2 we discuss related literature, including work on digital surface technologies such as tabletops, digital walls and interactive rooms. This review is complemented by the description of related approaches dealing with the interaction with these digital surfaces. Finally, related work about the design of collaborative digital workspaces, possibilities to combine real paper and digital information and aspects of bimanual pen and touch interaction are discussed.

Chapter 3 distills the results of an exploratory field study into the selection of design parameters that guide the development of an interactive room. The two main areas that are discussed include design parameters for collaborative spaces and specific parameters that distinguish horizontal and vertical digital surfaces.

1. Introduction

Chapter 4 describes the development of an interactive room consisting of multiple digital surfaces. The chapter discusses hardware solutions that we developed according to the previously defined design parameters. The specific solutions aim at enabling effective collaboration in the interactive room. We explain how existing digital pen technology can be applied to create large digital surfaces that feature high accurate input. Moreover, the chapter presents interaction techniques based on digital pen technology and interactive workspaces and an application that facilitates meeting activities. The chapter concludes with an evaluation of the interactive room prototype.

Chapter 5 builds on the first room prototype from Chapter 4 and discusses the advancement of the interactive meeting room based on the results of the first room's evaluation. The chapter provides details about hardware developments that enable rear-projected Anoto surfaces, approaches to combine pen and additional direct touch input and a solution that bridges the gap between real paper and digital documents. Moreover, we present advancements of the meeting application, including a novel menu design for multi-user tabletop workspaces.

Chapter 6 reviews the two interactive room prototype implementations referring to the design parameters that we postulated in Chapter 3.

Chapter 7 concludes the dissertation by revisiting the research objectives and how they have been addressed. We then summarize the contributions of this work. Finally, the chapter discusses potential future work in this area.

Related Work

Designing an environment that supports group work through interactive surface technologies has a deep research history in the field of Computer-Supported Cooperative Work (CSCW). The first examples of that work originate from extensions of single-user desktop computers. These Single Display Groupware (SDG) applications contain co-located interaction technologies with which multiple users share a single display [154] [13] [165]. Subsequent research focused on large interactive surfaces that support group work through their extended dimensions. The proposed solutions can be generally categorized into two classes: those using *digital tabletops* and others using *interactive wall* displays. There are obvious parallels in the base technologies upon which these surfaces are built; however, their spatial orientations afford different activities. Interactive rooms provide a larger research context in that they aim to incorporate both types of displays. Since each surface has its inherent strengths, those researchers combining them within one work environment aim at assigning specific activities to the appropriate technology.

The related work summarized in this chapter is meant to provide the reader with an overview of these enabling technologies, their combination and the interaction consequences of such setups. Section 2.1 examines digital surface technologies and includes detailed reviews of research on interactive tabletops, digital walls, interactive rooms and paper as a very specific interface in the context of interactive rooms. Section 2.2 reviews different approaches to interacting with these surfaces, starting with pen based solutions,

2. Related Work

then exploring the emerging field of direct touch interaction and the combination of pen-based input with direct touch interaction. Finally, Section 2.3 presents related approaches of designing workspaces for digital tabletops, followed by a discussion about the different aspects for horizontal and vertical surfaces.

2.1 Digital Surface Technologies

This section describes the related technologies on which an interactive room concept is defined. While each of the discussed technologies has been explored independently over the last years, their combination poses new challenges for research. In order to classify the different technologies, we consider the physical orientation (horizontal or vertical) as well as the interaction metaphor (static room environments versus mobile paper interfaces). The discussion starts with an introduction to horizontal tabletop surfaces in Section 2.1.1, followed by a comparison to vertical wall displays in Section 2.1.2. For this investigation, we concentrate on the tracking and visual output technologies that are used in the approaches. Among others, these include front and rear-projected displays, vision based tracking, capacitive racking and tangible objects. Based on these hardware technologies, Section 2.1.3 presents different research projects that attempt to incorporate them into a more complex interactive room context. In contrast to these interactive room approaches, we explore the design space of mobile paper interfaces in Section 2.1.4 since the affordances of paper make it suitable as an interactive surface itself as well as an interface to other surfaces.

2.1.1 Interactive Tables

An interactive tabletop is a horizontal surface that allows multiple users to work simultaneously on a shared digital display. There are various technologies that can be used to build an interactive table. While some were first explored a decade ago, others have emerged during the last few years [172] [33] [127] [166] [79] [69].

2. Related Work

Vision Based Tracking

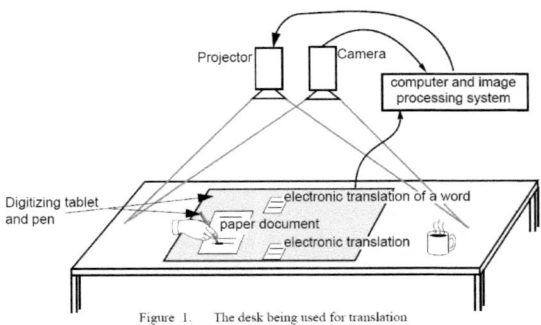

Figure 2.1: Wellner's *DigitalDesk* [110].

Back in 1993, Wellner's *DigitalDesk* [172] was the first project that investigated interactive tabletops as an extension to traditional desktop systems. He used an overhead mounted projector in combination with a camera to augment the surface of a table. The *DigitalDesk* was also the first prototype that showed the combination of real paper with a digital environment. With the overhead mounted projector, he could augment paper with digital information. Figure 2.1 shows the schematic setup of the *DigitalDesk*.

The vision based tracking for tabletops that was pioneered with the *DigitalDesk* was further explored by a variety of research projects [167] [128] [79] [178]. The technological background for these projects was based on the idea to use cameras to track the user to allow interaction with the tabletop. Similar to the *DigitalDesk* setup the cameras and projectors were mounted above the surface. More recently, we have recognized a change in setups as researchers have started to develop rear projected setups in which the camera is also mounted behind the surface. An obvious disadvantage of top projected setups is the effect that objects above the table's surface cast shadows. But in reality, this effect is less problematic than expected, as people are used to cast shadows in illuminated environments [6]. For rear projection setups, the

2. Related Work

table has to be built with a special projection surface that enables a high quality image and a stable surface for working. Additionally, the projector has to be installed under the table, which usually results in a box setup of the table. For group meetings, during which the participants normally sit around the table, the space for their feet is occupied by the projector. This is an ergonomic drawback that has to be considered when choosing between a top or rear projected table setup. Due to this special requirement for rear projected setups, top projection solutions were the first to be explored.

Figure 2.2: The *InfoTable* developed by Rekimoto and Saitoh demonstrates a top-projected table setup. With their prototype, they showed a possible combination of a table, wall display, and laptop computers. With their setup, they demonstrated the interchange of digital information among the different devices that are part of a spatially continuous environment [128].

Underkoffler and Ishii [167] used a camera above the table surface for their *Illuminating Light* setup. Rekimoto and Saitoh [128] developed a top projected setup for the *InfoTable* (cf. Figure 2.2).

The *EnhancedTable* by Koike et al. [79] has been used in two different versions: as a ubiquitous desktop and as a shared workspace. They applied two top mounted projectors for a higher resolution and three cameras as shown in Figure 2.3. Two cameras where used for finger/hand tracking, the third one for capturing images.

Andy Wilson developed *PlayAnywhere* [178] which used a combination of cameras and a projector in very compact setup for tabletop games. As shown in Figure 2.4, Wilson used a NEC WT605 short-throw projector together with two cameras on top of the table. With this setup, Wilson demonstrated shadow-based touch detection as well as an optical flow algorithm for manipulating objects. The setup is especially interesting as it provides a solution for a top projected table that is still portable. With a typical top projected setup, the mobility of the table is lost, because the projector is normally

2. Related Work

mounted in a fixed position on the ceiling. If the table is moved, the projection remains in place, resulting in a registration problem that constrains the system to a fixed position. With Wilson's *PlayAnywhere* setup, this problem is solved because the projector is installed on the table's surface instead of mounting it on the ceiling.

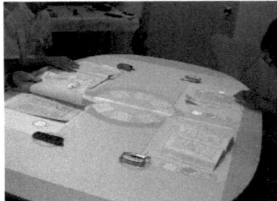

Figure 2.3: Koike et al. built the *EnhancedTable* that uses two projectors and three cameras mounted above the table's surface. Based on this setup, they showed possible implementations of a personal and a shared workspace [79].

The previously described interactive tables used cameras mounted above the surface for tracking. The other option for an interactive table setup is rear mounted cameras that view through the surface. The surface must be designed to allow the camera to see through and moreover has to support the projection from the rear.

Figure 2.4: *PlayAnywhere* from Wilson demonstrates a camera and projector setup for tabletop games. The special short-throw lens allows to place the projector directly on the table's surface. *PlayAnywhere* addresses issues that are typical of most vision-based table systems such as installation, calibration, and portability [178].

The most well-known example for such a rear-projected digital table is Microsoft *Surface* (cf. Figure 2.5). Designed as a closed box setup, all hardware components are placed inside the table's body beneath the surface. A projector is used for graphical output while four cameras pointed at the surface track objects near or on the screen. Microsoft uses an infrared tracking approach that is one of the state-of-the-art solutions for multi-touch enabled tabletops. The *Surface* is designed as a couch table with 56cm height and a

2. Related Work

display size of 53 × 107cm, featuring a 1024 × 768 resolution. In addition to multi-point detection, physical objects that are placed on the surface can be recognized. One scenario usage for the object detection feature is to transfer data from a mobile phone that has been placed on the surface. A main issue that Microsoft faces is the dependency on the environmental lighting conditions. If the room's illumination is too bright, the tracking performance decreases significantly. That is why the surface table is used in controlled light situations like hotel lobbies, stores, or casinos.

Figure 2.5: Microsoft *Surface* [1]is based on an optical tracking set-up, where four embedded infra-red cameras track the entire table. A special rear-projection surface and an embedded projector allow an optimal image. With the special projector, the engineers developed a relative low-sized table with a maximum height of 56cm. The *Surface* can track up to 40 simultaneous touches.

Another setup scenario for a rear projected table was shown with the *DialogTable* [170]. Installed in a museum's context, the *DialogTable* allows the users to virtually browse through the exhibitions, alone or in a group. The table is meant to stimulate discussions about the content through its multi-user interface.

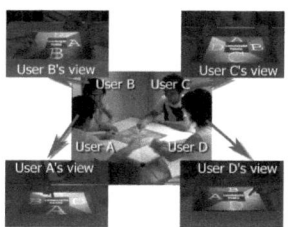

Figure 2.6: The *LumiSight* table enables user-differentiated views through its special screen material. Up to four different viewing angles are supported. *LumiSight* demonstrates an approach to create public and private spaces through its special display technology. The system combines two materials, a Lumisty film and a Fresnel lens. Together with the projectors and cameras, it allows to create a distinct view for each user and to capture input on the surface [96].

The *LumiSight* table from Matsushita et al. [96] is another example for

---
[1]www.surface.com

2. Related Work

a rear projected table setup, but with a special focus on user-differentiated views. Up to four users can interact with the *LumiSight* simultaneously, while each user has a distinct view on the surface. The surface is composed of a special refractive material that allows *LumiSight* to project different views for each side of the table. These user-differentiated views can be used to create private areas for each user on the surface, as the view is only clearly visible from one side of the table. Another possibility would be to automatically orient interface elements or text towards each user's position.

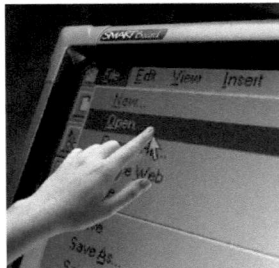 

Figure 2.7: SMART Technologies DViT frame turns screens into interactive surfaces. The small cameras are installed in the corners of the frame [151].

SMART Technologies developed the DViT [151] tracking solution. It is flat-panel overlay that enables touch interaction. Four cameras are embedded in a bezel installed on top of the display. When a finger is near the surface so that the camera can detect it, the correct position is calculated out of the four camera images. If multiple fingers are used, this technique suffers from occlusions and fails to accurately track the fingers positions. That is the reason why the DViT tracking technology is restricted to only two points of input. The advantage of the DViT setup is that the overlay form factor does not interfere with the display, resulting in no loss to the quality of the image. Moreover, the frame can be used on any flat display making it very versatile.

2. Related Work

A similar approach is used for the *NextWindow*[2] project, which is based on two optical sensors located at the corners of the screen. Objects close to the surface are tracked by the sensors that calculate their positions. Like with the SMART DViT, input is restricted to only two touch points.

Figure 2.8: The second generation of the *InteracTable*, developed by Streitz et al. [155]. This table was used in Fraunhofer's Roomware setup together with other interactive surface prototypes. For tracking user input, the *InteracTable* uses SMART DViT technology.

Both generations of the *InteracTable* [155] that was used in Fraunhofer's Roomware setup were based on SMART DViT technology. The first *InteracTable* used a rear projected surface with a DViT on top to enable pen and touch tracking. For the second generation of the *InteracTable*, a Plasma display of 70 cm × 125 cm was integrated into the table's surface, resulting in slimmer design of the table. The Roomware concept also included a smaller version of a table called *ConnecTable* [161]. These tables could be used by a single person or two tables could be jointed to build a larger unit for collaboration. The *ConnecTable* consists of a small interactive screen that allows pen-based input. The setup was designed for a standing position but had enough flexibility to adapt to different heights and tilts of the display up to fifteen degrees.

A similar approach to Fraunhofer's *InteracTables* was chosen by Ståhl et al. who designed the *Pond* [152]. This table is limited to single point interaction due to the overlay tracking technology. If more than a single point of input is sensed, the position is detected halfway between the two points. If multiple people work on such single point input surfaces, turn-taking mechanisms much be applied, otherwise the interaction will quickly become confusing.

---

[2]http://www.nextwindow.com

2. Related Work

Capacitive Tracking

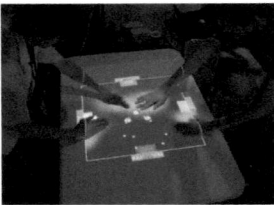

Figure 2.9: The *SmartSkin* table developed by Rekimoto. Due to the capacitive input sensing, not only direct contact with the surface can be detected, but also input in the proximity of the surface. Incontrast to vision-based tracking systems, all sensing elements are integrated within the surface. This makes the *SmartSkin* setup independent from surrounding light conditions [127].

In addition to vision-based sensing solutions, capacitive sensing technologies have been applied to large digital surfaces. Rekimoto's *SmartSkin* [127] uses a grid of antennas embedded in the surface. Through the grid layout, each touch can be detected with its corresponding x and y coordinates, there is no ambiguity of touch points. Since the antennas receive a signal if a user's hands are in the vicinity of the table, the mesh of transmitter/receiver electrodes also allows the system to estimate the distance of the user's hand from the surface. The closer the user comes to the surface, the stronger the signal becomes. Figure 2.9 shows the layout of the antennas and the *SmartSkin* table in use. The same technology was used in a smaller version to investigate gestures. The *SmartSkin* touch detection does not allow the system to identify who is touching the table or if the same or different people are touching the surface at multiple positions.

Figure 2.10: The *DiamondTouch* table. Based on an array of antennas embedded in the touch surface, the DiamondTouch can detect up to four different users simultaneously. The *DiamondTouch* moreover allows to identify the user, a feature that is still not available with other multi-touch systems [33].

This problem of user identification has been addressed by Mitsubishi Electric Research Laboratories's (MERL) *DiamondTouch* [33]. Based on an array of antennas embedded in the touch surface, the *DiamondTouch* can detect up

2. Related Work

to four different users simultaneously. The unique feature of the *Diamond-Touch* is its user identification. To distinguish different users touching the surface, each person has to be in contact with a special pad that is connected to the table. The antennas near the touch point couple an extremely small amount of signal through the user's body to the receiver. As each body carries a different signal, the application can distinguish between different people who touch the surface. *DiamondTouch* is so far the only interactive table that offers this feature. However, the system is different to the *SmartSkin* setup, because the x and y coordinates of touch points are decoupled. As a consequence, multiple points from the same person touching the surface result in ambiguity. In contrast, *SmartSkin* uses a grid of antennas where each crossing detects touches explicitly, whereas in the *DiamondTouch*, each antenna only transmits one signal. Multiple touch points from the same person on the *DiamondTouch* can also suffer from signal shadowing problems. This means that if two touches are on the same antenna, only one signal would be detected since each antenna only can offer one value. Moreover, the user always needs to stay in contact with the capacitive pads that are connected to the table, otherwise the circuit cannot be closed and the tracking does not work. Depending on the setup this restriction may cause problems. In a controlled meeting, for example, people are sitting at dedicated seats and normally stay there during the meeting. In this case, the contact to the pads that are normally integrated into the seats would be guaranteed. In a walk-up scenario like in public spaces or museum exhibitions in which people tend to stand instead of sit, the *DiamondTouch* would not work.

Although a vision-based tracking system offers more information about the nature of the touch, capacitive systems still allow to detect gestures and postures. Wu and Balakrishnan [179], for example, explored several multi-point and whole hand gestures and postures on the *DiamondTouch* table. In contrast to vision-based sensing setups, capacitive solutions like *SmartSkin* and *DiamondTouch* do not allow rear-projections. The reason is that the antennas that are embedded in the surface are not transparent. Therefore, this tracking technology is only used with front-projected setups.

2. Related Work

Tangible Objects

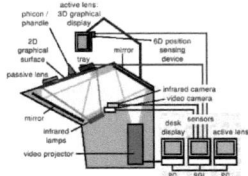 

Figure 2.11: The *metaDesk* offers tangible objects for interaction [166].

Along with the idea of using direct touch to interact with a digital table surface, researchers have investigated the potential of tangible objects as interfaces [166] [116] *Actuated Workbench* [69] [133]. Tangible objects are especially suitable for tabletops, since the horizontal orientation allows users to place them on the surface, an arrangement that is not possible with a digital wall setup. The physical objects are often augmented with digital data on the surface, which creates a visual transition from the real to the digital world. Ullmer and Ishii developed the *metaDesk* [166], which enabled users to interact with a digital campus model via tangible objects. Buildings, for example, are represented by tangible objects that can scale, move or rotate the map so that their position on the map is always correct. As illustrated in Figure 2.11, additional tangible objects like lens magnifiers or a ruler can be placed on the surface. They used two different kinds of lenses: a passive lens that showed a magnified view of the area beneath it and an active lens in form of a tablet PC that showed a 3D view of the campus.

As a subsequent project to the *metaDesk*, the *SenseTable* [116] was developed at MIT MediaLab. The digital table electromagnetically tracks the positions and orientations of tangible objects on its surface. With electromagnetic tracking instead of vision-based tracking, the objects can additionally change their state through physical modifiers and dials.

Rekimoto's *DataTiles* [129] showed another concept of tangible objects on tabletop. As depicted in Figure 2.12, Rekimoto used transparent glass

2. Related Work

Figure 2.12: The *DataTiles* developed at Sony CSL. The transparent tiles with embedded RFID tags display information when placed on the table. The physical user interfaces can be used independently or they can combined into more complex configurations [129].

tiles on the table that had different functions. With the *DataTiles*, dynamic content can be shown beneath the tiles so that the content appears to be held by tiles. He used different applications that were associated with the tiles, like playing videos or showing images. Some tiles have a control function like a curve dial that is supported by engraved guides.

The *Actuated Workbench* [114] detects objects on the surface via camera tracking that then act as interface for the system. Moreover, this table features electro-magnets that can be used to control the position of the tangible objects. This technology shows an interesting way of bidirectional communication, demonstrating input and output via tangible objects on a digital table.

Figure 2.13: The *reacTable* synthesizer tabletop. Fiducial marker tracking is used to identify objects on the rear-projected surface. For the marker tracking, a new set of fiducial symbols has been created. Moreover, the synthesizer application implements the TUIO protocol [73]. It allows to transmit information about tangible objects and multi-touch events on a table surface [69].

Another way of using tangible objects with digital tabletops is to apply fiducial markers on the bottom of the objects that can be tracked by a rear-mounted camera. The *reacTable* [69] uses this approach to build a music synthesizer that is controlled by tangible objects. The physical controllers are augmented with digital information that informs the system about the status of the objects and the current value of their parameters. Additionally,

2. Related Work

the tracking software *reacTIVision* [72] (upon which the *reacTable* is built) can sense direct touch on the surface. Together with the tangible objects, this system offers a powerful platform that shows the benefit of multi-modal input on digital tabletops.

Microsoft also integrated tangible interaction into their *Surface*[3]. Objects with fiducial markers on their bottom can be detected by the cameras beneath the surface. Microsoft has demonstrated mobile devices with fiducial markers communicating with their table. Kienzl et al. [74] developed an extension for fiducial marker tracking that allows to change the state of a marker. They demonstrate new possibilities of interaction on a tangible user interface for controlling real-time 3D visualization applications.

Rogers et al. [133] conducted a study to explore the benefits of tangible interaction with digital tabletops. They report that the integration of tangible objects into tabletop setups supported collaboration of groups working on a design task. The physical representation helped the participants in their study to finish their task more easily and with more flexibility.

2.1.2 Digital Wall Displays

Digital walls are the successors of analogue devices like chalkboards, whiteboards and paper flipcharts. They offer a shared display for groups and are commonly used in presentation setups. Another area in which we see digital walls emerging is in brainstorming scenarios. The technologies used for building upright interactive surfaces are more or less the same as those for tabletops. Nevertheless, different considerations are necessary for wall displays, as the physical setup of a vertical display has an effect on the way users interact with the surface. For example, writing with a pen is significantly different on horizontal and vertical surfaces. On a table, users tend to rest their arms on the surface while working with a pen. In contrast, the arm only occasionally touches the surface on a wall display. Moreover, in a horizontal setup, the hand and arm partially occlude the surface, whereas in a vertical setup, the whole body might be in front of the display. This again

---

[3] www.surface.com

2. Related Work

has an effect on the shadows casted when using a front projected setup. Dempski et al. describe some of these issues concerning interaction with wall mounted displays [32]. Size aspects, areas and distances for different modes of interaction as well as multi user concerns are discussed.

A different area of research explored the role of interactive walls in various surroundings. Some projects investigated the role of a large shared digital wall for planned group activities including brainstorming, data examination and presentations [117] [106] [55]. Russell et al. [135] [136] performed a detailed observation of these topics and also studied users' behavior in walk-up scenarios. Similar research dealing with ad-hoc interaction on digital wall displays has been published by Finke et al. [41], who tested a collaborative game in a public location. Further studies in this area support the notion that interactive walls installed in public spaces seem to influence the social interactions among people [50] [64] [34] [164].

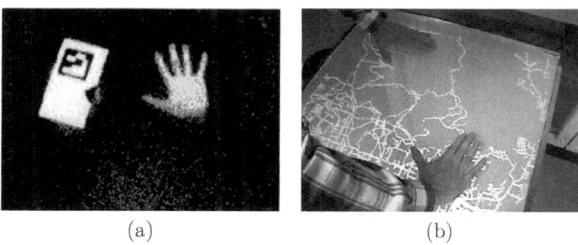

(a) (b)

Figure 2.14: Rekimoto's *Holowall* could detect direct touch and objects (a). Two handed manipulation of objects on the *HoloWall* (b) [98].

From a technological point of view, Rekimoto's *Holowall* [98] was one of the earliest implementations of a large interactive vertical surface. The *Holowall* uses vision-based input with a combination of infrared cameras and illuminators. Using a diffuse rear-projected screen, objects that come near the surface can be detected by the camera. Objects in front of the screen reflect IR light back toward the cameras on the rear, resulting in high contrast images that are easily handled by the vision system. With simple computer

2. Related Work

vision techniques like background subtraction, objects can be tracked across the surface. As shown in Figure 2.14(a), the system can detect not only touch points, but also arbitrary objects near the surface. Figure 2.14(b) shows bimanual interaction, one of the interaction techniques that has been demonstrated on the *HoloWall*. The main challenge with Rekimoto's approach is the even illumination of the surface through the infrared light from behind the screen. Rekimoto used an array of infrared LEDs around the camera to achieve an even distribution of light, but this solution restricts the maximum size of the screen. For larger displays, the arrays of LEDs is not bright enough. Nevertheless, Rekimoto's proposed system from 1997 is still one of the most often implemented vision-based tracking systems today. Microsoft's *Surface*, for example, is relying on exactly the same pairing of infrared illuminators together with infrared cameras.

Figure 2.15: Wilson's *TouchLight* uses a stereo camera setup to detect input on a Holoscreen. Infrared light sources that are placed behind the screen illuminate objects in vicinity. *TouchLight* uses a Holoscreen as projection surface. Due to the transparency of the screen, the whole environment is visible through the surface [177].

Before Microsoft announced *Surface* as their first digital table, Andy Wilson from Microsoft Research was already experimenting with infrared tracking technologies that led the way to *Surface*. With *TouchLight* [177], he presented a system based on stereo camera tracking to detect objects on a Holoscreen[4]. A Holoscreen is a transparent display with special holographic features that enable a rear-projection from a specific angle of 35 degrees. Without a projection, the HoloScreen seems transparent as the light from other incident angles than 35 degrees just passes through the screen. *TouchLight* uses this HoloScreen as a projection surface but also to detect objects in front of the screen. As the screen is transparent for the camera, all objects in front of the screen are visible. This is a main difference to Rekimoto's

---
[4]http://www.en.dnp.dk/get/472.html

2. Related Work

Holowall which used a diffuse screen and could only detect objects with a maximum distance of 30 cm. To distinguish between distant objects and objects near the surface, Wilson used a stereo camera setup. Each camera looks from a different perspective onto the screen. By calibration the cameras to the screen, a virtual image plane is defined at the screen's position. Objects approaching the screen would finally be in the same position in both camera views, whereas distant objects are in different locations in both views. By overlaying the two camera views, only objects in the same position in both images would merge. The infrared lights in the back of the screen would cause a reflection from objects near the screen, which adds up through the merging process. In addition to detecting touch points, a camera mounted behind the screen can capture snapshots of objects through the transparent surface.

A comparable commercial solution is the *ZCam*[5], a depth-sensing camera based on a combination of an infrared and a standard color camera. The technology is using the Time-Of-Flight (TOF) principle. Pulsed infrared light is emitted from the camera's position and reflected by all objects, which is then used to calculate a depth image of the scene. Similar to Wilson's approach of defining an interactive plane from which the input is recognized by the system, the *ZCam* could be used to gather information about the space in front of the screen. Point Grey Research offers the *Bumblebee*[6] cameras that are similar to the *ZCam*. The *Bumblebee* stereo camera is available in a two sensor and a three sensor version.

Another system using a stereo tracking setup is the *EnhancedWall* [108]. In this system, the stereo camera information is used for face tracking. The researchers propose using a person's gaze to control information on large wall displays. They mention the potential field of applications in public spaces.

In Fraunhofer's Roomware project, an interactive wall called *Dynawall* [155] was used together with the interactive tables we already discussed. They built one large interactive wall out of three SmartBoards. The drawback of this setup is that multiple people could only work on separated SmartBoards, thus making close collaboration difficult. The newer SmartTech DViT [151]

---
[5]http://www.3dvsystems.com
[6]http://www.ptgrey.com/products/stereo.asp

2. Related Work

technology is more advanced and can sense two points of input through the cameras mounted in the corner of the bezel. This means that two persons could work simultaneously on a single DViT equipped display, but only with a single input point each. Compared to state-of-the-art multi-point and multi-touch devices, this is still a very limiting restriction. The advantage of the DViT technology lies in the flexibility of the system, as it can be simply overlaid on an existing screen. Thus a variety of surfaces can be enhanced with the DViT tracking.

CityWall [119] is another setup that features a large multi-touch display installed in a central location in Helsinki. The researches captured videos of the public installation and examined them qualitatively as well as quantitatively based on human coding of events. They observed aspects like crowding, parallel interaction, teamwork, handovers and conflict management.

Figure 2.16: Jeff Han's FTIR based interactive wall [56]. The infrared light that is reflected from the touching fingers can be tracked by the cameras behind the screen. This technology is scalable and therefore suitable for large displays. Since Han demonstrated his first prototype setup, FTIR-based touch tracking has emerged as one of the most popular multi-touch technologies.

A recent solution for building a large interactive wall has been introduced by Jeff Han [56]. He uses Frustrated Total Internal Reflection (FTIR) to enable direct touch tracking on large surfaces. His primary area of interest is interactive walls, but the research community uses the FTIR approach to also build interactive tables. FTIR is commonly known for fingerprint image acquisition as used in security systems. The FTIR based setup differs from Rekimoto's *Holowall* [98] in the way touches create detectable spots for the camera. The tracking procedure itself remains the same for both technologies.

Recently, an emerging number of projects using FTIR light setup have

2. Related Work

been published or have already become commercially available. Smart Technologies, for example, extended their product palette from digital whiteboards to a digital table *SmartTable*[7] that uses FTIR in addition to their *SmartBoard* technology.

An alternative way of interacting with a digital wall display is with pens. This technology originates from traditional whiteboard and flipchart interaction, which was only pen based [117] [106] [55] [28]. In contrast to analogue whiteboards, most of the digital whiteboards that have been developed are only capable of detecting a single pen's input. This automatically leads to a turn taking behavior when working in a group.

Figure 2.17: The *Dynamo* setup featuring a public shared display [21].

In addition to pen interaction, different remote devices, such as laser pointers, hand-held computers, or wireless keyboards and mice have been proposed to control digital walls [105] [49]. Brignull et al., for example, studied the collaboration that happens in occasional encounters at their *Dynamo* public display [21]. The setup was meant to enable sharing of data among users, thus supporting the communication via the wall. Although the technology that *Dynamo* was based on did not support direct touch or pen interaction with the display, multiple users could interact via a multi cursor environment.

---
[7]http://www2.smarttech.com/st/en-US/Products/SMART+Table/

2. Related Work

2.1.3 Interactive Rooms

Interactive rooms aim at combining the previously discussed technologies in order to form a multi-display interactive workspace. At the time of this writing, an interactive room typically contains one or more digital tables and whiteboards, although this was not always the case. The first interactive room setups built in the 1980s were composed of multiple terminals in a shared space. The *Collab* system at Xerox PARC [153] was the first multi-terminal setup of this kind.

In the *ARIS* project [12], the interactive room used digital wall displays together with PDAs, laptops and graphics tablets on a table to create a shared space. To enable a richer collaboration among users, a 2D layout of the room supported managing the distribution of data and coordination of the collaborative work.

Figure 2.18: Fraunhofer's *i-Land* interactive room [155].

One of the most advanced interactive room setups has been realized with *i-Land* (cf. Figure 2.18), which combined an interactive table (*InteracTable*), a wall display (*DynaWall*) and electronic chairs (*CommChairs*) [155]. The room was designed to create a flexible workspace that could be rearranged to a certain extend if needed. The *CommChairs*, for example, could be moved

2. Related Work

in the room, because their display is embedded into the chairs. If two displays are physically joined, the digital desktops merge to a single desktop and allow for collaborative work. Moreover, images and documents can be transferred across surfaces in the *i-Land* room. Wooden blocks equipped with radio frequency identification (RFID) tags act as virtual object containers. The blocks themselves do not store any information about the data that is transferred, the whole information handling is processed in the background by the BEACH application framework [159] [160]. Each of the displays in *i-Land* includes an RFID reader that identifies the wood blocks and the associated data. Images or documents can be "stored" on the blocks, moved to a different display and finally retrieved again for further processing. The *i-Land* project focused on the design and hardware aspects of an innovative room for group meetings and discussions. Although issues like orientation problems on tabletop displays and gesture recognition were part of their project, application specific issues were only mentioned casually.

The *iRoom* project [65] at Stanford University had similar goals to the *i-Land* project at the Fraunhofer institute. *iRoom* featured a meeting space with large displays, wireless and multi-modal devices and a seamless mobile appliance integration. Several follow-up projects have been developed based on the *iRoom* setup, which runs a software framework called iROS. The Point Right project [66], for example, builds on the iROS framework to enable a system cursor that can be controlled directly and indirectly from any supported device and display in the *iRoom*. With this technique, users are able to interact with all of the displays in the room either via direct input or from a table centric position. Other projects designed for the *iRoom* are Multibrowser [67] and an application for architectural design meetings [42].

The *DiamondSpace* from MERL presents the vision of an interactive room that includes a digital table as a main control surface and several auxiliary wall displays to create a multi-surface space. MERL's approach is strongly based on the table centric setup and shows some interesting possibilities of space management from the table. One way of controlling multiple displays from a central table is to use the *world in miniature (WIM)* metaphor. Wigdor et al. [176] presented a solution where the WIM metaphor has been

2. Related Work

applied to the *DiamondSpace* to enable a table-centric management of the wall displays. Similar approaches to use the WIM model for multi-surface control have been further explored in research projects independent from the *DiamondSpace* setup [107] [122]. An alternative to the WIM concept has been proposed by Forlines et al. [44] who used the table to control different views of the same data on each wall display. The virtual cameras were defined by position and rotation in 3D space, which could be modified on the table.

Both described methods make use of indirect control over the peripheral wall displays. Previous research on tabletop displays has shown that the usual way of interacting with distant objects is to bring them into proximity, manipulate them and move them back when finished [140]. Indirect interaction techniques support this work flow by offering means of reaching distant objects. Laser pointers have been proposed as remote pointing devices for large wall displays [94], [103], [112]. The main drawback of these systems is the slow performance and weak accuracy that can be reached with laser pointers. Other approaches have attempted to improve target acquisition for mouse input through expanding targets [99], area cursors [70], object pointing [52], and semantic pointing [16].

Multi-user multi-surface environments extend common single-user desktop systems in two dimensions. Firstly, multiple persons can work collaboratively with a shared view of their environment. Tasks that include the interaction among participants can be carried out in a different way compared to single-user setups. Data handling and rights management [163] have to be reconsidered for a multi-user scenario in which all participants have the same view of data structures. Territoriality aspects become more important as soon as multiple users are sharing the same interactive surface [140]. Additionally, user identification and the possibility to recapitulate development processes are important features of a multi-user setup.

Secondly, multiple digital surfaces enable extended possibilities for collaborative work compared to a single-device scenario. Expanding the working environment through additional interactive surfaces permits different views on the same data set and multi-dimensional visualizations. Similar approaches are common in control rooms that have to offer a systematic overview of

2. Related Work

various data under different visualization aspects [31].

2.1.4 Mobile Paper Interfaces

In our proposed interactive room concept, paper is used as a bridging media. On one hand, paper can be used directly in the room in combination with the digital surfaces. On the other hand, paper can be used asynchronously when notes are made outside the room (before or after a meeting) and then later included in a session. This makes paper a potential media for asynchronous work environments.

This section examines various approaches to integrating paper as interface into a digital system. Section 2.1.4 discusses research projects that used different kinds of enhanced paper to bridge the gap between the physical and the virtual world. Section 2.1.4 is a brief summary of attempts to link the information of whole books with digital content.

Paper Interfaces

As studies from different domains suggest, paper is an important material early in the design processes [48] [91] [141]. Cook and Bailey [29] describe design tasks in which paper is still preferred over existing digital solutions. These tasks include communicating ideas, soliciting feedback, annotating designs, sharing at meetings, rapid sketching, ubiquitous sketching, brainstorming and refining ideas.

Early stages of architectural design are still dependent on traditional tools like sketching on paper. The *Visual Interaction Platform* (VIP 3) [2] [3] uses a combination of virtual and physical paper to offer an interaction style that preserves the naturalness of the traditional way of designing and provides access to new media at the same time. The VIP uses an LCD projector to create a large computer workspace on a horizontal surface on which a WACOM UltraPad digitizer tablet is positioned. Real paper is placed on top of the graphics tablet, and a non-inking pen captures the input. Visual feedback is projected from a ceiling-mounted projector onto the paper surface. With this setup, new kinds of interactions based on physical objects for analyzing

2. Related Work

volumetric scientific datasets have been investigated.

Figure 2.19: *Designer's Outpost* demonstrates a combination of paper Post-it notes with a digital whiteboard. The software behind *Designer's Outpost* allows to connect the physical notes to the digital world. For that reason, *Designer's Outpost* uses a combination of a front and a rear mounted camera. The front camera captures the contents on the physical notes while the rear camera captures the location of notes [78].

Designer's Outpost [78] [77] combines the affordances of real paper Post-it notes and a large physical workspace with the advantages of digital media. The aim is to support collaborative information design for the web. Tools like pens, paper, walls and tables are often used during the early phases of design for explaining, developing and communicating ideas. The *Designer's Outpost* offers a platform for a collaborative design process of websites (cf. Figure 2.19). Collected ideas are arranged as Post-it notes on a shared physical wall. The link between the physical and digital world is accomplished through the automatically created digital copies of the Post-it notes. During a creative meeting, ideas are written on real Post-it notes and arranged on a touch-sensitive smart board. A rear-mounted camera locates the position of the notes using a computer vision algorithm. A high-resolution camera in front takes snapshots of the Post-it notes, and a digitized copy of each note with the same information as the paper note is stored. Changing the position of a real note on the board also causes the digital note to be moved, as the rear camera detects the changed location. The pens that are included with the SMARTBoard can be used to annotate on the screen so that additional information for the notes can be entered. Tapping a note invokes an electronic context menu from which different commands can be chosen. For example, the digital copy of a real note can be deleted using this menu. Finally, links between notes can be drawn on the smart board with the interactive pen.

Paper in combination with digital content not only can be used as a capturing input device, but also can be enhanced with additional functionality

2. Related Work

so that it serves as a real interface tool. Coding structural information into a paper page and retrieving it through some kind of tracking technology changes a simple sheet of paper to a powerful resource for controlling complex processes. The *DigitalDesk* [110] [173] prototype was the first augmented desk system that combined real paper and digital content. An over-the-desk mounted camera tracks the user, who can interact with real documents on the table surface. A projector augments the paper documents with digital content according to the user's input. An example of one of the first paper interfaces is the *Desk Calculator* [172]. This system can be used in two different modes: either the calculator is projected on the table and the user can use it by clicking the projected buttons or a real paper version of the calculator lies on the desk that has the same functionality. The printed version works with an optical character recognition (OCR) that decodes the number on the paper that the user points at.

PaperWorks from Xerox [68] is a paper-based product for document storage and retrieval based on the *DataGlyph* technology [60]. *PaperWorks* uses forms that are a paper user interface to application programs. Similar to a dialog box that is a screen interface to a computer application, the form acts as a paper interface. Forms contain traditional printed information along with information encoded as *DataGlyphs*. Cover sheets are forms that are attached to each paper document that allow the user to specify the actions on the following document. A scanner or fax machine connected to a document services system, the XAX server, interprets the information encoded in the *DataGlyphs* on the cover sheet and invokes appropriate actions on the subsequent paper document. The XAX server offers some basic functionality for processing *DataGlyph* encoded documents, such as a server, a forms editor, and a client-server interface. More specific applications can be implemented on top of the XAX architecture. One such application, *Protofoil* [124], extends the XAX framework by offering an electronic filing cabinet that can be accessed by both paper and a computer workstation. Based on the same idea of specially designed cover sheets with embedded *DataGlyphs*, *Protofoil* provides users three basic services: document storage, document distribution, and document retrieval. Paper user interfaces enable the user to use remote

2. Related Work

services such as printing, mailing and faxing.

The *InteractiveDESK* project [5] shows a new approach to retrieve electronic documents through real objects such as paper documents or folders. Users of the *InteractiveDESK* can retrieve electronic documents by showing real objects that have links to the electronic documents. The paper documents serve as bookmarks for retrieving up-to-date digital versions of digital documents. The links are made by the users through interactions with the *InteractiveDESK*. The documents are tagged with a visual marker on their cover page that is recognized by the system. A ceiling-mounted camera detects any documents in its field of view. Occluded documents cannot be recognized by the system. Therefore it is important to arrange the documents carefully on the table. Moreover, only entire objects can be linked to their digital counterparts, parts of a document like an individual page cannot be processed. When a user puts a real object on the table, the *InteractiveDESK* recognizes the object and displays a list that holds the links to the electronic documents. The user then retrieves electronic documents by clicking the items in this list.

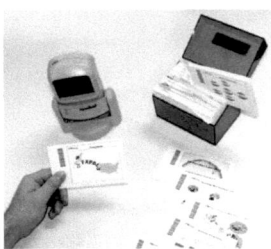

Figure 2.20: *Palette* is a system for controlling presentations through paper cards. Through the physical slides, flexible presentations are better supported than with digital slides only. The system is based on codes that are printed on each card. During a presentation, a new slide can be shown by reading the appropriate code with the card reader. However, the card reader is stationary and therefore limits the mobility of the presenter [109].

In addition to document retrieval systems, paper interfaces have been applied as supporting controls for presentations. For instance, the *Palette* [109] is a paper-based user interface designed for intuitive control of electronic slide shows. The presentations are created in PowerPoint. The finished digital slides are printed on special cards with a thumbnail view of the slide, text notes and a machine-readable code (cf. Figure 2.20). *DataGlyphs* [60]

2. Related Work

encode information on the cards. Each slide of the presentation can be accessed by simply sliding a card under the code reader located on a table. The encoded file and slide data provides the information about the current slide. The advantage of this system compared to traditional presentations is the ability to restructure the presentation at any point without the need to change the slide order in the presentation suite. Since single slides can be easily accessed the overview of the presentation is also enhanced. The *Palette* user interface supports new forms of giving presentations (such as collaborative presentations) and enables a spatial layout of the slides on a desk in preparation for nonlinear presentations. The drawback of the *Palette* system is the dependence on the bar code reader that has a fixed position on the table.

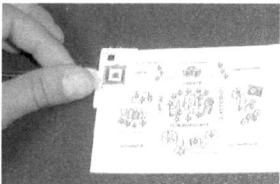

Figure 2.21: *PaperButtons* improve the *Palette* system through physical buttons that can be applied to each slide. The buttons on a slide invoke functions for controlling the presentation such as show, start, pause and play [118].

PaperButtons [118] overcomes this problem by extending the *Palette* system with "paper buttons". With *PaperButtons*, a user can engage actions in a computer by touching a button on a piece of paper. When used in the context of the *Palette* system, a button applied to a card replaces the previously used bar codes (cf. Figure 2.21). Buttons can invoke any operation known by the presentation system such as displaying a slide, starting and pausing an embedded media clips and controlling animation. To overcome the restriction of a fixed bar code reader in the *Palette* system, the *PaperButtons* send their state information to the linked server wirelessly. The sender button, which is placed on the card, consists of four basic components: a switch, an encoder for the identification signal, a power source and an emitter. Radio frequency (RF) components are used to transmit the signal. The corresponding button receiver (RF receiver and decoder) is attached to a PC running the *Palette* presentation system. Multiple *PaperButtons* with different functions can be

2. Related Work

attached to a single *Palette* card. One card can therefore be a fully equipped paper interface for the presentation.

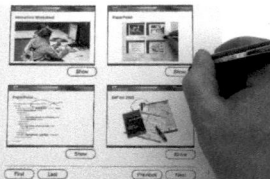

Figure 2.22: *PaperPoint* uses Anoto pens and printouts of the slides in order to control a presentation. The slides include special areas with buttons that can be clicked with the Anoto pen. In order to provide interactivity with the pens, the Anoto pattern must be printed on each slide [147].

PaperPoint [147] [148], introduced by Signer et al., also aims at supporting presentations through paper printouts of Powerpoint slides. In contrast to the *Palette* and *PaperButtons* approach, the interaction with the paper cards is achieved through Anoto technology (see Section 2.2.1). The cards feature two layers, one consisting of the Anoto pattern, the other shows the printout of the slide and some additional buttons for interaction (cf. Figure 2.22). Events triggered from a card are communicated to the presentation system. The *PaperPoint* printouts of the slide handouts contain various buttons for interacting with the PowerPoint application. A "Show" button at the bottom of each slide can be used to present the current slide. Navigation through the slides can be either linear by touching the "Next" and "Previous" buttons, or the user can directly access a slide by pointing with the Anoto pen on the appropriate card. Additional functions include switching to the first or last slide of the presentation and annotation of single slides. Annotations can be directly seen on the card, as the Anoto ink-pen leaves a trace while writing. A digital counterpart of the annotation is stored together with the correspondent slide in the *PaperPoint* system (cf. Figure 2.23).

PaperIcons [126] allows users to access digital content through paper user interfaces in the context of a clipart gallery. A printed clip art book allows fast random access to a digital clip art gallery. Jun Rekimoto uses a paper on top of a graphic tablet in combination with 2D bar codes to demonstrate his Pick-and-Drop metaphor. The bar codes are used to uniquely identify different document pages, the selection on a page is defined by the pen-sensitive tablet. The combination of pen coordinates and the ID from the

2. Related Work

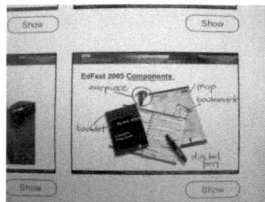 

Figure 2.23: Annotation on PowerPoint slides with *PaperPoint* [147].

bar code, tracked by a ceiling-mounted camera, identifies the corresponding digital object.

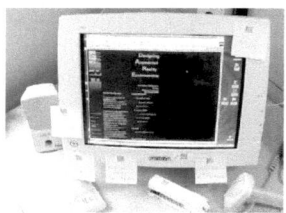

Figure 2.24: *WebStickers* is a bookmark management system. Special Post-it notes with bar codes contain the bookmarks that are linked to bookmarks in the web. To activate a bookmark, the sticker is scanned with a bar code reader [89].

WebStickers [89] shows an approach that combines paper and digital information in the form of bookmarks to the WWW. Digital bookmarks collected in lists are replaced by stickers carrying the same information (cf. Figure 2.24). Using readily available technology like standard bar code readers and adhesive stickers, *WebStickers* enable users to take advantage of their physical environment when organizing and sharing bookmarks. Moreover, the project investigates methods of handling different types of information based on how long they are used. Three different information types were identified: ephemeral, working and archived information. The physical representation of these different types must be appropriate enough to reflect their nature in the physical world. Therefore, *WebStickers* composed of Post-it notes with aging glue, represent ephemeral bookmarks. For bookmarks that are expected to have a long life or being frequently used, other kinds of physical tokens can be used.

2. Related Work

A similar approach can be found in Hewlett-Packard's *Cooltown* project [76] [123]. Users can link digital bookmarks to not only paper documents, but also any kind of physical object by attaching a printed tag.

Figure 2.25: *IconStickers* uses bar codes on stickers as representations of desktop icons. The stickers can be arranged in the user's workspace like other physical objects. When scanned with a bar code reader, the sticker activates the according program on the virtual desktop [150].

Instead of administrating bookmarks, the *IconStickers* [150] project investigated arranging a virtual desktop with physical objects. Paper icons, associated with the corresponding digital desktop icons, can be easily created and placed in the real world. Digital icons that are dragged onto a special icon representing the *IconStickers* manager program are printed as their physical counterparts on the label printer (cf. Figure 2.25). A unique bar code identifies the printed label, a small image and the name of the digital icon are also printed as a hint for the user. Scanning a bar code on an *IconSticker* with a bar code reader invokes the associated program on the computer the same way as if it would have been double-clicked with the mouse. Therefore, *IconStickers* are a more general approach of linking digital information with real paper as arbitrary programs can be accessed.

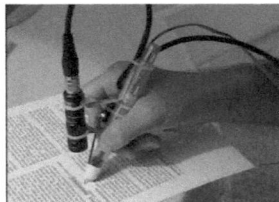

Figure 2.26: *PaperLink* shows a solution for invoking commands through the scanning of words on a paper printout [4]. The content on the page serves as a command interface for the digital application. The system is similar to scanning bar codes in a supermarket which are digitally linked to a product and price information.

PaperLink [4] uses the *VideoPen*, a highlighter pen combined with a small camera, to augment paper with electronic features (cf. Figure 2.26). Computer vision techniques allow the recognition of marks (such as written words)

2. Related Work

that are associated with digital content. *PaperLink* focuses on linking paper based commands to existing digital information instead of storing written input.

The *Origami* project [120] [121] from Xerox provides an alternative solution that maps real paper documents to digital information. Conventional HTML web pages are stored in postscript format and embedded hyperlinks are preserved. The converted postscript documents can be printed and placed on the *DigitalDesk* [110], where they are tracked by the ceiling-mounted camera. Pointing on a link on the paper document invokes the digital link to be displayed on the desk next to the document. Therefore, users can print their web pages and still obtain full hyper link functionality.

Finally, *PaperClick*[8] and *Wiziway*[9] are commercial solutions that use printed symbols linked to web pages to manage the connection between physical and digital world. *PaperClick* is based on a linear bar code representation of the tags that are read by a bar code reader. Alternatively, mobile phones with integrated cameras can be used to scan the tags and access the related information directly on the phone. *Wiziway* uses different tags in the form of small pictograms that are printed on the paper documents that then serve as physical link to the digital content.

Interactive Books

Figure 2.27: *Books with Voices* is a paper interface that allows to access video interviews through their transcripts [77]. The user gets a fast overview by reading parts of the transcript and can access further information through the linked video.

Retrieving information out of books has been the focus of several research projects. Approaches differ concerning the technology employed as well as the applications that are finally supported. *Books with Voices* [77]

---
[8]http://www.paperclick.com
[9]http://www.wiziway.com

2. Related Work

features a paper interface for fast random access to digital video interviews (cf. Figure 2.27). Digital video interviews augment paper transcripts that can be accessed through PDAs. The enhanced paper pages are tagged with linear bar codes that can be read by the bar code scanning device applied to the PDA.

The *A-book* [92] is a laboratory notebook used to investigate how to manage information with both physical and electronic manifestations. The project aims at biologists and archivists to support them in their daily work. The research group built two working prototypes that test different technical and interaction strategies. Writing with standard ink on paper is possible in both cases, the *A-book* captures a digital copy of the written input associated with the correct page and marked with a time-stamp. It consists of two parts, one for capturing the handwriting, the other for augmenting the real paper with digital information. Placing a paper notebook on a WACOM graphic tablet, the writing on real paper is captured in form of strokes. A PDA is used as an interaction lens linking the physical and electronic documents.

The PDA is equipped with a WACOM 4D mouse sensor that is used to track its position and orientation with respect to the paper page. The "magic lens" can be placed on the paper notebook and shows a combination of digital overlay information and the captured handwriting. Interaction with the *A-book* involves creating new content by writing on the paper notebook with an inking pen that is tracked by the graphics tablet. This written input can be read without any technology like in a conventional paper notebook. Additional information can be entered with a non-inking pen via the PDA. Existing written text can also be highlighted, linked or annotated with digital information using the PDA as an interaction lens. The overlaid information can be accessed later on by moving the magic lens over the paper notebook. To achieve a consistent visualization, the occluded text on the paper notebook is substituted by its digital copy on the PDA screen.

The *MagicBook* [15] is another interactive book that is based on AR-ToolKit marker tracking. A *MagicBook* is a regular book with printed texts and pictures on each page, enhanced with markers that serve as link to the digital content. A head mounted semi-transparent display is used for

2. Related Work

the presentation of supplementary digital information. Using the ARToolKit tracking software [10], the augmented three-dimensional models appear in the correct position and rotation for the specific user. Switching from semi-transparent to a non-transparent display is also supported. Based on the *MagicBook*, several applications, ranging from architecture and scientific visualization to general entertainment, have been implemented.

Figure 2.28: *Active Book* demonstrates the link from a book to additional background information on the web. The resources that are linked to a paper page can be sounds or animations that are accessible through the web page. For interacting with the *Active Book*, a combined bar code reader and mouse device, called *FieldMouse*, is used [149].

The *Active Book* [149] works with a *FieldMouse* as input device. The *FieldMouse* is a combination of an ID recognizer like a bar code reader and a mouse which detects relative movement of the device. The interaction with the *FieldMouse* requires to first detect the current page by scanning the bar code. The relative position on the current page is provided by the mouse part of the device. Pages of the *Active Book* are stored as clickable maps in the Hypertext Markup Language format (HTML). By pointing-and-clicking with the FieldMouse at a specific location on the page, the coordinates are transmitted to the system and the linked web resource is accessed via the clickable map (cf. Figure 2.28). For each page of the *Active Book*, a HTML map representation with links to different resources exists. The current page is identified by a bar code printed on each page. Therefore, the whole page of an *Active Book* is interactive, and input is not restricted to only the tagged areas.

The *Interactive Textbook* [80] project is based on the augmented desk interface system *EnhancedDesk* [108]. When opening a page in the real book, the system automatically retrieves digital content from a database and projects

---

[10]http://www.hitl.washington.edu/artoolkit/

2. Related Work

this content next to the textbook. The current page is identified by a two dimensional bar code. The user can directly interact with the digital content to perform tasks such as changing the parameters of an experiment.

2.2 Interaction with Digital Surfaces

This section presents different approaches that enable users to interact with the digital surfaces described in the previous section. When compared to traditional desktop computer environments, work in an interactive room that consists of large digital surfaces creates new demands on the interaction design. The setup must be able to handle multiple users and must allow for interaction with multiple displays simultaneously. Moreover, a practical system must support interaction that maps to the affordances of the hardware. Thus, the selection of the appropriate input technology complements the choice of the hardware for the digital surfaces in the room. Section 2.2.1 examines digital pens as input devices for digital surfaces. Different pen solutions that have been used in research projects are compared. Section 2.2.2 discusses direct touch as input for digital surfaces. Due to the rich qualities like multi-point input, gestures and postures that direct touch offers, it has been extensively explored by researchers. Finally, Section 2.2.3 discusses projects that have explored the possibilities of bimanual interaction. Our examination focuses on the different tasks that could benefit from bimanual interaction as well as hardware requirements for this modality of input.

2.2.1 Pen Based Interaction

Pens have been used as tools for interacting with horizontal as well as vertical digital surfaces in various research projects. The affordances of a pen make it a suitable input device for tasks like writing or sketching. Users are well practiced with traditional pen use, and can easily translate their knowledge to the digital surface with minimal cognitive impact. Moreover, pens provide a precise tool for pointing and can further include extensions like buttons or pressure sensors. Pens as input devices for digital surfaces have been initially

2. Related Work

designed in two versions: as stylus for interacting with small displays like PDAs or Tablet PCs and pens that capture the input on digital whiteboards. While the first kind of pen is rarely suitable for interacting with large digital surfaces, the digital pens designed for working with a whiteboard can also be used on horizontal surfaces; therefore, we will perform a more detailed examination of these digital whiteboard pen technologies in this section.

There exist some commercial solutions that allow pen interaction on large digital surfaces. The *Mimio*[11] pen is a commercially available product based on ultrasonic technology that captures handwritten notes made on large whiteboards. Special pens in combination with a receiver provide positional information. Rogers and Lindley [134] used this technology to enable pen interaction with a tabletop. The *Mimio* pen solution is restricted to a single pen and only works if the pen is directly in contact with the surface. Moreover, it was initially designed for vertical displays and not for horizontal tabletop setups. As the tracking relies on ultrasonic signals that are emitted from the pen and captured by the receiver at the side of the surface, objects in the line of sight can block the signal. While this rarely happens on a wall setup (unless one rests his palm or hand on the surface), it is more common on a tabletop display. People tend to rest their arms on the surface and put objects on the table, both of which can interfere with the ultrasonic tracking. A comparable product is offered by *eBeam*[12], which also uses ultrasonic signals for pen tracking.

An alternative solution is graphic tablets. WACOM[13] is the most popular producer of graphic tablets on the market. Their technology is based on active digitizers, which use electromagnetic signals that are reflected by the tablets' pen. The pen can include electronic switches for changing the properties of the reflection. These switches are used for pressure sensing in the pen's tip as well as buttons on the pen's barrel. The digitizer in WACOM tablets is located behind the screen, which allows for maximum visibility. Moreover, the tracking technology enables above-screen tracking, which is commonly used

---
[11] http://www.mimio.com
[12] http://www.e-beam.com
[13] http://www.wacom.com

2. Related Work

for hover interaction. In contrast to a resistive digitizer, active digitizers only capture pen input, whereas resistive systems can also be used with direct touch. The main restriction of active digitizer based graphic tablets is their maximum size. A state-of-the-art WACOM Cintiq is available in a maximum 21-inch screen size, which is of course too small for a multi-user digital whiteboard or tabletop.

Figure 2.29: The *Escritoire* foveal display for digital tabletops. The setup combines different pen input and display resolutions [7]. *Escritoire* is designed for common tasks such as document viewing and annotations on a tabletop. The higher resolution projector is used to display documents in a quality that is sufficient for reading.

A combination of both described digital pen technologies has been shown with the *Escritoire* [7]. This digital table uses an A0 sized digitizer with a *Mimio* tracking installed for tracking the surrounding area. The two pen tracking technologies are supplemented with two projectors that create a foveal display. Precise interaction occurs in the center of the table where the higher resolution of the digitizer is combined the higher projected resolution. Contextual information can be interacted with in the surrounding regions, which feature a lower resolution tracking through the *Mimio* with a large but lower resolution projection. The *Escritoire* allows to work bimanually with both pens on the two different areas of the surface.

 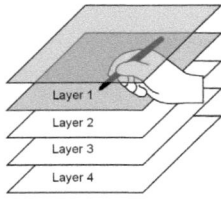

Figure 2.30: 3D pen interaction above a digital table [158].

2. Related Work

3D pens have been explored for their enhanced functionality in conjunction with large digital surfaces. In contrast to the hover state that a WACOM tablet offers, 3D tracking provides a richer interaction above the surface. One example has been demonstrated by Subramanian et al. [158] who used a magnetic tracking system together with a pen. With this approach, they could track the position, orientation and the roll of the pen above the surface. They constructed a layer model above the surface and showed a prototype drawing application with different functions assigned to different layers. One layer could, for example, be responsible for the stroke width, another for the shape of the pen tip. Figure 2.30 shows their setup with the corresponding layer model.

Intensive research has been invested to develop digital pens that work in combination with enhanced paper. *Intelligent Paper* from Xerox [37] integrates physical paper documents and digital content in combination with a special pen. The pages are standard sheets of paper that are covered with printed marks that are invisible to the human eye but visible to the pen. The marks contain information about the unique page ID and the location on the page. *DataGlyphs* [60] were suggested as a possible solution for the printed pattern. *DataGlyphs* are an unobtrusive method of embedding computer-readable data on surfaces such as paper using a special printed pattern. They are a pattern consisting of forward and backward slashes representing ones and zeros. Encoded information that is invisible to the human eye can be extracted by a GlyphPen scanning device. *Intelligent Paper* is made up of three elements: support, input device and communication infrastructure. Support means that each physical page is identified by a code page ID, which uniquely identifies the specific page among all other existing pages. An input device, called a pointer, recognizes its location on the page as soon as the user touches the surface with the pen. The communication infrastructure is responsible for sending the (page ID, pointer location) pair over the web; the page ID is decoded as a network address, and the pointer location is interpreted by a program at this address. Furthermore, *Intelligent Paper* proposed the use of the Adobe Acrobat suite of products to build an electronic counterpart of the paper document with embedded links for every physical

2. Related Work

page. Possible actions with the *Intelligent Paper* include triggering of output actions, using the pointer as a mouse, selecting content and annotating. Pointing actions on the paper document, for example, could be mapped to virtual mouse actions on the display. By pressing a button on the pen, mouse clicks can be emulated for selecting specific objects on the page. The pen is a full replacement for the mouse, the paper substitutes the screen surface. The technology behind the *Intelligent Paper* relies on two layers of printed ink, the first serves as code layer that is not visible for the user whereas the second layer is typical ink layer.

The *Paper++* project [111] used paper documents with a grid of linear bar codes printed with conductive ink. The grid is nearly invisible. A special inductive pen decodes the bar codes into positional information. The resolution of the inductive pen tracking is not sufficient to support pen-based writing.

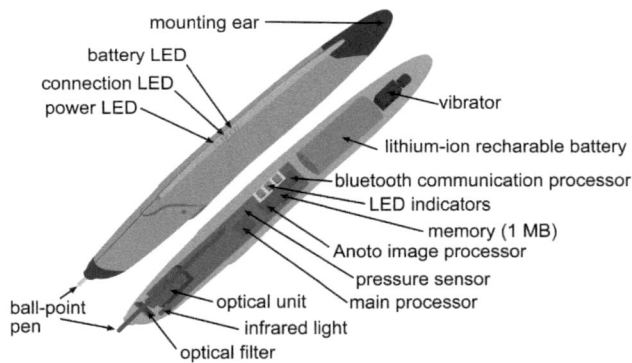

Figure 2.31: Anoto pen technology.

The Swedish company Anoto[14] developed the *Digital Pen and Paper* technology. At the time of this writing, this technology features the highest tracking resolution on enhanced paper available. The main tool for interaction is

---
[14]http://www.anoto.com

2. Related Work

a pen with a small infrared camera integrated in the tip that derives the pen's position on a unique high-resolution dot pattern. Figure 2.31 depicts the components of an Anoto pen. The Anoto pattern consists of tiny dots that are slightly displaced from a regular grid (cf. Figure 2.32). By setting the dots with offsets in horizontal and vertical position from the grid, each dot encodes two bit of information. The combination of several dots makes a unique sequence that defines the position on the paper. To enable stable tracking, the digital pen has to see at least a collection of six by six dots. In practice, the camera in the pen's tip manages to see this minimum 36 points with a surprisingly high frequency. Once the dots are recognized, the pen not only sends its coordinates, but also additional information about the current page ID and a pressure level.

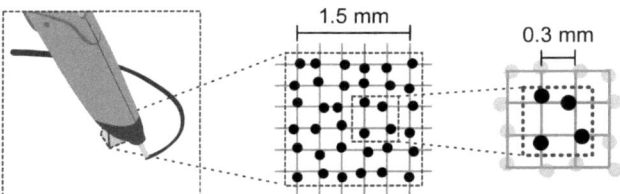

Figure 2.32: The Anoto dot pattern.

The Anoto digital pens are available in two different types: a USB and a Bluetooth streaming version. Figure 2.33 shows the two different versions of data transfer from the Anoto pen to the PC. The USB pen, which is commonly used for storing a digital copy of one's handwriting, can only be synchronized with the PC when placed in a docking station. Once the pen is connected to the PC via the docking station, all stored data from the pen is transmitted in a single step. Afterwards, the memory in the pen is emptied. The second version of Anoto pen not only stores handwriting in the pen, but also allows one to stream data in real-time over Bluetooth to the PC. With this streaming input, the user can get feedback from the PC in real-time. Moreover, this real-time streaming makes the Anoto technology suitable for

2. Related Work

direct interaction on large digital surfaces. Currently, three commercial pens with Bluetooth are available from Nokia (SU-1B), Logitech (io-2), and Anoto (PenIT).

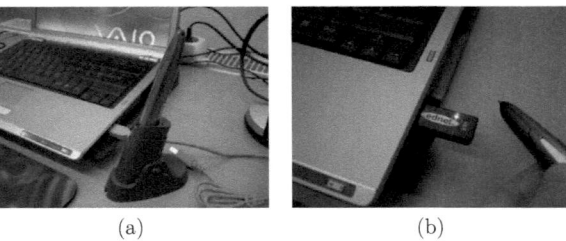

(a)   (b)

Figure 2.33: Anoto pens are available in two versions: a USB only version (a) and a Bluetooth streaming version (b).

Since the Anoto technology was made available, researchers have been thinking about novel ways to use it for capturing users' input. The fact that the pen works in combination with real paper makes it portable and therefore allows scenarios in which graphic tablets or tablet PCs are not usable because of their weight and dimensions. In addition, paper can be seen as another interface to the digital world, as it is still used in the form of printouts. The problem with paper printouts is the loss of synchronization with the digital counterpart. To address this problem, Anoto technology has been applied in several research projects as a bridging technology between real and digital world.

PapierCraft [88], for example, is a gesture-based command system for interactive paper. It enables users to manipulate paper printouts of their documents while updating the digital document simultaneously. The Anoto pen technology is used to access the user's input from the paper and consequently apply it to the digital source. Figure 2.34 shows the command for copying an image from a paper document and inserting it into a digital document.

2. Related Work

Figure 2.34: The *PapierCraft* gesture-based command system for interactive paper [158].

ButterflyNet [182] is an application based on the *PapierCraft* infrastructure. Real paper is combined with digital content in the background via the Anoto technology. In this case, the application aims to support field biologists. With an additional digital camera, biologists could take picture of samples, link them with their note in the paper notebook and finally synchronize the content of the notebook with the PC to obtain a digital copy of the notebook. The digital notebook enables actions that are impossible with the paper version, like sharing of data for example.

Another scenario to use Anoto technology has been demonstrated by the *PaperPoint* project [148]. Printouts of PowerPoint slides can be used with their system to control the presentation by simply clicking on the appropriate slide. They also integrated a sketching functionality within the system that allows one to annotate slides during the presentation by drawing on the appropriate slide's printout.

2.2.2 Direct Touch Interaction

The most common and obvious way to interact with a digital surface is with direct touch interaction. Observing people in setups that include digital walls or tables reveals that the first intention is to touch the surface and discover the effect. The first system that supported a direct touch surface was Wellner's *DigitalDesk* [110]. He used a vision based tracking system to detect the user's hand and further enabled interaction with the table's surface. Since

2. Related Work

this first prototype, a lot of research has been invested into direct touch interaction. Different approaches have been chosen, but all of them with the same goals: to find a stable tracking solution that is comfortable to use, scalable in size, precise and fast enough to allow fluid interaction. In this sense, direct touch offers a novel complexity of input to a computer system. A mouse or stylus provide single point interaction, whereas touch based systems deal with several points simultaneously. Moreover, touch based systems are not restricted to multi-point input, although this is still the most common way of using these systems so far. Depending on the underlying tracking technology, a richer interpretation of the input can be processed. Examples include gestures and postures that enable more complex methods of interaction than single point input technology. These enhanced possibilities create high expectations from the user's side. We are used to touching and manipulating objects in the real world, and we expect a similar behavior in the digital world. While many research projects have addressed this issue, direct touch interaction is still a compelling and open area of research. This section aims to give an overview of past research in this field and a summary of the state-of-the-art.

Generally, direct touch technologies can be divided into two sub categories: vision based tracking systems and capacitive tracking systems.

Vision-Based Tracking

Proposed solutions for vision-based systems differ in various aspects. For example, some systems track bare hands, while others employ easily tracked markers. Dorfmüller et al. used a glove with infrared (IR) retro reflective markers to detect finger positions in a chess game application [36]. In a similar setup, they use infrared beacons to detect hand and head positions in combination with a BARCO projection table [35]. Kim and Fellner applied fingertip markers that were clearly visible in a black light environment on a rear-projected screen [75]. Retrieving a high contrast image of the fingertips, they controlled 3D objects by hand gestures. IR retro reflective markers

2. Related Work

in combination with stereovision tracking produced convincing results documented by Ribo et al. [130].

Markerless approaches appear to be more intuitive and closer related to natural working situations. Several approaches have tried to handle the technological obstacles that constrain accurate tracking results. Most problematic are changing illumination conditions and moving backgrounds. Hardenberg and Berard implemented a system that claims to be stable under arbitrary conditions [169]. Similar results are reported by Chen et al. who implemented a two-handed drawing application that is able to interpret several different hand gestures [27]. Nakanishi et al. included this system in the *Enhanced-Desk* and *EnhancedWall* setup [108]. A finger controlled drawing application called *SmartCanvas* was proposed by Mo et al. [100]. They use a stereo camera setup to detect surface touch information. Hand gestures are interpreted to achieve different drawing modes and a color chooser. Finger based drawing at pixel accuracy is described by MacCormick and Isard [90]. Sato et al. introduced a finger-tracking system with an infrared camera used on an augmented desk [138]. They studied the usage for sample applications like web browsing or the manipulation of 3D objects. Rehg and Kanade [125] presented early results in hand tracking, with which they controlled a 3D mouse interface. In their system, a kinematic hand model mapped real hand postures to the virtual space.

Tracking user interaction on wall displays requires different considerations than tracking interaction on table-based setups. Capturing hands or fingers trough a camera mounted on the user's side of the screen may not be suitable due to self occlusion. Cameras placed behind the screen or close to the surface seem to be the most promising configurations. As previously described, Rekimoto et al. built the *HoloWall*, an upright surface that allowed tactile interaction [98]. Using a diffuse rear-projected screen, IR LEDs and a camera with IR pass filter, they achieved reasonable tracking results. Figure 2.35 shows the schematic setup of the *HoloWall*. Not only hands and fingers could be tracked by the system, but also any object near enough to the surface. Reflecting the IR light, those objects appeared with high contrast to the vision system. An approach for arm tracking situated in a restrictive

2. Related Work

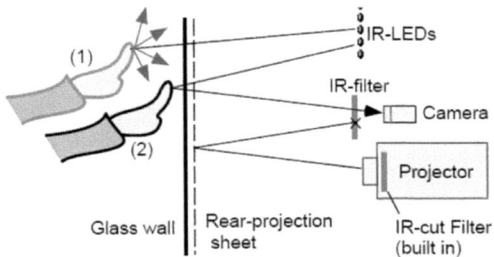

Figure 2.35: Rekimoto's *HoloWall* [98].

environment was presented by Leubner et al. [87]. Their tracking was based on the assumption that the user's arm is the only object in the camera's view, so that no occlusions with dynamic objects could appear. The setup could be used to control the mouse cursor within a connected software system. Further instructions like mouse button clicks could be given by voice commands.

State-of-the-art vision tracking systems are mainly based on two different approaches: diffused illumination (DI) and FTIR as described by Han [56]. Rekimoto's *HoloWall* [98] was the first setup that demonstrated a DI setup. The first working prototype of a FTIR based setup was shown by Jeff Han [56]. The following comparison is meant to provide more insights in similarities and differences of these two technologies.

Both approaches aim at the same goal, which is to provide visible spots of the regions where a user touches a surface that can be further tracked by a rear-mounted camera. For both setups, the projection normally happens from the rear, although a front-projection would be also possible. In order to avoid interferences with the projected image, the camera is equipped with an IR-pass filter that only lets the IR part of the light spectrum pass through. The projection is therefore invisible to the camera. Both setups, DI and FTIR, use infrared light to illuminate the touched areas on the surface. The

2. Related Work

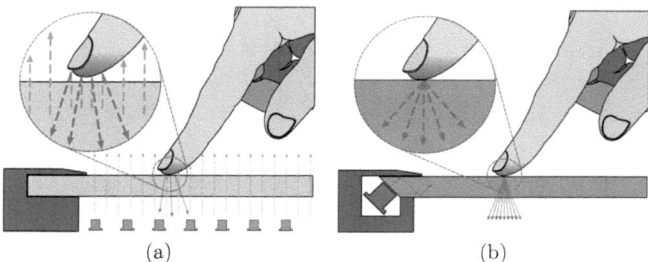

Figure 2.36: Diffused illumination (DI) setup (a), FTIR setup (b).

enabling technology behind this effect is the main difference between DI and FTIR based tracking systems. As shown in Figure 2.36(a), the DI version uses infrared illuminators behind the screen pointing at the surface. Objects that come near the surface tend to reflect the light, which results in a visible spot that can be tracked by the camera. To assure that only objects near or on the surface will reflect the light and thus become visible to the camera, the surface must be diffuse. Depending on the diffuseness, the depth in front of the screen in which objects can be seen can be regulated. Another challenge with DI setups is the requirement to spread the light evenly across the screen surface. If an even distribution of light is not guaranteed, hot spots will influence the tracking quality. For that reason, DI setups normally use several light sources to avoid hot spots.

One recent example of a table based on DI is Microsoft's *Surface*[15]. The exact number of light sources in *Surface* has not been announced by Microsoft, but for a stable solution, more than one illuminator will be used.

In contrast to DI technology, FTIR does not need light sources mounted behind the surface. Rather, this technique relies on the fact that light that is coupled into a transparent acrylic plate will stay inside due to internal reflection. As soon as a finger touches the surface, the path of the light is frustrated and will leave the acrylic material on the opposite side of the hand.

---

[15] www.surface.com

2. Related Work

The reflected light produces a visible spot. This procedure works with visible as well as infrared light. The visible version is well known from exit signs, for example, where the text is engraved into the surface, which triggers the FTIR effect. This causes the engraved text to glow. For tracking touches on interactive surfaces, infrared light is normally used instead of visible light.

Overcoming the restrictions of vision based approaches, Paradiso and Strickon experimented with a scanning laser rangefinder [157]. Their tracking results are not disturbed by ambient light or multiple users in front of the screen. Improving their system, they implemented a knock sensitive setup on a glass surface [115]. This approach seems especially interesting for transparent surfaces.

Capacitive Systems

Capacitive tracking is another solution to detect touches on an interactive surface. Projects like Rekimoto's *SmartSkin* [127] and MERL's *DiamondTouch* [33] showed implementations that worked for digital tabletops. The main drawback of these capacitive systems is the opaque surface that prevents a rear-projection setup. On the other hand, the *DiamondTouch* offers the functionality to distinguish the users who touch the surface, a feature that is still not available with vision based systems. Capacitive touch screen technology has been used with a variety of commercial kiosk systems. These products use a transparent glass surface with a special coating that stores a small continuous electrical current across the screen. Oscillator circuits that are located at the corners of the screen measure the capacitance of a person touching the screen. Since the touch sensing relies on the changing current across the surface when a finger touches it, gloved fingers, pens or styli will not work with this technology. However, most of these systems are only capable of sensing a single touch point. One of the reasons for the single point restriction is that the changes in the current are only detected in a specific direction instead of at each point on the surface. Moreover, the measurements are based on changes that refer a baseline signal. Once the screen is touched, the baseline changes and a further touch measurement would use the wrong

2. Related Work

baseline.

However, this major restriction can be overcome by modifying the setup of capacitive sensing. With the *iPhone*[16], Apple developed a commercial product that uses multi-touch capacitive tracking. The sensing circuits of the *iPhone* are arranged in a coordinate system which allows to detect multiple simultaneous touches. This approach has been pioneered by *Fingerworks*[17] who developed the *TouchStream LP* keyboard and the *iGesture Pad*. For enabling multi-touch tracking, they applied an array of capacitive sensors to the surface. Wayne Westerman provides a detailed description of the underlying data processing [174]. The basics of this technology have been used for the development of the *iPhone*. Since it is still based on capacitive tracking, gloves or styli are not working with the *iPhone*. Another solution for a capacitive multi-touch screen has been marketed by the company N-Trig[18]. They support user input from both pen and capacitive touch in a single device. For the pen tracking, they use an electrostatic stylus and an active digitizer that is embedded in the screen. The N-Trig technology has already been integrated into commercial products such as the Dell Latitude XT tablet[19].

2.2.3 Bimanual Interaction

The research on interaction with digital surfaces has a strong focus on *natural* and *intuitive* techniques that allow the user to perform actions with a minimum cognitive load. Since the first implementation of direct touch interactions, it has been seen as a potential technology that allows ease-of-use combined with a high grade of flexibility. But when we think about the way people naturally interact with their hands, we'll find that single point input systems, for example, do not reflect our input capabilities at all. Multi-point and multi-touch systems go one step further and enable the simultaneous input of several points, thus getting closer to a *natural* system. Considering the way people work in reality, bimanual work plays an important role.

---
[16] http://www.apple.com/iphone/
[17] http://www.fingerworks.com/
[18] http://www.n-trig.com
[19] http://www.dell.com/tablet

2. Related Work

That is the reason why numerous research projects have investigated and measured the benefits of bimanual interaction for a variety of tasks [9] [22] [23] [24] [40] [127] [8] [62] [85] [113]. By leveraging input from both hands, system designers can increase the input bandwidth from their users and add rich and natural interactions to their applications. When designing for bimanual input, system designers must choose among the many input devices available for each hand. Comparisons among various input devices (such a mice, pucks, stylus, and touch-tables) are plentiful [47] [61] [71] [104]. Taken as a whole, this body of research indicates that individual input devices excel in certain measures and lack in others.

The previous work on bimanual input can generally been divided in to two categories: those that define or extend models and frameworks for bimanual input, and those that apply those models and frameworks. We now review each in turn.

Models and Frameworks

Most work in bimanual interaction has been influenced by Guiard's Kinematic Chain model [51], which proposes general principles for asymmetric bimanual actions. During two-handed interaction, both hands have different roles that depend on each other with respect to three rules: the dominant hand (DH) moves within the frame of reference defined by the non-dominant hand (NDH); the sequence of motion generally sees the NDH setting the reference frame prior to actions with the DH being made within that context; and that the DH works at a higher level of precision than the NDH in both spatial and temporal terms.

Follow-up research has extensively investigated different facets of these hypotheses, such as the importance of visual and kinesthetic feedback for bimanual tasks [8] and differences between symmetric [85] [113] and asymmetric [25] [26] [61] bimanual input. Kabbash et al. [71] studied four techniques for performing a compound drawing and color selection task using a unimanual technique, a bimanual technique where each hand controlled independent tasks, and two bimanual tasks where the DH depended on the

2. Related Work

NDH. They suggest that asymmetric, dependent tasks are most effectively performed using two hands.

Several research projects have sought to apply these findings and to investigate interaction design and input devices for bimanual tasks.

Interaction Design and Input Devices

Different input devices have been evaluated regarding their suitability for bimanual tasks. The use of bare hands for gestures and self-revealing tasks has been studied by Kruger [81] in VIDEOPLACE. Matsushita et al's. *Holowall* includes bimanual object manipulation [98]. *SmartSkin* [127] is an interactive surface enabling bimanual interaction for different tasks, such as map panning and zooming. Several projects have explored the benefits of two-handed control [22] [40] [47] [180] using *DiamondTouch* [33].

Kabbash et al. [71] performed a comparison among a mouse, a trackball, and a stylus for bimanual tasks. Their findings support Guiard's claim that the NDH is best suited for imprecise tasks. Forlines et al. [47] conducted a study that compared bimanual mouse and touch input on interactive tabletops. A combination of a PDA in the NDH and a mouse in the DH was investigated by Myers et al. [104].

Matsushita [97] and Yee at al. [181] implemented mobile devices supporting pen and touch input. In both cases, touch input complemented pen input. Cutler et al. investigated the use of a glove and pen on the *Responsive Workbench* [30]. They found that the combination of a glove for the NDH and a stylus in the DH worked best for asymmetric tasks that reflected the natural qualities of each input device. The stylus with its thinner tip and more precise point of touch fits better for high precision tasks.

Researchers have explored bimanual interaction for a variety of tasks that can be performed more efficiently compared to a sequential single-handed input. Potential tasks include menu control [9] [14] [84] [179], desktop interaction such as selecting [23], scrolling [24] [93] and cursor control [10] [40], map navigation [61] [127] [146] [166] and sketching [22] [43] [84].

Hinckley et al. [61] explored the performance of puck and stylus as well

2. Related Work

as touchpad and TouchMouse combinations for bimanual interaction. They found bimanual benefits for map navigation tasks. Formerly sequential actions were chunked by the simultaneous use of two devices were therefore performed more quickly. Kurtenbach et al. [84] tested two-handed interaction with Toolglass menus with a graphics-editing program. They used WACOM tablets with two pucks as input devices to evaluate their design approach that aimed at maximizing the screen space for application data while providing an increasing quality of input.

Compared to relatively small surfaces such as Tablet PCs or graphic tablets, the necessity of visually linking the tasks of both hands on a tabletop becomes increasingly important. Switching the attention between left and right hands results in highly sequential performance and neutralizes or reverses the advantage of bimanual interaction [8] [71], a design based on both descriptive principles and predictive models is especially important for large surfaces.

2.3 Digital Workspace Design

The horizontal layout of a table along with the possibility of multi-user interaction requires new workspace design concepts that have been researched under a variety of different aspects. Assuming that the hardware supports interaction with the table's surface, the main attention has been focused on the application design for digital tabletops. The following summary shall provide an overview of the most important features and related published approaches.

2.3.1 Digital Tabletop Interfaces

As related work on interactive tabletops has shown, it is possible to use standard Windows applications on a horizontal surface [40]. But such an approach will never explore the full functionality of a tabletop, since the input is restricted to a single cursor and the output is tailored for viewing from only one distinct orientation. In an interactive tabletop setup, multiple

2. Related Work

users expect to interact simultaneously without restricting their workflow to turn-taking. Studies about traditional tables and the interaction of groups around them have shown that table surfaces encourage people to use physical objects simultaneously [162] [140] [82]. This behavior must be supported by the design of a digital tabletop by providing mechanisms that allow for concurrent input. With a horizontal surface, people tend to develop new forms of collaboration and communication when working with applications that are tailored for this kind of surface [132].

Designing the application for a digital table requires considering multi-user aspects that are substantially different to conventional WIMP (Windows, Icons, Menus and Pointing devices) concepts. With a table setup, people will naturally sit or stand around the table. Once people sit at different sides around the table, individual views onto the surface vary, creating the problem of orientation of visuals on the table's surface. This is the reason why traditional Windows interfaces cannot be simply ported onto the table, because they rely on a distinct orientation. A lot of research into the field of tabletops has been invested on this issue already [82] [140] [175] [46] [45] [58]. The DiamondSpin tabletop groupware [145], for example, supports the development of such applications for tabletops. Among others, it provides a feature to replicate the system menu for each user at the table and place it at an appropriate position on the surface. Projects like the Personal Digital Historian [168] [143] and the UbiTable [142] show implementations based on the DiamondSpin toolkit with different duplicated personal menu layouts. The menus provide the tools for multiple users to interact with the table. This process also involves the digital artifacts that are manipulated by the group. Since multiple users work simultaneously, the concurrent access of objects must be handled. The DiamondSpin groupware allows for this collaborative interaction so that users can manipulate objects and enlarge them to gain shared access. A different approach has been explored for the InteracTable within the i-Land project [155]. Their table is based on the BEACH software [160] [156], which allows for the making of copies of an object for each user and further manipulating the object through these references. In contrast to the collaborative manipulation of objects on the shared

2. Related Work

surface, hand-over techniques have been investigated for tabletops. In such applications, only one user has the right to work with an object. To grant access for other users, the object must be passed on. Four different hand-over strategies have been explored with the release, relocate, resize, and reorient techniques [131]. All four techniques suffer from the strong dependency of the hand-over action on the user currently owning the object. Without the action initiated by the owner, the object is not accessible for the group. This workflow is considerably disturbing fluid interaction. As Scott's studies on territoriality in collaborative tabletop workspaces suggest, the management of data on the table leads to the effect of partitioning in the user's personal space [140]. This observation has influenced the implementation of separated workspaces for digital tabletops. DiamondSpin, for example, allows for the creation of *personal* and *public spaces* that are visually demarcated in the application. But Scott also revealed that visible boundaries of the workspace might have a negative effect on the territorial behavior on a tabletop.

With a single large display that is visible to all users in the room, a lack of privacy exists. There are possibilities to arrange the space of the surface in a way that each user has at least a visual boundary of his workplace [101] [140]. But there are only a few prototypes that allow for real privacy. The *LumiSight* table uses orientation dependent views on the surface, for example [96]. On the other hand there is a natural constraint to work in the proximity space of another user. This is supported by the work of Scott [140] who noticed that users avoid reaching into the personal space of others.

Front-projected tabletop systems suffer from shadow and occlusion problems once a user reaches with his hand over the surface. But interestingly, the assumed problems are not affirmed in practical tests. Ashdown observed with the *Escritoire* setup [6] that shadow and occlusion problems turn out to have less effect than expected. This is due to the fact that people are used to cast shadows in illuminated rooms. They are not surprised if the same happens while interacting with a front-projected table. Moreover, if they occlude information on the surface with their hands, it is again a familiar effect that also appears with physical objects.

When building a table for collaborative work, the physical size is of course

2. Related Work

an important factor. The size of the table is related to the size of the group that is expected to use the table for their work. Ryall et al. [137] conducted an interesting experiment that gives valuable insights about the correlation of table and group sizes. They identified three main effects: first, the table size had no effect on the speed a task could be completed. Second, the group size effected collaboration; smaller groups collaborated more strongly than larger groups. Finally, they noticed that other users respected personal spaces so that they did not reach into their proximity. This is in tune with the findings reported from Scott [140].

2.3.2 Comparing Horizontal and Vertical Surfaces

Due to the different physical orientation of horizontal and vertical surfaces, the user's perception of the workspace will vary. Hence the design parameters from digital tabletops cannot be directly applied to wall displays.

Rogers and Lindley [134] report about the effect of physical affordances of an interactive workspace on the social interactions and collaborations. On the tabletop, they observed that users would switch more roles, explore more ideas and have a stronger perception of the other user's actions. In contrast, horizontal displays tend to disturb the collaboration aspect in groups as the physical distance between the person at the whiteboard and the rest of the group becomes larger.

Through the changes in collaboration between horizontal and vertical displays, the role of the users during a work session is altered. The fluid role changing that Rogers and Lindley [134] observed on tabletops changed to a "one person as presenter" situation when they used a digital whiteboard. The same behavior of one person taking the lead and the others stepping back was noticed by Russel et al. [135]. Since most interactive whiteboard solutions are still designed for single person usage, turn taking is required in these environments. But looking at the way people work with traditional whiteboards [162] suggests that this turn-taking behavior would not change even if the technology would support multi-user interaction. This is again in tune with the findings of Rogers and Lindley [134] who observed that

2. Related Work

it is generally difficult to notice what other people are doing at the wall without stepping back. Moreover, people felt uncomfortable working too close together at the wall display.

A vertical display is well suited for presentation tasks as all viewers have the same view on the displays. In contrast to a tabletop setup, there are no rotational problems with a vertical display. Although the exact task will depend on the context of the work group, there is a tendency towards using the digital whiteboard for displaying information that is relevant for everyone in the room. This is coherent with the role of a single person taking control over the display instead of multiple persons working simultaneously. This person is normally the presenter, which is also communicated through his standing position in contrast to the sitting position of the users at the table. If the whiteboard is used in a creative task together with an interactive table, Rogers and Lindley [134] noticed that the connection of the person at the whiteboard to the table group was disturbed. The whiteboard requires the user to turn his back at the others while his body occludes parts of the display, making it harder to follow his actions. To re-establish the connection to the group, a specific effort was necessary. In a presentation situation, this might be less of a problem, because everyone is paying attention to the presenter instead of working on a different task simultaneously.

Aspects about the design of a digital whiteboard are described by Guimbretière [53] in his work about large interactive walls. He reports that they faced three major challenges when building a wall for brainstorming sessions: First they had to find a command mechanism that allows for working with the wall with a minimum distraction from the task. Moreover, they describe the need for a novel space management to support creative sessions without the limitations of a conventional analogue whiteboard. And finally, a digital whiteboard will only be accepted when the latency is minimized and the user can experience fluid interaction.

For the user interface of vertical surfaces, traditional WIMP designs

2. Related Work

known from desktop systems have been ported. Products like the SMART-Board[20], for example, offer WIMP style applications for their digital whiteboard. Although rotation is not an issue for a vertical display, the placement of UI elements is a key factor for the design. Unfortunately, the commercial software solutions for interactive whiteboards are following a too traditional WIMP implementation, which leads to obvious problems on large surfaces. The top located task bar, for example, is hard to reach on a SMARTBoard, and for smaller persons it may be even impossible to reach.

2.4 Summary and Open Research Issues

This Chapter 2 aims to provide an overview of existing technologies that can be used to build an interactive room that supports activities in a meeting and brainstorming context. It was first shown that related digital surface technologies have been explored in a variety of research projects that either dealt with digital tabletops or digital wall displays.

2.4.1 Digital Surface Technologies

The combination of these technologies in a single room has been demonstrated by only a few prototypes that were restricted by the technical limitations of their time. The approach presented in this dissertation is to use state-of-the-art technology to create a multi-display space for collaboration. This process involves the selection of enabling technologies that facilitate the exploration of novel interaction paradigms. The solutions for large digital surfaces that are presented in this thesis build on the related work presented in Section 2.1. Our approach focuses on the affordances of horizontal and vertical surfaces in a combined setup and the influence on group activities. The contributions of our work in this area are:

Novel technical solutions for digital surfaces. We introduce a new digital tabletop solution that can be integrated into a real-world environment (Section 4.2). Through the modification of existing tables, we are

---

[20]http://www2.smarttech.com/st/de-DE/Products/SMART+Boards/

2. Related Work

able to support traditional workspaces with the extension of digital systems that can be used on demand. The same technology is applicable for vertical surfaces such as digital whiteboards.

High accurate and scalable tracking. With the adaption of Anoto technology for large surfaces, we present a new approach for turning traditional surfaces into user interfaces (see Section 4.2.3). The described development provides precise enough input data for capturing handwriting. Moreover, the solution is scalable without the disadvantage of decreasing resolution. We show different possibilities of using this technology for designing tabletops, digital walls, tangible palettes (Section 4.2) and paper interfaces (Section 5.3.2).

Applications supporting multi-user multi-surface setups. We present a software framework that enables the integration of new devices into a multi-surface enhanced environment (Section 5.6). To allow collaboration within this environment, the framework supports simultaneous input from multiple co-located users. Built upon this framework, we show a prototype application that supports meeting activities.

2.4.2 Interaction with Digital Surfaces

The interaction with the digital surfaces was further discussed in this chapter including pen-based input, direct touch and bimanual work practices. Instead of using these input technologies in isolated solutions, we argue for a combination of adequate input devices. Considering the strengths of each input technology, the goal is to explore the benefits of a combined scenario within the interactive room context. We complement the related work in this field through the following contributions:

Multi-surface setups with user identification. Based on our hardware developments for digital surfaces, we present a scenario that supports multi-user pen interaction with the identification of each user. The solution is not restricted to a single surface but can be used across the entire room (Section 4.2).

2. Related Work

Pen and touch combinations. We introduce different attempts to combine the digital pen technology with direct touch-based input. Our solutions include new Anoto and DiamondTouch, Anoto and shadow tracking and Anoto and FTIR combinations (Section 5.2.2). We further present a set of design principles intended to guide developers of bimanual user interfaces in Section 5.3.1.

Comparisons of workspace concepts for digital surfaces. With our interactive room application development, we show two different approaches to manage a collaborative workspace. One implementation is based on separated personal workspaces (Section 4.4) while the other builds on a common shared space concept (Section 5.4).

Novel user interface designs. Since the interaction with large direct digital surfaces is strongly influenced by physical restrictions, we introduce a new menu design for tabletops (Section 5.4.2). The key design criteria are to avoid occlusions created by the user's hand and to adapt the menu placement to the user's handedness and position on the tabletop. We present an adaptive menu placement method based on direct touch and pen tracking that allows correct menu placement around the table. As an extension, we propose adding a gesture input area for fast interaction which can be partly occluded by the user's hand.

2.4.3 Integration of Paper

The objective of our work is to build on the experiences that have been published about the technologies and interaction with digital surfaces. From these findings we intend to derive the features for the design of a space that combines a digital tabletop and several digital walls for collaborative work sessions. The connection between the table and the wall displays should be achieved through tangible objects that afford the interaction with these surfaces. As finally discussed in this chapter, paper can be used as a special interface in digital environments. Related solutions build on different hardware technologies and show a variety of application domains. Our concept

2. Related Work

involves the integration of paper with two main purposes: Firstly, to support the unobstructed interaction with the system which is possible through the inherent quality of paper. Secondly, to facilitate the surrounding activities of the work sessions, like note taking in advance and after the session. The contributions described in this thesis include:

Bridging the Gap Between Paper and Digital. Finally, we present a new paper-based interaction device which enables a seamless usage of a digital pen for manipulating real printouts and for controlling a digital whiteboard. Based on this concept, we show new interaction techniques including *Pick-And-Drop*, *Sketch-and-Send* and *Present-and-Interact* in Section 5.3.2.

Conceptual Framework

In the previous chapter we analyzed technologies that can be used as components in interactive rooms. Since the aim of this dissertation is to explore the design space and the fundamental interaction paradigms within collaborative interactive spaces, the scope of our work goes beyond the simple combination of related technologies. Consequently, this chapter defines a selection of design parameters that guide the development of an interactive room. In order to gain a better understanding of the requirements and potentials for interactive workspaces that arise from real meeting situations, we carried out an exploratory field study at a big Austrian steel company. The field study has been focused on the collaborative interactions between the participants and how these are mediated by the documents and tools used as well as the physical setup of the meeting room itself. The field study included six meetings and workshops of the company's IT-service division with internal and external customers. The meetings took between 1 and 3 hours and covered topics such as business process modeling, requirements specification, evaluation of mock-ups, and project coordination. Both participants and locations varied across the meetings. The data collection included the notes taken manually during non-participant observation in the meetings as well as qualitative interviews with the chairs before and after the meetings. In order to structure the data collection and allow for comparison across the meetings a self-devised protocol was used. The protocol draws on cultural-historical activity theory and provides a set of questions aimed to identify

3. Conceptual Framework

(1) core activities addressed in the meeting, (2) relevant stakeholders and communities as well as (3) actors involved, (4) rules and values guiding the interaction, (5) specific actions performed, (6) the artifacts and tools used, (7) physical properties of the meeting venue as well as (8) problems and breakdowns occurring in the meeting. Based on the data collected, a set of preliminary design challenges was formulated. Afterwards the outcomes were validated against the judgment of the meeting chairs as well as prior research on synchronous collaboration. The following sections provide a synopsis of the design parameters for a new collaborative interactive space concept that emerged from our analysis.

The discussion should motivate the design decisions we made for our prototype implementation as well as provide a guideline for similar projects. Section 3.1 describes design parameters that frame the concept of an interactive space. Based on that, Section 3.2 explores differences and specific requirements for horizontal and vertical surfaces.

3.1 Collaborative Space Design Parameters

The design of an interactive space involves considerations about the affordances of its components, the accommodated tasks as well as the overarching activities. This section presents a selection of design parameters that aim at assisting the development of such spaces.

3.1.1 Multiplicity and Heterogeneity of Tasks

Even though workshops and meetings are usually focused on a limited set of topics, they regularly encompass a multiplicity of heterogeneous tasks. For example, one and the same session might entail phases of presenting, brainstorming, decision-making, collaborative modeling, and planning. As each of these tasks requires different types of collaborative behavior, a meeting room has to be adaptable according to the changing needs. While during a presentation it might be useful that the presenter can guide the participants through a set of documents, other tasks such as collaborative modeling might

3. Conceptual Framework

require active contribution to the development of a shared artifact by all participants. The change from one task to another often occurs spontaneously based on the situational demands emerging in the meeting. Consequently, interactive spaces for meetings and workshops have to account for the diversity of tasks at hand. During a meeting, the participants share data across a variety of media and with different interaction styles. Documents in the form of paper notes, flip charts and digital documents are shared through different means. For example, physical artifacts are directly shared through copies that are handed to each participant, whereas digital sharing often happens via e-mail or portable storage media. However, the processes involved with sharing artifacts are cumbersome. For traditional paper documents, copies must be prepared or produced during the meetings which distracts from the main task. With digital documents, current systems barely support the simultaneous viewing and editing of data in combination with mechanisms for fluid exchange of results. Moreover, security issues often hinder a seamless exchange of data in a shared environment. As a consequence, the design of a collaborative work space has to aim at simplifying the integration and exchange of media. Moreover, there is a need for seamless mechanisms that allow to control the space as well as the access of data within the space. Furthermore, it has to be possible to switch between different tasks and to save the current system status to come back to a task later on.

3.1.2 Fostering the Creation of Shared Documents

Shared documents play a fundamental role in collaborative working environments as they foster the creation of a shared understanding, support the coordination of activities and provide a shared memory for the group. The creation of shared documents also fosters the objectification of thoughts and ideas, a process highly relevant for creative and constructional tasks. However, one of the main obstacles of current collaborative work systems is that the technical tools are cumbersome and hinder collaboration and engagement rather than enhancing it. Thus, meetings are often based on traditional paper documents in order to avoid these obstacles. This is in contrast to the fact

3. Conceptual Framework

that the content in the background is increasingly digital. Hence a collaborative space requires the collective access, manipulation and storage of digital media so that a seamless integration into a meeting is guaranteed. In order to foster the joint creation of documents, concurrent document manipulation should be enabled and documents should be readable by all attendees simultaneously.

3.1.3 Integration of Individual and Shared Spaces

Most collaborative tasks also include subtasks to be carried out by the different participants in parallel. Accordingly, all participants have to have access not only to a shared but also to an individual workspace where they can retrieve, create and store their own documents. In order to integrate individual and collective activities, a smooth transition between individual and shared spaces has to be ensured. Along with this requirement, the integrity of the personal workspace must be ensured. For example, the notes taken in a personal space might not be intended for the eyes of the other participants. Current meeting situations are often limited by either supporting a shared view for all participants (normally through a presentation display) or allowing each participant to create a personal space (generally through a mobile computer for each person). However, in both cases social interactions and fluid exchange of data are not well supported. Moreover, the transition from personal to shared space is hardly supported or too cumbersome to be effectively integrated into the workflow. Thus, a collaborative meeting environment must provide concepts that allow for the creation of shared and personal spaces and the fluid transition between them. Moreover, the use of multiple documents in a shared space requires to support natural pointing gestures and direct manipulation of objects in order to prevent misunderstandings.

3.1.4 Multiple and Interrelated Documents

The set of documents used in professional workshops and meetings are often quite extensive and heterogeneous in nature. For example, software mockups, requirements specifications and business process models might be used in parallel. In addition, these documents are often highly interrelated and relevant information is often spread across the various resources. Therefore, it is important to provide interfaces that allow to access these documents for further use within the collaborative space. Since documents exist in various different file formats, directly importing them into another application first requires the development of appropriate interfaces. However, due to the diversity of existing formats, this can be a challenging task. Furthermore, the use of multiple and interrelated documents requires interaction metaphors that allow for easy navigation across documents, a feature that assumes the knowledge about the structure of the document.

3.1.5 Multi-Modal Input and Task Assignment

In a collaborative environment that takes advantage of several display and input technologies, the natural affordances of each device have a strong influence on the division of activities during a meeting. For example, different tasks will be carried out on surfaces that allow for concurrent input in comparison to single user systems. Moreover, the social context may have an influence on the choice of an input device for a certain task. For instance, writing on a surface can be accomplished in different ways: either with a pen, using a finger or with other devices. However, writing with a finger will not be appropriate during a business meeting where the social context requires a more formal behavior. Moreover, the capabilities of the interactive space will have an implication on the assignment of tasks. While a table is suitable for collaborative work with a high degree of group interaction, a wall display is more likely used for presentations in front of a group. Therefore, a collaborative space must provide support for the natural activities that are anticipated by its components.

3. Conceptual Framework

3.1.6 Consistency of Input Devices

Once an interactive space includes several digital surfaces that allow for multi-modal input, it is important to avoid frequent switching of input devices. If the available input devices are not used consistently, people will be confused and distracted from their activities. Switching between a variety of different devices distracts the natural workflow because the attention is focused on the handling of the devices instead of the process itself. Moreover, in more complex setups that include several input devices, searching for the right device may cause additional performance penalties. One key factor for the successful integration of input devices into an interactive room is the support of fluid interactions. A common approach is to associate different input devices with different activities, like wireless keyboards for text input and pointing devices for selecting and manipulating digital objects. Ideally, a consistent integration of devices with a minimum of necessary switches is desired.

3.1.7 Visibility and Transparency of Actions

During collaborative tasks, people tend to monitor the activities occurring in the group. On the one hand, this monitoring behavior is important to create awareness about the personal space that is available in the collaborative room. This personal space, which is demarcated from the group space, is used for private activities. On the other hand, the awareness about the activities of the group is an essential parameter for successful collaboration. In order to be able to monitor these activities, they have to be visible and transparent. Visibility is necessary to recognize an action, while transparency informs about the nature of an action and the used resources. For example, in a meeting where each participant uses a laptop, the visibility might still be guaranteed because one can see and hear if another person currently writes on his laptop. But the transparency is not provided, since it is not obvious what kind of action the person performs on the laptop (unless one can directly see the screen). Especially in scenarios with limited resources that have to be shared in a group, the awareness is increasingly important. Therefore,

3. Conceptual Framework

a successful collaborative system that should enhance workflows requires a high degree of visibility and transparency.

3.1.8 Integration into Overarching Activities

Meetings and workshops usually do not constitute an end in itself, but are part of more overarching activities such as project work, or other ongoing work processes. Hence, it is important that meeting attendees can easily access previous information and store the results of the meeting for further processing. The access to one's own information is especially relevant when different organizations are attending a meeting. Moreover, it should be possible to access data from meetings without being connected to the interactive room. Most activities in the periphery of a meeting will be performed on traditional desktop computer systems. Hence, it is required to provide access to the meeting content via these interfaces.

3.2 Considerations for Horizontal and Vertical Displays

To complement the selection of design parameters for a collaborative space, this section presents essential parameters dealing with the differences between horizontal and vertical surfaces.

3.2.1 Surface Size and Group Size

The size of a digital surface has a direct implication on how it will be used within a collaborative space. For example, 1×1m large tabletop suggests that a group of two people can comfortable work on it, whereas it will be too small for six people. Depending on the task assignment, a vertical display may be rather used for presentations than for collaborative work. In this case, a smaller size of the surface is appropriate. However, as mentioned in the previous design parameters, tasks in the collaborative space will change over the course of a meeting. Hence, an interactive digital whiteboard should

3. Conceptual Framework

not only offer a single user presentation surface but also support group activities. Moreover, the heterogeneity of tasks complicates the design of digital surfaces. For example, in a loosely-coupled collaborative task, more space for personal territories will be required compared to tasks that require tight cooperation. If the size of a surface is too small for a task, frequent reordering and partitioning of the personal space will happen. On the other hand, if the provided space is too large, people will be disengaged from the group. For both types of surfaces, horizontal and vertical, the size is in direct correlation with the number of users. Therefore, an approximate number of people that should be supported is helpful for the successful design of the space.

3.2.2 Offering Custom Functionality

Similar to traditional tables, a digital tabletop affords activities that are not directly related to the digital workspace. For example, people tend to place objects such as paper documents, laptops or coffee mugs on the surface. Hence an appropriate space concept must include areas that can be used for storing additional items. This can be considered in the design in two different ways: either by providing peripheral space that is not used for the primary digital workspace or by allowing to place artifacts directly on the digital surface. The first solution requires to add additional space to the table's surface that should be in reach for all users. This requirement may additionally complicate the design of the table. For the second solution, the table's surface must be stable enough to allow for placing objects on it. Moreover, objects on the surface should not interfere with the input mechanisms of the system. Another consideration when placing objects directly on the digital surface concerns the interference with the display. For front-projected systems, the projection is still visible, although it will be distorted by the objects on the table. With rear-projected setups, objects on the surface occlude the displayed content in this area. However, an additional scenario would allow to turn the digital workspace off and use the tabletop like a traditional table. The design of vertical surfaces is less complicated since people will not expect to place objects on the surface due to its orientation.

3.2.3 Arranging Content within Reach

Designing applications for large interactive surfaces is challenging since traditional WIMP concepts do not automatically apply. For a system that accommodates different display sizes, a key design criterion is to place content in the user's reachability. In contrast to desktop applications, large surfaces that are controlled through direct input devices require a different design of the screen space. In a collaborative space, factors such as varying group sizes, seating arrangements or task activities have an influence on the spatial layout of content. The goal is to ensure that the necessary content is in reach of the user. This requirement is the same for digital tabletops as well as digital walls.

3.2.4 Accounting for Different Orientations

Horizontal surfaces that allow the users to arrange their seats around the table create another problem; in addition to the challenge of placing content in the vicinity of the user, the orientation might be wrong seen from the opposite side of the table. To account for rotational issues, content should be transformable in order to correct the orientation on demand. Considering a rectangular table shape, four orientations towards the according edges of the table might be sufficient. In more specialized setups, continuous rotations might be preferable. For the design of interface elements, the goal is to design controls that are either rotation invariant (radial menus with according icons, for example) or that adapt their orientation in relation to the user. In contrast to horizontal surfaces, vertical displays are not concerned by rotational issues since the display's orientation is similar to traditional desktop screens. Nevertheless, directly porting WIMP interfaces to a digital wall should be avoided. As mentioned in the previous design parameter, different layout requirements for large vertical screens are imposed due to the size and input mechanism of the display.

Interactive Meeting Room Prototype

This chapter presents our development of an interactive meeting room that includes multiple digital surfaces. The contribution of this chapter includes a detailed description of the room's actual realization and the considerations that influenced it. Furthermore, we present achievements in the development of large interactive surfaces based on Anoto tracking technology and a meeting room application that facilitates typical meeting activities through interactive tabletops and wall displays. This chapter is also intended to provide an example for developers of similar real world setups.

Our development process was based on an initial survey of current meeting practices, followed by a requirements analysis and the actual implementation of a prototype. We then evaluated the prototype system and identified improvements for a redesign that is described in Chapter 5. The organization of this chapter is according to this development process. We begin in Section 4.1 by detailing a survey of current meeting practices in a partner company. A set of design parameters that we formulated based on the results of this survey can be found in Chapter 3. The aim of Section 4.1 is to provide more details about the activities that we observed during the meetings and the related artifacts and tools in order to motivate the implementation of our proposed solution. In Section 4.2, we describe the underlying hardware components, particularly the construction of a tabletop and whiteboard based on Anoto digital pen technology. Along with this description, we provide details about Anoto technology that can be used for future projects in the domain

4. Interactive Meeting Room Prototype

of large interactive surfaces. Based on the hardware description, we explore the interaction with our room prototype in Section 4.3. In Section 4.4, we present a solution for designing the digital workspace and the according user menus in the interactive room. Furthermore, we describe how typical meeting activities are facilitated through the interactive room in Section 4.5. Finally, we discuss the results of an evaluation that we carried out to identify areas of improvement; these points serve as input for the redesign that is described in Chapter 5.

4.1 Meeting Activity Survey

Interactive rooms incorporate different digital surfaces such as tabletops, digital walls and portable devices in a single space to facilitate work processes [155] [65]. However, no single design of such a room and its applications can fulfill the requirements of a wide-range of likely activities. For example, a workspace for presentations and customer meetings will pose different demands on the system than a creative brainstorming session. Considerations about the room design must involve various situation specific facets such as work group size, group characteristics, required tools or media used during the meeting. To meet the numerous and changing requirements of an interactive room, defining use cases can help specify the activities that should be supported. For our first prototype setup, we decided to support meeting scenarios in an office context. This scenario includes three main activities: presenting, brainstorming and summarizing results.

Our first step in developing an interactive room that supports meetings through digital surfaces was to gain more insights into the activities we aimed to support. Toward that end, we observed several meetings in our partner company Voestalpine as described in Chapter 3. The sessions included not only meetings with outside customers, but also internal company meetings. The most typical meeting contained four people, and the largest meeting we observed involved six people. Many of our observations confirmed our and other understanding of current work practices; however, the implications of these practices on our interactive room concept is important. The goal of

4. Interactive Meeting Room Prototype

our prototype is to support these practices and to provide a single combined solution to the numerous activities. Details about the survey and a collection of derived design parameters can be found in Chapter 3. In the following sections, we present additional meeting practices that we observed during the survey and an abstraction towards requirements for our interactive room implementation.

Meeting procedure. The general procedure of a meeting typically starts with a customer or group leader presenting a contextual overview. This overview is followed by a discussion that is based on this initial presentation and often involves a brainstorming session. The presentation can serve as an agenda for the meeting, which requires a schedule to be visible all the time during the meeting. During the discussion portion of the meeting, different kinds of media are used, most commonly paper printouts and context specific data from the company's content management system. At the end of the meeting, agreements are summarized and new appointments are arranged.

Sharing and hand-over of control devices. Interruptions to the meeting occur when the control device (in most cases the mouse) is shared among several users. Since there is only a single control device for the presentation computer, hand-over and turn taking strategies must be adopted by the group. We observed that these strategies were hampered by physical restrictions of the workplace, such as short cables. Additionally, the presenter frequently exhibited a controlling behavior, often keeping control of the input device instead of sharing it with the group.

Flipchart handling. Flipcharts are an essential tool in meetings, and are used throughout the whole process. However, interaction with a flip chart is far from ideal. As only one page is visible at a time, flipping back and forth through the pages is a common practice. The large pages make this navigation cumbersome, and quickly switching pages is difficult. To extend the functionality of the flip chart, pages are ripped off and pinned to the wall; however, the rearrangement of the pages on the wall is difficult. During a meeting, it is sometimes necessary to access previous flip charts, which are in most cases not available. At the end of a meeting, the single pages of the flip chart are captured with a digital camera to preserve them, adding an extra step. This practice also enables the electronic sharing of the pages via email or the insertion of the pages into the meetings notes.

Paper and digital documents. Paper is still very important for meetings. Documents that are digitally available are often used in form of printouts during the meetings. The digital documents are projected on the wall, while the paper printout is used to make annotations. This leads to a gap between paper and digital documents. Furthermore, paper has a special importance for contracts and signatures.

Single copy document. If there is only a single printout of a document, the discrepancy between the digital source and the printout is minimized. All changes are annotated on the same document, which solves the problem of different meanings of a note. Despite these benefits, the use of a single document hampers the group's interaction with and the view of the document. This results in a permanent rearrangement of the document on the table. Especially small and large documents are cumbersome to use.

Multiple copy document. Multiple copies of the same document enable all users to have the ideal view of the document. Moreover, there is no interference if more than one attendee wants to work on the document. However, multiple copies lead to consistency problems. Since each person works on their own copy, annotations are not automatically synchronized. Groups need to take additional care to ensure that each attendee works on the same page of a document. Presentations change from "all look at the same page" to "everyone looks at his copy". At the end of a meeting, annotations must be merged to guarantee that no information is lost.

4. Interactive Meeting Room Prototype

Private notes. Note taking is an integral part of meetings. Public notes are often written in a protocol style that is later shared among the participants of the meeting. In contrast, private notes are not meant for the group, the view should be restricted to the author. This requires some kind of private space for note taking that has a limited view for the group. This is especially true in customer business meetings, during which confidential notes are required.

The results of the observation should provide an understanding of traditional meeting practices and the involved activities. It is noticeable that potential distractions to communication and engagement in meetings are caused by the inadequacy of the tools and the meeting environment. Consequently, the knowledge about these shortcomings can be used to design a space that better supports meeting practices. In the following, we are going to discuss the results of the activity survey in consideration of the design parameters from Chapter 3. Based on that discussion, we define requirements for the interactive room.

The typical meeting procedure that we observed involved an initial presentation, followed by a group discussion with occasional brainstormings and a final summary of the agreements. These parts of a meetings are quite diverse and demand for different capabilities of a meeting room and tools. The design parameter in Section 3.1.1 (Multiplicity and Heterogeneity of Tasks) encompasses them and emphasizes the fact that the change from one task to another often occurs spontaneously.

Requirement 1: Support of common meeting activities including the presentation of content, brainstorming ideas and summarizing results.

During a meeting, the control device was shared among users which led to interruptions and turn-taking strategies. The introduction of multiple input capabilities for the interactive room addresses this problem. However, the suitability of a device for a specific task (Section 3.1.5) and the consistency of input devices (Section 3.1.6) must be considered.

Requirement 2: Input facilities for all users along with a shared view on information and collaborative editing functionality.

4. Interactive Meeting Room Prototype

The handling of the flipchart revealed several shortcomings that are caused by the tool's physical restrictions. In addition to the difficulties of flipping through the pages, the content created on a flipchart is cumbersome to transfer to digital applications. The same applies to any analogue input such as notes on paper or annotations on a design printout.

Requirement 3: Digitizing user generated content for further usage in the room.

Documents in meetings are often printed in advance and handed out to each participant. This creates a media gap between traditional paper and digital documents. Moreover, the discrepancy between using a single copy and multiple copies of a paper documents has an effect on the persistence of annotations and the group interaction.

Requirement 4: Bridging the gap between analogue and digital media.

By simply providing digital documents, the problem is not entirely solved because issues like orientation (Section 3.2.4) or reachability (Section 3.2.4) have to be considered. In addition, documents used in meetings are often heterogeneous in nature (Section 3.1.4) which requires appropriate exchange interfaces.

Requirement 5: Interfaces for data exchange (import/export) with external sources.

Depending on the current task, persons of a group work either collaboratively or individually during a meeting. This yields for the creation of territories that support private and public areas. As described in Section 3.1.3, individual and shared workspaces facilitate this need.

Requirement 6: Workspaces that provide public and private areas.

Considering these six requirements, we present our concept of an interactive meeting room. The proposed setup in the following section shows one possibility for building such a room. Alternative hardware solutions are possible, and will be discussed in Section 5.2.

4.2 Hardware

The development of our interactive space concept involved extensive tests with different hardware components. We aimed at building on experiences that related research already made in this area (see Section 2.1.3). However, we noticed that existing hardware solutions are often limiting the users in a way that real world scenarios cannot be realized. In respect to the six previously identified requirements for a collaborative interactive space, we chose a two step approach to create our system: If feasible, we applied existing technologies. Otherwise, we explored possibilities to develop new technological solutions for our needs. In this sense, we focused on possibilities to extend existing furniture with interactivity. One of our achievements in this area was the development of large interactive surfaces based on Anoto tracking technology. In Section 4.2.2, we describe the enabling base technology. In the following Section 4.2.3, we show how this technology can be used to develop large interactive surfaces.

4.2.1 Interactive Surfaces

According to the equipment that is commonly used in meeting rooms, we chose to include the following components in our interactive room:

- A digital tabletop,
- a digital whiteboard and
- a presentation display.

The digital tabletop is used because every traditional meeting room is equipped with a table. Commonly, group activities are centered around the table, thus the size of the table has to fit the size of the meeting group. In addition to using the table as a workspace, items such as coffee cups, mobile phones or notebooks are often stored on the table's surface. Moreover, a meeting room traditionally offers a presentation display, often complemented by a flipchart. While the presentation display facilitates showing content (e.g.

4. Interactive Meeting Room Prototype

at the beginning of a meeting), the flipchart is used to create content during the meeting that can be summarized for a final presentation. In order to provide both devices, we decided to equip our interactive meeting room with a presentation display and an additional digital whitboard. The presentation display is basically identical to a traditional version that uses a projector for showing content. In addition, our presentation display is linked to the other components in the room that allows accessing the current presentation from the tabletop or the whiteboard. The digital whiteboard in our interactive room replaces the traditional flipchart.

Figure 4.1: The interactive room consisting of a digital tabletop, a digital whiteboard and a presentation display.

The digital whiteboard is installed as a replacement for the traditional paper flip chart. The activities that are assigned to the digital whiteboard include presenting and brainstorming. Our digital whiteboard implementation targets the Requirement 1 through the support for these two activities and Requirement 3 through the digital surface. For the projection we used a mirror setup that allows to rear-project the whiteboard. The interaction with

4. Interactive Meeting Room Prototype

the whiteboard is based on a Mimio[1] ultrasonic tracking device. Mounted on the left side of the whiteboard, it can capture input across the 112cm × 84 cm surface.

The central element of the interactive room is the digital tabletop (cf. Figure 4.1). For the interactive table in our room concept, features of a traditional table should be available along with modifications that allow for an interaction with digital data. The following specifications describe the table's properties:

- A large surface that allows for the viewing of digital information but also can be used as a traditional table surface
- Space for four to six users
- Multi-user input on the surface
- Accurate input that allows for basic handwriting and sketching
- Identification of the user
- Integration of tangible objects

There are basically two different display-based hardware solutions that can be used to build an interactive table: a front projected or a rear-projected setup. LCD or plasma screen-based solutions as used by Streitz et al. for the InteracTable [155] were not relevant in our case, because they were too limiting in size and shape factors. Compared to a front-projected solution, rear-projected setups typically require a more complex hardware setup. For example, the projector must be placed beneath the surface which requires additional space. Moreover, the projection surface must be appropriate for rear-projection while guaranteeing enough stability (since there is no table construction under the projection layer that helps to stabilize the surface). These considerations led us to the design of a front-projected setup for our first interactive table. The decision is also targeting the first two points of the previously mentioned table's properties list: featuring a table that allows

---

[1] http://www.mimio.com

4. Interactive Meeting Room Prototype

for the use as a digital input surface and as a traditional table which offers space for four to six users.

Through additional feedback from our company partner, we identified another important feature that the table design had to address. As the domain was focused on meetings, people would sit most of the time around the table, with occasionally exceptions when someone walks to the whiteboard or joins the side of another person. For a sitting position, however, appropriate space for the feet under the table is very important, as staying in an awkward position at the table for an extended period of time has a negative effect on the user's comfort. These ergonomic issues are supported by a front projected setup, but they are hard to satisfy with a rear-projected setup if users should be able to sit around the table.

The interactive room development was supported by the furniture company Team7 with two objectives: modifying existing furniture to allow interactivity with digital content and designing custom furniture tailored to the needs of a distinct setup. This collaboration enabled us to experiment with different possibilities for the interactive table, leading to a first prototype in form of a 175cm × 90cm table that could be further extended to a 250cm long surface. The characteristics of this table were chosen based on the requirements that we presented in the previous section. In particular, we addressed Requirement 1 by providing a tabletop that allows for creation of content, Requirement 2 by facilitating multiple users and a shared view on information, Requirement 3 through digitizing user generated content and Requirement 6 in form of public and private areas on the surface. For this purpose, we modified the table to support projections onto the surface through a front-projected setup. In order to allow users to interact with the table, we extended the surface with a high accurate input solution based on digital pens. In the following section, we discuss the details of this technology and the possibilities for applying it to different surfaces.

4. Interactive Meeting Room Prototype

4.2.2 Anoto Digital Pen Technology

The digital pens from Anoto are suitable input devices for interactive environments in all respects. Since they have been designed for digitally capturing notes on real paper, they can be used to bridge the gap between traditional paper and the digital world. Moreover, the pens allow to stream the data in realtime to a connected computer. This feature makes the Anoto pens applicable input devices for controlling interactive surfaces. As mentioned in Section 2.2.1, the pen includes a small infrared (IR) camera to track the region near its tip. An additional IR-LED illuminates the area for the camera. In order to derive its position on the surface, the camera captures a unique high-resolution dot pattern. The position is coded into the structure of the dots in form of unique sequences. The small dots (100 μm in diameter) are arranged with a spacing of approximately 0.3 mm on a square grid. With slightly displacement from the grid, each dot is in one of four possible positions. To enable an accurate tracking result, the camera has to see at least an area of 6 × 6 dots. With the four possible displacements, 2^{72} unique combinations exist ($4^{6\times 6} = 4^{36} = 2^{72}$). Once the camera recognizes a valid pattern, the pen records the following data:

- Pen ID
- Page ID
- Pen Up/Down/Move Event
- Position (x,y)
- Timestamp
- Pressure intensity

If the pen model is capable of streaming data in realtime (Nokia (SU-1B), Logitech (io-2), and Anoto (PenIT)), the information can be directly processed by a connected device (computer or mobile device). In this mode, the pen streams the data via Bluetooth to the device. The alternative option

4. Interactive Meeting Room Prototype

is to store the data on the pen's internal memory in order to process it later. In this offline version, the pen has to synchronize with the computer either over Bluetooth or via the USB docking station. Both versions, the online streaming and the offline, can be applied in a multi-user setup. Theoretically, there is no limit to how many people interact simultaneously. However, only seven devices can be connected to a single standard Bluetooth receiver. By increasing the number of Bluetooth receivers, the maximum number of pens on one computer can be scaled. The pens are equipped with a force feedback module that creates vibrations. This feedback is used to notify about tracking errors and about special user interface elements called *magic boxes*. Once a user clicks on such a *magic box*, the pen vibrates several times in accordance to the function of the *magic box*.

In the following section, we are going to describe how the Anoto technology can be used to enable interactivity with different kinds of surfaces.

4.2.3 Anoto Tracking for Large Surfaces

One main advantage of the Anoto tracking technology is its scalability. Since the tracking relies on the dot pattern that is tracked by the integrated camera, conventional surfaces can be turned into interactive surfaces by overlaying them with the pattern. The pen's tracking accuracy is constant independently of the pattern size. This means that the pattern area can be scaled to large sizes without causing tracking resolution penalties. However, the development of such large patterns requires some knowledge about the technical specifications in order to ensure compatibility with the Anoto tracking system.

Real-Time Streaming vs. Offline Pattern

There exist two different versions of pattern: streaming and offline pattern. The streaming version enables the appropriate pen models to transfer the tracked data in realtime to a connection device. The offline version requires the user to click with the pen on a special *magic box* that triggers the data transfer from the pens internal storage to the connection device. Depending

4. Interactive Meeting Room Prototype

on the Anoto pattern, the pen either captures data in offline or streaming mode. This means that a streaming pattern cannot be used in offline mode and vice versa. For the development of interactive surfaces that support direct user feedback, the streaming pattern is suitable. For asynchronous note taking before or after a work session, the offline mode would be appropriate.

Pattern Sizes

The algorithm behind the Anoto pattern is capable of calculating a unique pattern area of 60 million km^2. The pattern is divided into smaller, identifiable parts called pattern pages. The *pages* are the smallest entity of a pattern. *Pages* are grouped into *books*, which are grouped into *shelves*, and each shelf belongs to a *segment*. In a *segment*, all *pages* have the same size, all *books* hold the same number of *pages*, and all *shelves* hold the same amount of *books*. Each page is identified by its page address that consists of four numbers: *segment.shelf.book.page*. A typical example for a page ID is 70.0.10.0.

The maximum available pattern size that the company Anoto delivers is A0 (841mm × 1189mm). Due to our requirement to equip a 175cm × 90cm table surface with the Anoto pattern, we experimented with the stitching of multiple pages. This procedure allows to create an arbitrarily large pattern area. However, this approach has some side effects. First, the pen shortly vibrates when it is moved from one page to another. This behavior cannot be changed, but in practical implementations we noticed that users hardly recognize this vibration feedback. Second, each change of the page results in a "Pen Up" event which initially prevents a continuous movement of the pen. Our implementation of the Anoto streaming driver is handling this restriction by suppressing this event. Finally, a stitched pattern requires a more complex calibration of the system, since each page is based on the same relative coordinate system. As a consequence, the coordinates derived from the dot pattern repeat across the stitched area several times. Therefore, our calibration algorithm accounts for this drawback by calculating the final position as a combination of page address and relative position on the page. The resulting coordinates are unique absolute values across the whole

4. Interactive Meeting Room Prototype

stitched area.

Printing the Pattern

The resolution quality requirement for printing the Anoto pattern is 600 dpi. A lower resolution would decrease the tracking performance. It is important that the ink used for printing the pattern has the correct spectral wavelength characteristics. Since the Anoto tracking relies on reading a black and white difference image, the printed pattern must appear black in the near IR spectrum of the camera. This means that the ink should absorb the wavelength band between 800-950 nm in order to appear as black color for the camera. A black toner containing carbon (black standard toners normally contain carbon) fulfills this requirement. For the paper, white or bright colors are suitable.

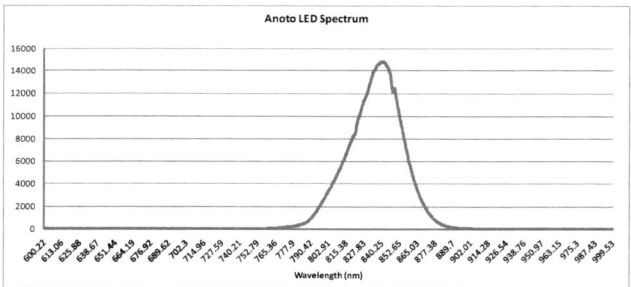

Figure 4.2: The infrared spectrum of the Anoto pen.

As the pattern has to appear with a high enough contrast on the background, the paper should have high reflection in the IR wavelengths between 800-950 nm (see Figure 4.2). However, glossy surfaces are not suitable, since they reflect too much IR light in a small spot with a strong falloff. For the camera the center of the spot appears white and the boundary very dark. Both effects interfere with the tracking, as the dot pattern is not visible in these areas.

4. Interactive Meeting Room Prototype

Advantages of Anoto Tracking for Large Surfaces

The advantages of using Anoto technology to enable interaction with surfaces are manifold. The accuracy of the tracking is independent of the surface's size. There is no difference between the resolution of an A5 and an A0 sized area, for example. The pen provides its ID with the data stream, thus a device identification is possible. This is an important feature especially for multi-user systems. The tracking technology creates stable and accurate results under varying light conditions. Moreover, the pattern can be cut into arbitrary shapes which makes the Anoto technology very versatile. Finally, a main advantage of Anoto tracking for large surfaces is the simplicity and flexibility of the setup. Since all technology is integrated into the pen, the surface only has to fulfill the quality requirements of the dot pattern. In contrast to other tracking solutions such as optical or capacitive tracking (see Section 2.2.2), the surface itself contains no technology with the Anoto solution.

4.2.4 Anoto Tracking for Mobile Controls

In 4.2.3 we presented our approaches to apply Anoto pen tracking to large front- and rear-projected surfaces. However, Anoto tracking offers another possibility for interaction with surfaces: mobile tangible palettes. Since any surface can be made interactive by simply overlaying it with the Anoto dot pattern, this technology is potentially suitable for mobile controls. The advantages of using Anoto pen tracking on mobile palettes are manifold:

- Palettes are lightweight (they are composed of paper and optional acrylic covers)

- Palettes do not need technology integrated into the object itself (all technology is in the pen)

- Flexibility of different shapes and graphic designs

- Cheap and fast to produce (if a design update is required, the new palette is simply printed)

4. Interactive Meeting Room Prototype

- No switching of devices required (the same pen works with the palette and the large digital Anoto surfaces)

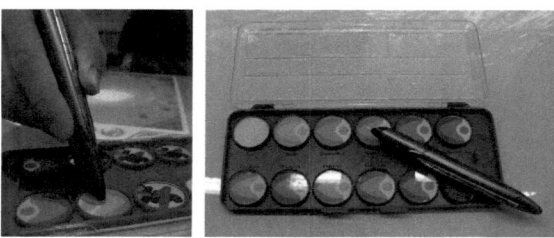

Figure 4.3: Examples of color palettes that are based on Anoto technology.

In contrast to digital surfaces based on Anoto tracking, tangible palettes must work without the visual feedback through projections onto the pattern. Therefore, we overlay the pattern with graphic designs as shown in Figure 4.5 that inform the user about the functionality of different areas on the palette (e.g. buttons). As described in Section 4.2.2, the tracking relies on the high resolution dot pattern that has to be printed in black ink on a IR-reflecting surface. For the IR-camera in the pen the dot pattern has to be readable through overlaid graphics, otherwise the tracking fails. To ensure that graphics on top of the pattern are transparent for the IR-camera, they must not be printed with black toner or other toners that interfere with the IR absorption range of the camera. Figure 4.4 (a) shows an example of color areas printed without black toner on top of the Anoto pattern. For the IR-camera, the color areas are transparent (Figure 4.4 (b)).

In order to protect the pattern from scratching, we explored different material combinations. The most robust solution is to use scratch resistant acrylic on top of the pattern. As mentioned in Section 4.2.3, a maximum thickness of 4mm should not be exceeded. To protect the backside of the pattern, we apply another layer of acrylic so that the pattern is clamped between the two acrylic plates. An alternative would to laminate the pattern print. This results in a slimmer and lighter construction.

4. Interactive Meeting Room Prototype

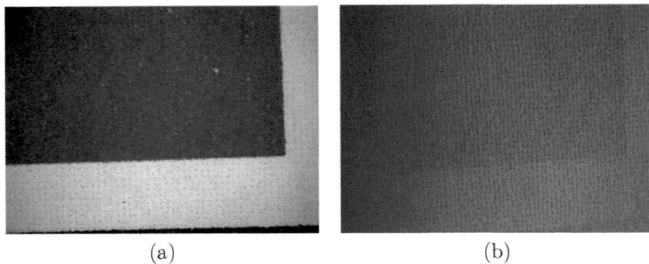

(a) (b)

Figure 4.4: Designs that are overlaid on top of the Anoto pattern must be printed without black toner (a). Graphics that are printed with CMY colors only do not interfere with the black dot pattern (b).

4.3 Interaction with the Room

In this section, we present our considerations about the interaction with the digital meeting room. For the first prototype, we used the six requirements that we presented in Section 4.1 for defining appropriate interaction techniques.

4.3.1 Interaction with Digital Pens and Palettes

For the design of the first interactive room, our research focused on digital pens as the primary input devices for the tabletop and the whiteboard. The tangible palettes that we presented in the previous section allow to change the properties of the digital pens. We note that for the first prototype the palettes could only be used on the table since the digital whiteboard used Mimio pens instead of Anoto pens. In the following, we are going to discuss some interaction related characteristics of tangible objects in digital room settings.

Previous studies suggest that tangible objects can enhance collaboration among groups, as the perception of the others' actions is naturally supported [133]. Although these studies have been based on tabletop setups, we thought

4. Interactive Meeting Room Prototype

Figure 4.5: Tangible palettes are used for changing pen properties such as color and stroke width.

of an extension to our interactive room concept. As demonstrated by Streitz et al. [155] in the i-Land project, tangible objects can also be used to transfer data between surfaces. They used wood blocks that could be recognized by every surface and linked data to the blocks. Consequently, they could transfer data through the physical placement of these blocks.

In our concept, we designed tangible palettes as control interfaces for the digital surfaces in the room. The functionalities assigned to the palettes are shortcuts for frequently used actions or tools that allow for a fluid interaction with the system. By defining the number of available palettes, different parameters of the collaboration can be influenced. First, if options are only available on a unique palette, a group has to share that object which again leads to stronger collaboration. Second, multiple palettes with the same function will require a distribution across the table or the whole room with respect to the screen estate and reachability. Compared to a digital menu, a hardware

4. Interactive Meeting Room Prototype

palette is a very natural control object. It can be easily accessed and also removed on demand. Moreover, the tangible aspect makes it easy to share and hand over. As explained in the hardware section, the palettes are based on the same Anoto technology that is integrated into the table's surface. The single color and stroke width areas of the palette include the Anoto pattern in the background of the printout. The overlaid graphics are the visible hint for the user to distinguish between different functions that are invoked by the area. There is no interference between these printed graphics and pen positioning. Figure 4.5 shows the two palettes for picking different colors and stroke widths on the tabletop.

4.3.2 Interaction with Digital Content

The diversity of materials that are used during meetings leads to a variety of problems. For example, annotations must be merged not to get lost, as discussed in the initial meeting activity survey (Section 4.1). Or documents that exist only in a single copy influence the collaboration in a group through limited view and access. Moreover, the combination of paper and digital documents creates a media gap. Different workarounds, such as taking digital photos of the results of brainstormings after meetings, have been established to address these problems. In our first prototype development, our approach was to create a digital environment that supports meeting activities to an extend that allows participants to exclusively work in the digital world without the need to switch to the analogue anymore.

4.4 Workspace and Menu Design

In the course of the interface design development for our interactive meeting room, we mainly concentrated on the design of workspaces and appropriate menu designs. The workspaces in our concept are areas for each user that allow working with the documents and digital artifacts in the room. The menus complement the workspaces by enabling the selection of tools, accessing different options and triggering actions.

4. Interactive Meeting Room Prototype

4.4.1 Personal Workspace Concept

Figure 4.6: The application on the tabletop features separate personal workspaces and a large shared space.

For our first interactive meeting room, we designed personal digital work spaces for each user. Figure 4.6 depicts the setup with three personal spaces and the public space. In contrast to a shared large workspace as described in Section 5.4.1, personal workspaces are clearly delimited from the public table space. This public space is defined by the area that is not occupied by the personal workspaces, similar to the background of a desktop computer with overlaid windows. The design of the personal workspaces therefore builds on an established concept. Consequently, we designed the basic layout and functions of the personal workspaces similar to traditional desktop user interfaces (cf. Figure 4.7). Each workspace features a work canvas that can hold different types of media such as whole documents, cropped snapshots of a document and free form annotations. For additional space, the workspace can handle multiple pages, each accessible through its tab control on top. In contrast to the shared workspace concept in Section 5.4.1, the pages within the personal workspace cannot be resized.

4. Interactive Meeting Room Prototype

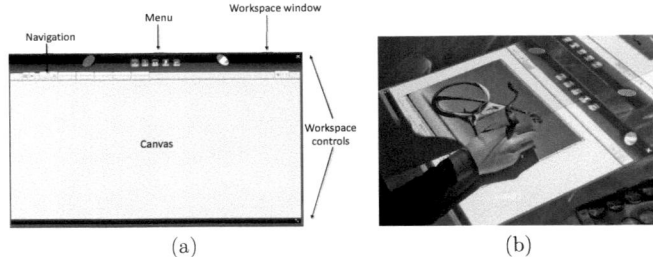

Figure 4.7: The personal workspace design is based on a classic window layout with a menu area, navigation tabs, a page canvas and window controls for transforming and closing the workspace (a). A workspace in use during a design session (b).

Figure 4.8: Workspaces can be continuously resized (a) and rotated (b).

However, the whole workspaces itself can be resized, rotated, moved and shown/hidden on demand as depicted in Figure 4.8. The rotation allows to present the workspace to other users who might otherwise have an upside down view of it. This interaction metaphor extends traditional desktop windows that are only resizable, but not rotatable. Both manipulations, resizing and rotating, are continuous; this allows to precisely transform the workspaces.

But this precise transformation has a major drawback: we recognized in

4. Interactive Meeting Room Prototype

our evaluation of the room that this continuous rotation is practically hindering the smooth handling of the workspaces (see Section 4.6). A selection of the most common angles would be preferable. For resizing, a continuous scale makes sense, since the workspaces are frequently scaled to the exact size of its page's content. When a workspace is dragged towards an edge of the table, it automatically orients itself in this direction. Workspaces can be moved by dragging the frame or clicking an empty spot on the table which immediately places it at this position.

Each workspace is assigned to a digital pen, which means that each pen can only activate the corresponding workspace. In this way, each user has control over his personal workspace. Opening the workspace happens by pointing with the pen at an empty position on the table. The workspace is shown at this position. Moreover, the workspaces are automatically oriented towards the nearest edge of the table when activated. In most cases, this is the direction of the user who activates the workspace. For hiding a workspace, the user has to press the appropriate button in the workspace's toolbar.

In contrast to the multi-user environment on the tabletop, the digital whiteboard supports single-user input only. For that reason, the workspace is designed with a fixed view window instead of the flexible workspace layout used on the tabletop. Figure 4.9 shows the digital whiteboard with the Mimio tracking device on the left and the main toolbar on the right side.

4.4.2 Physical and Digital Menus for Personal Workspaces

For our first interactive room design, we implemented two different menu options that allow the user to control parameters for the digital pens and interact with the workspaces and documents on the tabletop. The first type is a digital menu that is integrated in the personal workspaces. According to the workspaces' desktop window layout, the menu is designed like a traditional toolbar. As depicted in Figure 4.10, it provides controls for changing the pen's mode from sketching to transforming, taking snapshots and exchanging documents with the shared space on the tabletop or the whiteboard. In addition to these functions, the workspaces include feedback areas for the current color

4. Interactive Meeting Room Prototype

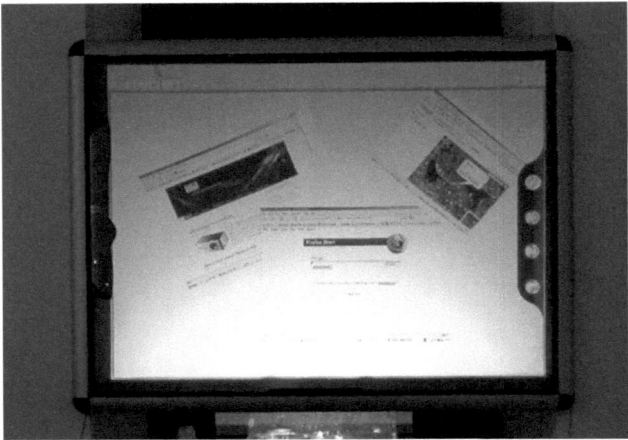

Figure 4.9: The digital whiteboard provides a single-user workspace that is controlled with a Mimio pen.

and stroke width. Due to the specific assignment of each workspace to a pen, the feedback is only valid for this pen.

However, we did not include the menu for selecting colors and stroke widths in the digital menu. These controls are accessible through our second type of menu, the tangible palettes. As described in Section 4.3.1, the palettes are designed like real paint boxes in order to mimic their physical archetype. Thus, whenever users want to change their drawing color, they simply pick a color from the modified paint box as they would do using a brush (cf. Figure 4.11).

4.5 Meeting Activities in the Interactive Room

The interactive room with its tabletop, the digital whiteboard and the presentation wall is designed as a collaborative workspace for meetings. The basic supported activities include presenting content, importing, manipulating

4. Interactive Meeting Room Prototype

Figure 4.10: The digital menu is integrated in the personal workspace. It offers functions for switching the pen's mode and for interacting with the other devices in the room.

and sharing data. Some actions are performed by the attendees of a meeting, while others are presenter tasks. The manipulation of data, for example, is an activity that can be performed by both groups. In order to enable groups to collaboratively work in the room, all hardware components are interconnected. This allows to share data not only between users on one and the same surface, but additionally between surfaces. For example, documents can be exchanged between the tabletop and the whiteboard. Moreover, the work environment in the room can be adapted to fit the group's size by defining the number of personal workspaces on the tabletop. In the following sections, we present details about the different activities that are facilitated through the interactive room.

4.5.1 Presentations

Since presentations are generally based on documents that are externally prepared and finally shown in a meeting, the interactive room offers a very

4. Interactive Meeting Room Prototype

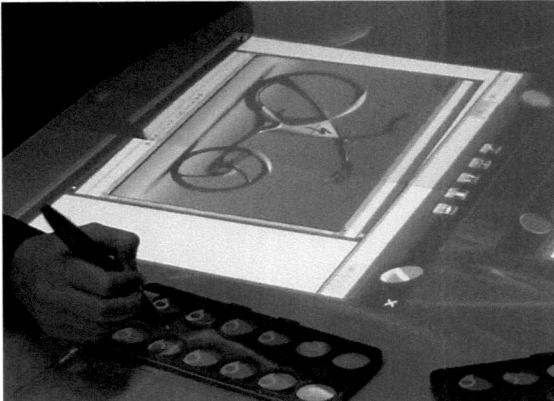

Figure 4.11: The color and stroke width selections from the tangible menu are visible in the digital workspace's feedback area.

general interface for presenting content. Presentations can be held on a mobile computer that the presenter brings to the meeting; there is no restriction concerning supported file formats since the presentation runs in the native application on the presenter's computer. For the audience that attends the presentation, the screen is replicated on the presentation wall. The presentation wall is a traditional non-interactive projection screen. For navigating a presentation, all common devices such as mouse, keyboard or wireless presenter can be used.

4.5.2 Data Import

The interactive room supports an additional way to interact with presentations. Users can take a snapshot of the current presentation and include it in their workspace. To enable the snapshot functionality, the snapshot server application must be installed on the presenter's computer. Once a user makes a snapshot, this application captures the current presentation

4. Interactive Meeting Room Prototype

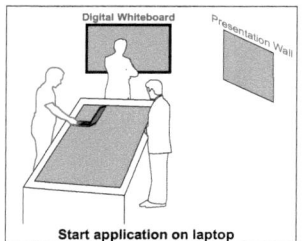 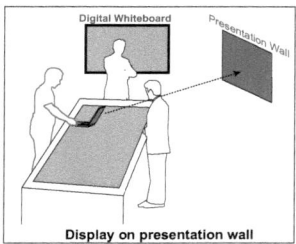

Figure 4.12: Presentations are started in the associated application. The screen of the presentation computer is shown on the presentation wall.

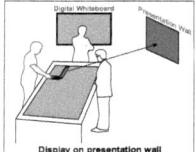 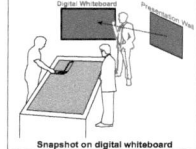 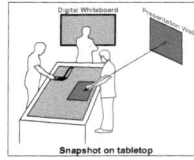

Figure 4.13: Snapshots of the current presentation screen can be requested from the digital whiteboard and the table.

screen and shares it with the requesting workspace. The user interface for taking snapshots is integrated as a menu function in the personal workspaces on the tabletop and on the digital whiteboard. The whole process of taking a snapshot is depicted in Figure 4.13. Snapshots on the tabletop and on the digital whiteboard are included as manipulatable artifacts that can be further rotated, scaled and moved.

4.5.3 Data Manipulation

The personal workspaces on the tabletop and the digital whiteboard support free form annotations. Like with traditional pens, users can simply sketch ideas or extend existing documents with notes. For example, a snapshot from a presentation can be annotated in the personal workspace. The visual style

4. Interactive Meeting Room Prototype

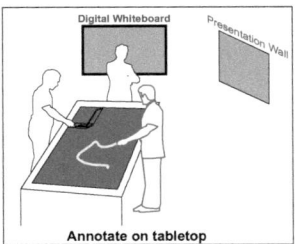 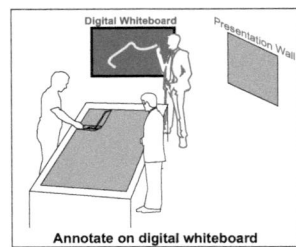

Figure 4.14: Annotations allow to take free form notes on the table and the digital whiteboard.

of the annotations depends on the pen's current color and stroke width. As described in Section 4.4, these parameters can be changed through the tangible palettes. Because the Mimio does not support tangible palettes, annotations on the digital whiteboard have a predefined color and stroke width.

4.5.4 Document Sharing

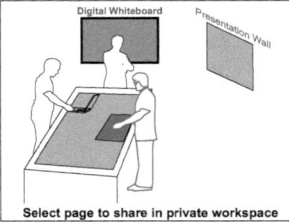 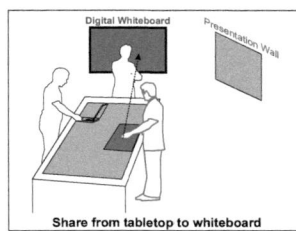

Figure 4.15: Data from the table can be transferred to the whiteboard by sharing it from a private workspace.

For sharing documents, we implemented three different interaction techniques. First, documents can be shared between the tabletop and the whiteboard. As Figure 4.15 depicts, a page must be provided from one of the

4. Interactive Meeting Room Prototype

personal workspaces in order to share it from the table with the whiteboard. The page is then available on the digital whiteboard for further manipulation.

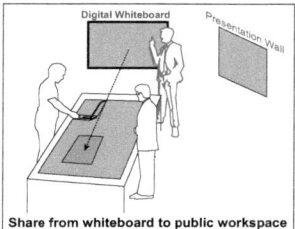 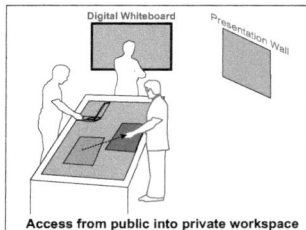

Figure 4.16: Pages from the whiteboard can be shared with the public space on the tabletop. The sharing is initiated by the user at the whiteboard.

Second, pages from the whiteboard can be shared with the tabletop (cf. Figure 4.16). The action must be triggered from the whiteboard's side. For example, the presenter can decide to share the current slide of a presentation with the group through this channel. The page is then available in the public space of the tabletop. In order to access the page from the public space, users at the tabletop make a copy of the document to their private workspace.

Finally, pages can also be exchanged between the personal workspaces on the table as shown in Figure 4.17. For this purpose, a page must be offered by a workspace which transfers it to the public space on the table. Another user has access to the page by retrieving it from the public space in form of a copy. The page will then appear in his personal space while the original page remains in the public space.

4.6 Evaluation

After the implementation of our first interactive room that was based on the results of our initial meeting survey (Section 4.1), we conducted an observational evaluation. The study was based on the following objectives:

Objective 1. Investigate the functionality of the delimited workspaces in a

4. Interactive Meeting Room Prototype

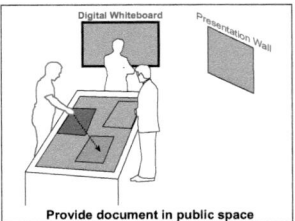 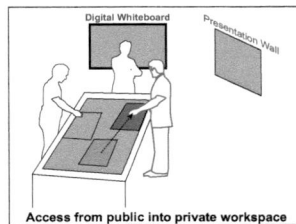

Figure 4.17: Documents that are shared on the tabletop must be moved to the public space. From there, all users have access to the document for further use in their private workspace.

group activity.

Objective 2. Explore the task assignment and labor division between the tabletop and the whiteboard.

Objective 3. Analyze the appropriateness of using digital pens and a Mimio device for user input.

Objective 4. Survey the handling of the tangible palettes.

Objective 5. Study the partitioning of the table's space for digital and analogue usage.

Objective 6. Explore the role of public and private spaces in the room.

Evaluation Design

We invited groups of three people from our partner Voestalpine. These groups were all assigned the same task that they had to solve with the support of the interactive room. The task was to design a communication room that includes similar hardware as the current room (tabletop, digital whiteboard, presentation wall). The group was not restricted to only integrating the existing hardware into their design, they could extend the room concept with any hardware they considered as necessary.

4. Interactive Meeting Room Prototype

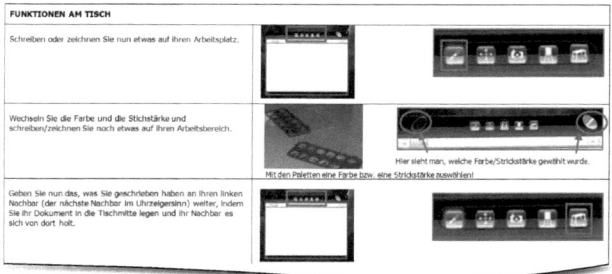

Figure 4.18: Part of the tutorial that the group had to walk through before performing the real task in the room.

In order to familiarize the group with the functions and features of the interactive room, the evaluation started with a tutorial. During that phase, the group was introduced to the functions in a step-by-step sequence. The tutorial was divided into the following sections: workspace configuration, table functions and whiteboard functions. The tutorial was designed in a way that each participant had to perform the task to be familiar with the functions afterwards. The whole tutorial took about 30 minutes. Figure 4.18 shows an example part of the tutorial.

In total, we tested six groups with two observers taking notes during the process. In addition, we video taped the sessions for later review. After each session, we interviewed the group. In the first part of the interview, the group reported on their experience with the environment. After that, they were asked to complete a questionnaire. The questionnaire comprised the six objectives that we defined for the study. In particular, we asked about the interaction with and between the digital surfaces, the design of the user interface and the features of the application.

4. Interactive Meeting Room Prototype

Evaluation Results

The evaluation provided valuable feedback about the strengths and shortcomings of our implementation. From the notes that were taken by the observers during the meetings we mainly created an understanding about the physical environment of the room and the effect on the group work. We concentrated on the usage of the surfaces, the pen input devices, tangible palettes and additional work material that was used during the sessions. We also observed the interaction with the digital workspaces and the public space on the table. In combination with the answers form the questionnaires, we developed a comprehension about the pros and cons of our implementation. The following summary describes our results.

Tangible palettes. We provided only a single color palette and one stroke width palette to explore the collaboration effect in the group. The participants noted that they had problems to share the palettes, as they were often out of reach or currently in use by another person. Moreover, the palettes occupied screen space which resulted in a shortage of space on the table. The tangible palettes seemed to hamper fluid interaction on the tabletop. The participants requested to include additional color and stroke width picker into the graphical user interface of each workspace.

Input devices. Using two different input devices for the table (Anoto pens) and the digital whiteboard (Mimio pen) caused interruptions of the interaction fluidity. It happened that users tried to write with their Anoto pens on the whiteboard. The Mimio pen was also brought to the table, which hindered the interaction with the whiteboard, as the pen first had to be fetched from the table. A single input device for the table and the whiteboard was requested by all groups.

Private notes. The workspaces were occasionally used to take private notes. However, these notes were still visible for all other participants. A method to restrict the view of private information should be integrated into the tabletop interaction.

4. Interactive Meeting Room Prototype

Storing objects. Although the table's surface is designed to allow for the placement of physical objects (no interference with the tracking occurs), we noticed that the groups quickly removed objects from the table. The reason was the cluttering of the surface, which resulted in a decreasing quality of the interaction. Physical objects occluded the workspaces and the data spread across the table. Although the workspaces and the data could be rearranged, the objects were impeding interaction. It was also interesting to observe that the additional space next to the table's interactive surface was not used for storing objects. This may be due to the remote position at the end of the table which was out of reach for most users.

Shared space. The shared space on the table can be used to exchange data between participants. The way the application is designed, annotations can only be made in the personal workspaces. This resulted in a suboptimal work flow, as collaborative annotations were only minimally supported. The typical process we observed was to move data into the personal workspace, modify or annotate it, and finally move it back to the shared space to grant access for the other users. This was especially difficult if the table was already covered with a lot of data. Since there was no direct channel to transfer data from one workspace to another, the data had to be searched in the shared space. The tendency to group objects in a side areas of the table to create new space could be observed during the majority of the meetings.

Visibility of data in the shared space. Documents in the shared space are often hard to see as they get occluded by other documents. This makes the retrieving of documents for the personal workspace difficult. Moreover, it creates confusion about the available documents on the table. A group or arrangement function would be required.

Table centric work. Working with the whiteboard involves to physically walk there and interact with the surface. While this is a natural process in a presentation scenario, we gathered feedback that suggested to

4. Interactive Meeting Room Prototype

also implement a table centric control of the whiteboard. This would allow the group to stay seated at the table but with a direct access of the whiteboard. Summaries during a meeting, for example, could be controlled on the table but shown on the whiteboard.

Whiteboard functionality. The design of the whiteboard offers a fixed view window. Like in the traditional paper flipchart case, pages are too small for certain tasks and would need to be extended. This could be implemented in form of a scale and move function of an infinitely large page on the digital whiteboard.

Workspace handling. Workspaces can be shown/hidden, resized, moved and rotated. The rotation allows to orient the workspace with a preciseness of a single degree. We observed that users generally need fixed rotations such as 45, 90 or 180 degrees. They often tried to approximate these rotations through stepwise rotations which resulted in a too complex process for this simple task. A selection of three or four predefined rotations would be sufficient. We observed that the scale function was used to present work to the group. This process normally involved a combination of rotoate and scale operations so that the group had a good view on the workspace. We moreover noticed that workspaces were generally rotated to be correctly positioned for the user who worked with it. Although it would have been possible to sketch in a workspace that is upside down, the participants preferred to correct the view before working with the workspace.

Delimited workspaces. Each workspace is visualized with a border that frames its area. The feedback about delimited workspaces was positive, as the users had control over the space they could use to work with. It was important for them to know how large their personal space was.

Labor division. The workspaces are often used to divide labor among the group. For this purpose, the functionality of the workspaces was used to specify the way the work was split. For example, one group assigned

4. Interactive Meeting Room Prototype

the task of taking snapshots to one user while another user was taking notes in his workspace.

User identification. All groups explored the possibility to use different colors for different users to distinguish the ownership of created information. This was especially useful in the shared space if multiple documents had to be a assigned to users at a later point during the meeting.

Direct touch interaction. The interaction on the table is based on the digital Anoto pens. For annotating and precise pointing, this input device was automatically accepted by the users. However, some tried to manipulate the workspaces with their hands. They noted during the final interviews that they would prefer direct touch interaction for handling the workspaces and moving documents on the table, as this a more closely mapping to the real world than using a pen for these tasks. The pen, on the other side, is a perfect tool for annotating and high accurate input. Consequently, a combination of both techniques would be preferred.

4.7 Conclusion

The evaluation of our prototype interactive room suggested that the concept of combining a tabletop, a digital whiteboard and a presentation wall in a single space has the potential to improve work processes. However, some of the design decisions turned out to hamper the interaction instead of simplifying it. The delimited personal workspaces, for example, were well accepted, but the work flow between them via the public space was not optimal. The shared space was lacking the functionality to make annotations, this feature would have increased the collaboration among the group.

The affordance of the digital whiteboard as a presentation area with correct view for all participants (in contrast to the rotational problems on the table) makes it a perfect supplement for the table's workspace. In this sense, a table centric approach that allows to access the whiteboard from the table

4. Interactive Meeting Room Prototype

would be a potential extension for the room setup. Nevertheless, for certain tasks the traditional way of working at the whiteboard would still be preferable. From an application's perspective, the table centric approach has to account for additional interaction processes. Especially when a mixed scenario with one person working at the whiteboard while another one accesses the whiteboard from the table is planned. In this case, simultaneous tasks can be confusing and must be changed to sequenced processes. For example, if the presenter writes on the whiteboard, a user at the table should not be able to simultaneously change the page.

Furthermore, we identified the need for a combined pen and touch interaction. It is still not solved how the exact task assignment of pen and touch will look like, but we already gained some insights as described in Section 5.3.1.

Concerning the integration of tangible palettes, we argue for the affordances of the objects that can be easily regulated through the visual design. The feedback we collected suggests that more redundant methods for the interaction would complement the usage of the tangible palettes. Finally, the negative commented limitation of single objects for multi-user collaboration offers new possibilities for control management. Actions that should be restricted to a single user control in a collaborative environment could therefore be assigned to the tangible palette. This naturally manages the single user aspect while simultaneously maintaining the feedback for the group.

Interactive Meeting Room Redesign

In this chapter, we describe the improvements of our first interactive meeting room prototype (see Chapter 4). We used the results of the evaluation as presented in Section 4.6 to further develop parts of the interactive room. In particular, we advanced our concept in four aspects: First, we extended the support of input devices form pen only to additional touch input. In order to simplify the integration of new input devices, we implemented a flexible input framework. Second, we included real paper documents as an extension to the purely digital workspace from the first prototype. Third, the workspace concept based on personal workspaces for each user was replaced by a single large shared workspace. For this step, novel menu design concepts were developed to support the interaction with our meeting room application. Finally, we unified the pen devices by using Anoto technology for the tabletop, the whiteboard and the interaction with real paper instead of using a combination of Anoto and Mimio pens. This included the development of rear-projected Anoto surfaces; an achievement that allows for the flexible combination of front and rear-projected large interactive surfaces.

At the beginning of this chapter in Section 5.1, we define the project goals for these four areas of refinement in more detail. In Section 5.2, we give an in-depth description how to develop rear-projected Anoto surfaces and how to combine touch with digital pen input. Based on these hardware developments, we discuss the enhanced interaction possibilities with the redesigned interactive room. In particular, we provide results of a formal experiment in

5. Interactive Meeting Room Redesign

Section 5.3.1 suggesting that combined pen and touch input excels pen and touch used separately. In Section 5.3.2, we present interaction techniques that are based on the integration of real paper documents in a digital environment. Moreover, we further develop the design of the room's digital workspace and illustrate a novel menu design for tabletops that facilitates a single shared workspace for multiple users in Section 5.4. Analogical to the discussion of typical meeting activities support in the first room, we present the redesign's equivalent in Section 5.5. Finally, we describe the reimplementation of the meeting room software with the focus on a more flexible framework design in Section 5.6. We propose a unified input framework that aims at simplifying the integration of different input devices in interactive room setups. Based on that framework, we show a possible implementation of a meeting room application.

5.1 Redesign Project Goals

With the 2nd generation interactive room, we present a redesign of the initial room implementation. According to the feedback we collected about our first design (see Section 4.6), we defined the following goals to better support the activities within the room:

Support user interaction. Interaction with the system as well as among the group members strongly depends on the interface design. With our first setup, we observed that visually separated workspaces on the large tabletop were not efficiently supporting the work flows. Thus we based our new design on the concept of a single workspace that allows for simultaneous interaction with equally shared rights for each user. Since this paradigm shift from multiple delimited workspaces towards a single shared workspace requires an adaption of the user interface, we also redesigned the graphical user interface.

Simplify device integration. One of the main problems with designing multi-user applications is the lacking support of the underlying operating systems. Since current operating systems are not capable of handling multiple points of input, an abstraction layer between the device driver and the application is necessary in order to provide multi-user functionality. However, custom applications will still not be able to interpret multiple inputs simultaneously. For that reason, multi-user applications also have to be adapted for this kind of input. In the course of redesigning the application for the interactive room, we developed a unified input framework. This framework allows to integrate new input devices through a simple interface. For each new device a specific device driver must be implemented that communicates the events from the device to the event handling of the application.

Minimize the media gap. In a collaborative working environment, users import data, share it and further need to export artifacts from a session. Therefore the simultaneous interaction on shared documents is an essential feature of the interactive room. However, our first generation prototype did not completely support these activities. Moreover, in a real world environment different kinds of media are used throughout meeting sessions. Documents can exist in a digital form or as a real paper document. As both types are commonly used, the appropriate support within the room for bridging the gap between analogue and digital media is desirable.

Minimize input device switching. Due to technical restrictions during the development of the first generation room, a Mimio tracking device was used for the digital whiteboard. At that time, the Anoto tracking technology could only be used on front-projection setups. Using Mimio pens for the whiteboard and Anoto pens for the tabletop resulted in frequent switching of devices and discontinuity of work flows. Therefore, we aimed at a solution that would minimize the need of switching input devices. Through further research, we discovered a material that allows us to use Anoto pens in combination with a rear-projection setup. Hence the same digital pens can be used for interacting in the meeting room.

5. Interactive Meeting Room Redesign

Extend import and export interfaces. One of the key criteria of the interactive room is the ability to access data from third party applications. This includes functions to import data into the system as well as export documents from a session. Since our use case scenario is based on meeting and brainstorming sessions, Microsoft PowerPoint is the most popular format for presentations. Our first version of the room featured support to include snapshots from arbitrary applications through a screen capture interface. However, this approach requires the user to install and run the server application in order to enable the snapshot functionality. To overcome this drawback, extended data access functionalities have been integrated into the second generation. First, the snapshot feature is based on a VGA signal grabber[1] that allows to capture the output of a connected computer. No additional software must be installed on this computer. Second, PowerPoint can be directly imported into the system. The session can be also exported to PowerPoint again. Finally, a VNC[2] viewer allows to show any program from a server computer within the system.

Support multi-modal input. Designing interactivity with digital surfaces requires carefully selecting the appropriate input devices. For a usable system, it is important to meet the user's expectations concerning the actions that should be supported and the related input devices that should be used to accomplish them. While a digital pen might be the perfect device for sketching or writing, direct touch might be better suited for moving or resizing documents, for example. The goal for the interactive meeting room was to explore the possibilities of combining pen and touch input for tabletops and walls and to identify the tasks that are best supported by each of them.

---
[1] http://www.epiphan.com/products/frame-grabbers/vga2usb/
[2] http://www.realvnc.com

5.2 Hardware

According to the previously described goals for the room's redesign, we discuss two specific developments in this section. First, we advanced the application domain of Anoto enabled surfaces from front-projected opaque surfaces as described in Section 4.2.3 towards rear-projected surfaces. This allows the creation of a broader range of Anoto enabled displays, especially the development of rear-projected digital whiteboards that replace the previously used Mimio tracking system. Second, we extended the input modalities from solely pen interaction to pen with additional touch interaction.

5.2.1 Rear-projected Anoto surfaces

The digital whiteboard in our first interactive room prototype featured a rear-projected surface with Mimio pen tracking as described in Section 4.2. However, we noticed that using different pen devices for the whiteboard and the table hampered fluid interaction in the room. Moreover, the tracking system restricted the whiteboard to single-user input. Hence, we aimed at a digital whiteboard that uses the same Anoto input technology as the table in order to unify the input devices. In the following, we present our research of combining Anoto tracking technology with a rear-projected surface.

Since the Anoto pen tracking technology is designed to be used with traditional paper, materials that allow for rear-projections are not initially supported. We faced this problem when we tried to print the dot pattern on different surfaces such as transparent foils. The optimal base-material should reflect the IR light that is emitted from the pen's integrated IR-LED. For the camera in the pen's tip, the area appears as a bright surface with a black high contrast pattern on it. If the material is too transparent or too glossy, the contrast between background material and dot pattern is not high enough to ensure stable pen tracking. A transparent surface would not reflect enough IR light and therefore appear as a dark background with nearly invisible black dots on it (Figure 5.1 (a)).

5. Interactive Meeting Room Redesign

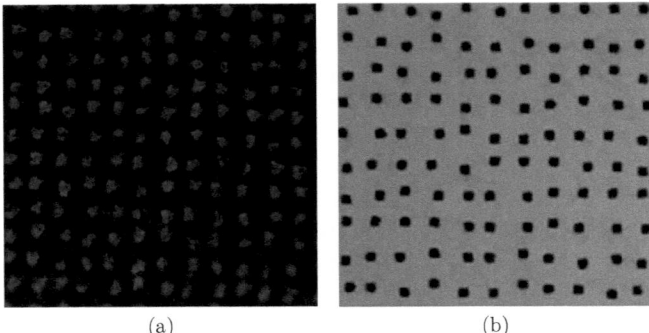

(a) (b)

Figure 5.1: Sufficient contrast is necessary for the Anoto tracking. Closeup of a transparent foil that does not reflect enough infrared light (a). For comparison, the HP Backlit UV supports Anoto tracking (b).

We found a solution that allows to apply Anoto pen tracking to large rear-projected surfaces. The tracking is realized by using a large Anoto pattern printed on a special rear-projection foil. This foil diffuses the illumination from the rear projector resulting in an image with no visible hotspots at the front of the screen. HP Colorlucent Backlit UV foil is used in order to produce an image with sufficient contrast for the embedded Anoto pen camera to recognize the dot pattern (Figure 5.1 (b)). This provides translucency for projection while being opaque enough to enable the Anoto IR-tracking.

For comparison, Figure 5.2 (a) depicts the layer composition for a front-projection setup where the Anoto pattern is printed on traditional paper. The surface is covered with a thin acrylic panel (0.8mm thickness) to protect it from scratches. As long as the cover layer is thin enough (max. 4mm), a stable tracking result is ensured. Thicker layers would interfere with the tracking. In contrast, Figure 5.2 (b) shows the rear-projection version with the Anoto pattern on the foil. The dot pattern on the backlit foil is placed between two acrylic panels. The panel in the back has a width of 5mm and guarantees a stable and robust surface while the panel in the front has a

5. Interactive Meeting Room Redesign

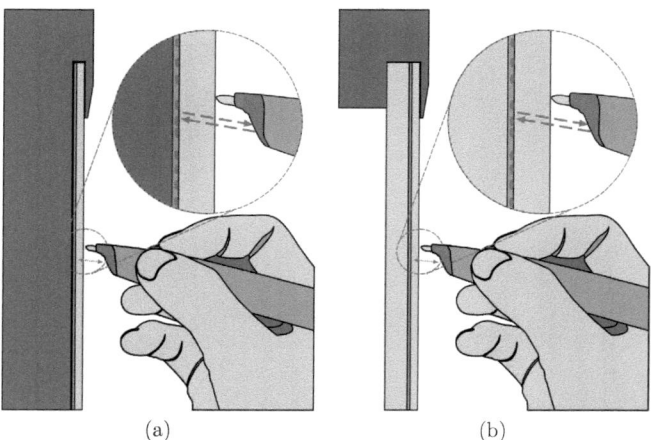

Figure 5.2: The front-projected layer composition (a). Anoto pattern for a rear-projected interactive surface (b). *Image courtesy of Jakob Leitner.*

width of only 0.8mm to protect the pattern from scratches. Figure 5.3 finally depicts the whiteboard as it is used in the interactive room.

We note that it is possible to use Anoto overlays on transparent foils. However, this requires two major modifications: First, the pattern has to be printed with an infrared reflecting ink. Since the background of a transparent foil appears black to the pen's camera, the approach is to reverse the whole tracking mechanism. Therefore, the dots of the pattern have to reflect infrared light while the background is black; instead of black dots on a white background, this provides an inverse image for the camera with white dots on a black background. The second modification concerns the tracking algorithm that has to extract the dots from this new reversed source. With this two changes, it is possible to use transparent Anoto overlays, but the production of the special reflecting pattern and the modification of the pen's firmware currently prevent its application.

5. Interactive Meeting Room Redesign

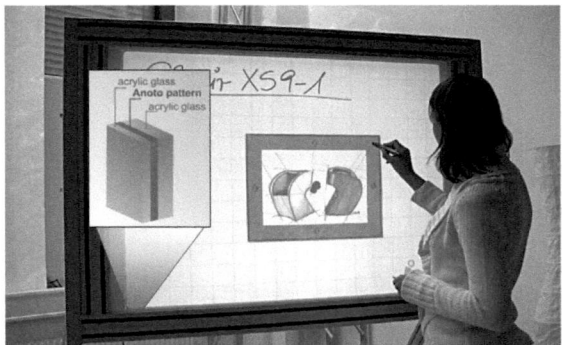

Figure 5.3: Example of a rear-projection whiteboard. The Anoto pattern, printed on HP Colorlucent Backlit UV foil, is embedded between two layers of transparent acrylic.

5.2.2 Combined Pen and Touch Input

In Section 5.3.1, we argue for a combined pen and touch solution that leverages the individual strengths of both devices. From a hardware perspective, the combination of pen and touch input on a large coincident surface has hardly been investigated. One possible solution are touchscreens overlaid on tablet computers that allow for simultaneous pen and touch interaction. As an example, the small-scale capacitive multi-touch screen from N-Trig[3] has already been commercialized. It supports user input from both pen and capacitive touch in one single device. For the pen tracking, they use an electrostatic stylus and an active digitizer that is embedded in the screen. The N-Trig technology has also been integrated into commercial products such as the Dell Latitude XT tablet PC. However, these systems limit the users through their restricted scalability; N-Trig only provides overlays in the size of a laptop screen, for example. In contrast, our focus for combining pen and

---

[3] http://www.n-trig.com

5. Interactive Meeting Room Redesign

touch input was to explore solutions for large interactive surfaces like tabletops and walls. Since we used Anoto technology for the pen input, a variety of compatible touch input technologies were possible. We present three different approaches, starting with a combination of a DiamondTouch table and Anoto tracking, followed by a front diffused illumination setup and finally a FTIR and Anoto combination.

Anoto and DiamondTouch

The first approach we explored for combining Anoto pen tracking with direct touch interaction is based on a DiamondTouch table from Mitsubishi Electric Research Laboratories (MERL)[4]. As depicted in Figure 5.4, the hardware design composes of two components only: the DiamondTouch table and an Anoto dot pattern as overlay. Since the DiamondTouch uses capacitive sensing technology, the pen tracking is completely independent from the touch tracking with this setup. Moreover, the DiamondTouch requires front projection; for a front-projected setup, the choice of possible Anoto pattern base materials is larger than with a rear-projected setup (see Section 4.2.3). Hence we experimented with different types of materials to overlay the DiamondTouch surface with the dot pattern. A print on transparent self-adhesive foil works well since the surface of the DiamondTouch is opaque and reflects enough IR light to support stable Anoto tracking. Another solution is to use the same HP Colorlucent Backlit UV foil that we already applied for Anoto based rear-projected setups. In combination with the DiamondTouch table, the rear-projection characteristics of the foil are not important. However, the foil has a matte side that supports touch interaction really well. Due to the smooth surface, moving gestures can be performed fluidly with minimum friction. Especially for extended activities, this quality for direct touch interaction is important. With both materials, the capacitive touch detection is not influenced through the overlaid pattern.

In addition to the simple two layer construction of the setup, the combination of Anoto pen tracking and touch tracking on the DiamondTouch has

---

[4] http://www.merl.com

5. Interactive Meeting Room Redesign

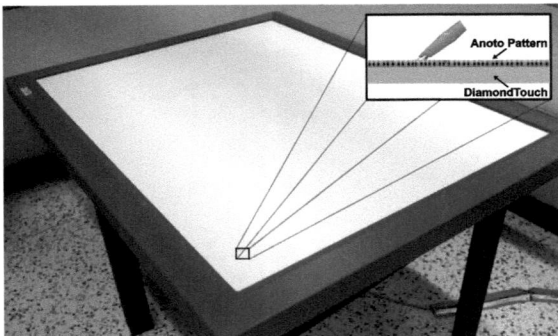

Figure 5.4: Direct touch and pen tracking surface as a combination of Anoto and DiamondTouch technology.

another advantage. As described in Section 2.1.1, the DiamondTouch supports user identification. Up to four users can be distinguished by the system. The Anoto pens also provide unique identification data (see Section 4.2.2). In combination, Anoto pen and DiamondTouch touch tracking support user identification on both levels. As long as the users remain on their connection pads for the touch tracking and do not exchange their Anoto pens, this system is the only one with the capability to relate the pen input to the touch interaction. In contrast, with vision-based touch tracking systems the identification of users has still to be solved.

Anoto and Diffused Illumination (DI)

An alternative solution to combine Anoto pen tracking with direct touch input is to use an optical tracking setup. With DI, the camera on the backside of the projection surface tracks objects that approach the screen by using brightness differences. We experimented with a rear DI setup where the infrared light sources are placed behind the screen (cf. Figure 5.5 (a)). Objects near the surface reflect parts of the infrared light and can be tracked by the

5. Interactive Meeting Room Redesign

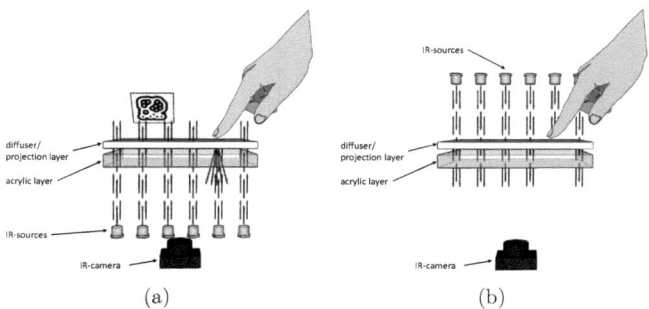

Figure 5.5: Comparison of rear and front DI tracking. With rear DI, the light is on the camera's side of the screen and tracks reflections from objects in front of the surface (a). Front DI uses the light on the user's side, resulting in shadows of objects that are between the light source and the surface (b). *Image courtesy of Jakob Leitner.*

camera. However, one of the main issues we encountered was the proper illumination setup. We based our setup on Rekimoto's *Holowall* description [98], that resulted in serious hot spots caused by the infrared lights behind the screen and only very limited areas of brightness. For that reason, we used a variation of the rear DI setup where the infrared lights are placed on the users side of the screen (cf. Figure 5.5 (b)). This approach is commonly known as front DI. In contrast to the rear DI solution, front DI relies on the shadows casted by objects near the screen.

For the front DI screen construction, we use HP Colorlucent Backlit UV foil as a projection screen with the Anoto pattern printed on the foil. For tracking touch input, we mount a WATEC WAT-502B camera behind the screen. The camera captures a gray surface and objects coming near the surface will appear as blurred shadow. As Figure 5.6 shows, only objects directly touching the surface are recognized as sharp outlined shapes.

The ambient light does not disturb the setup, but rather enhances the quality of results as there are enough IR components in the day light spectrum. The texture of the reflection surface is not relevant as long as enough

5. Interactive Meeting Room Redesign

Figure 5.6: The environmental light causes the user's hand to cast a shadow on the diffuse screen. The bottom row shows the correlation between the object's distance from the screen and the resulting contrast in the image. Useful tracking information can be filtered from a distance between 0mm and 40mm.

light is reflected towards the direction of the screen. The bottom row in Figure 5.6 shows the correlation between the hand's distance from the screen and the contrast of the captured image. Under weak lighting conditions, the IR part of the environment light will not be strong enough to provide stable results with the described setup. The shadow casted on the diffuser surface decreases in contrast and therefore the tracking becomes weaker. Since the environmental light was not sufficient to guarantee for a stable hand tracking, we reconsidered our approach and decided to develop a setup based on these four points:

- Create a high contrast shadow by light from the back of the scene

5. Interactive Meeting Room Redesign

- Brighten unwanted shadow regions by adding light from the front
- The front light is reflected by the user's body and supports a clear contrast shadow if the body blocks the back light
- The combination of front and back light is crucial, the angle of the front light defines the distance for interaction

Figure 5.7: Light from the back casts a high contrast shadow of the user's whole body on the screen (*left*). Infrared lights at the back of the user and on top of the screen guarantee an optimal lighting condition for the hand tracking (*right*).

Figure 5.7 (*right*) illustrates our general hardware setup that enables a stable tracking in an IR light scenario. The light illuminating the scene from the back casts a high contrast shadow of the user's body on the screen. As Figure 5.7 (*left*) depicts, without additional light from the front the resulting contrast image seen by the camera would include the full body shape. Notice that the IR lights at the front of the panel do not interfere with the tracking results of the digital pens.

Given the situation that the user's hand is near enough to the screen to cast a shadow, we distinguish between two cases concerning the hand's position relative to the body. If the user moves his hand directly in front of his body, only a small amount of light from the back influences the shadow. The main part of light from the back is blocked by the user's own body. At

5. Interactive Meeting Room Redesign

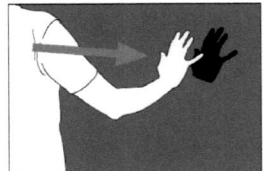 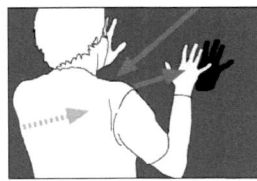

Figure 5.8: If the user's hand is beside his body, the shadow is casted by the light from the back (*left*). If the hand in front of the body blocks light from the back, the shadow depends on the reflected front light (*right*).

the same time, the body acts as an indirect light source that is responsible for casting the shadow onto the screen as shown in Figure 5.8 (*right*). This reflection of light from the user's body happens automatically because of the light sources placed in front of the screen. In the other case, when the user's hand is beside his body, the light from the back is responsible for the shadow (cf. Figure 5.8 (*left*)).

For a stable tracking result, we propose a setup with IR light as depicted in Figure 5.7. Tracking the shadow worked better in our setup than the reflection alternative. Our setup is refined by positioning the light in front of the user and also behind. Through this constellation, shadow tracking is independent from environment light conditions. In fact, surrounding light improves the tracking result. Choosing the appropriate angle for the front light is important to define the distance for interaction and finally, additional light from below the screen stabilizes the tracking result.

Anoto and Frustrated Total Internal Reflection (FTIR)

An alternative possibility to combine Anoto pen tracking with direct touch tracking is to use the FTIR effect (see Section 2.2.2). The simplest way to get started with FTIR is just to use a layer of polycarbonate augmented with a frame of IR-LEDs. With this approach however, users often must press hard on the surface in order to trigger the FTIR effect. Additionally when dragging a finger on the surface, such as to perform a motion gesture,

5. Interactive Meeting Room Redesign

friction may decrease the FTIR effect caused. Therefore, many researchers use an additional layer (compliant surface layer) on top of the polycarbonate material to improve the sensitivity of the surface. These compliant surfaces typically compose of a soft and transparent material which is placed between the polycarbonate sheet and a diffuse (projection screen) layer. Figures 5.9 (a, b) highlight the relevant layers of our final composition. When pressure is applied on the surface, the coupling of the diffuse top layer and the bottom polycarbonate surface triggers the FTIR effect; this effect is intensified by the middle compliant surface layer (Figures 5.9 (a)). As shown in Figure 5.9 (b), the digital pen tracking is enabled through the dot pattern printed on the top projection layer.

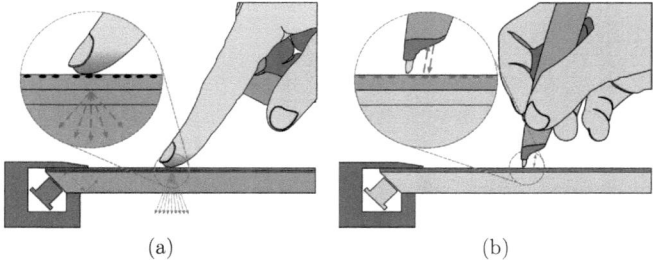

(a)   (b)

Figure 5.9: The three layers needed to track the finger touches: projection screen (top), compliant layer (middle) and polycarbonate (bottom) (a). For the Anoto tracking, only the top layer is relevant (b). *Image courtesy of Jakob Leitner.*

Finding the correct material for a compliant surface is crucial. When experimenting with different materials we noticed two problems that can occur with the layer: either it does not set off a strong-enough FTIR effect, or it sticks to the surface, constantly triggering the FTIR effect even after a finger has been removed. This would completely destroy the effect of FTIR triggered through the user's finger. The best results for the compliant surface

5. Interactive Meeting Room Redesign

were achieved with SORTA-Clear 40[5] and ELASTOSIL RT 601[6] silicone, both materials being relatively hard (Hardness Shore A $>= 40$), non tacky and very clear. Once hardened, both silicone layers can easily be removed from and reattached to the polycarbonate surface. However, using silicone as a compliant surface poses one problem. As the material comes as a gel, it must be poured evenly over the surface, which can prove a difficult task. ELASTOSIL RT 601 is less viscous and hence easier to pour, resulting in fewer bubbles in the vulcanized layer.

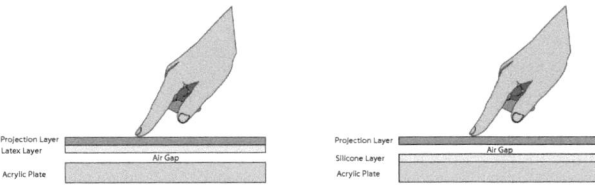

Figure 5.10: With the latex version (*left*), the projection and the latex layer must be combined; the air gap is between these two and the acrylic plate. In the silicone version (*right*), the air gap is between the projection surface and the combined silicone and acrylic layer.

As an alternative to silicone for the compliant layer, we found that a thin layer of latex also works perfectly. This has a huge advantage over silicone layers as it does not have to be poured, reducing the production time of the combined layer setup significantly. Additionally latex is easier to handle, faster and cheaper to produce and more easily accessible as a mere off-the-shelf component. Moreover, latex does not stick to neighboring layers, as with other alternative compliant surface materials, so latex can be combined with a wider variety of projection layers. In contrast to the construction with silicone, the latex must be combined with the projection layer; with an air gap between the latex and the polycarbonate base plate. In the silicone version we have exactly the opposite requirements. Figure 5.10 shows this difference between the latex and silicone layer construction.

---

[5] http://tb.smodev.com/tb/uploads/SORTA_CLEAR_40_32707.pdf
[6] http://www.wacker.com/

5. Interactive Meeting Room Redesign

Using either the latex or the silicone version, the layer composition that technically enables to combine Anoto pen and FTIR based touch tracking has a constraint. Since both FTIR and Anoto pens are based on an IR-tracking setup, the pen is also detected by the FTIR-camera as a touch input. This most likely will lead to undesirable results. In order to detect only touch points, the pen has to be masked in the image that is processed by the touch tracking software.

We propose two different solutions that address this problem. Firstly, we present a computer vision approach that makes use of pulsed infrared light. Secondly, we demonstrate a hardware solution that uses an IR longpass filter to distinguish between pen and touch IR wavelengths. We then compare the two solutions and discuss advantages and disadvantages of the two approaches. Finally, we highlight the steps necessary to upgrade existing touch surfaces.

For our setup (90cm × 67,5cm) we use 154 LEDs (SFH485P) with a peak wavelength emission at 880nm. The LEDs are placed along all four edges of the 6mm thick acrylic plate. The touch points are captured with a single PointGrey Firefly MV (320px × 240px, 120Hz). In order to eliminate the projected image in the captured frames, we apply an IR-pass filter in front of the camera's sensor. The Anoto digital pen technology uses an infrared camera and a flashing IR-LED. The pen tracks with a speed of 75Hz.

Computer vision approach

The idea of the first approach is to continuously take reference images to detect external IR-light sources like the digital pens or ambient light sources. For this approach, the LED-frame is pulsed synchronously with the camera using an additional electronic circuit similar to [1] and [38]. The clock signal for the pulse is generated at tracking framerate (120Hz) by the camera. This pulse causes a JK-flipflop to switch between its low and high state at half the input frequency. These switches between low and high state are amplified through a transistor and are used to drive the LED frame. The frame is now synchronized with the camera, resulting in alternate captured images with the led-frame *on* and *off*. Figure 5.11 shows two consecutive frames with the

5. Interactive Meeting Room Redesign

enabled pulsing effect.

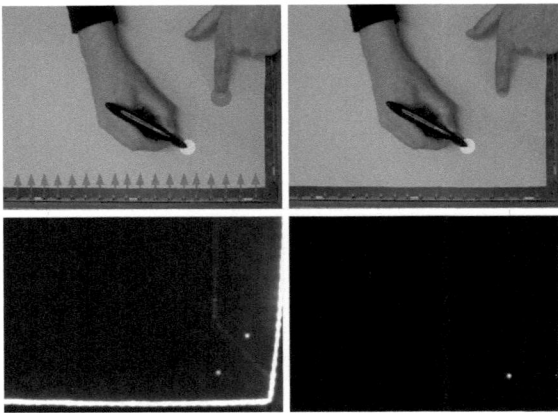

Figure 5.11: Two different states of the LED frame. In the tracking frame, pen and touch input are both visible for the camera (bottom left). The reference frame shows pen input only (bottom right). *Image courtesy of Jakob Leitner.*

By subtracting the reference frame (LED frame *off*) from the tracking frame (LED frame *on*), active IR light sources such as light-pens can be eliminated. Since the position of the light-pen might change slightly over two consecutive frames, expanding the masking area is recommended.

If the IR-light from the pen would be visible in each reference frame, the described approach would reliably exclude the blobs created by the pen. However, the pen's IR-LED is also pulsed with a frame rate of 75Hz. The pen emits a light pulse with a duration of $200\mu s$ every 13.3ms. As described before, the light starts as soon as the pen touches the surface. This happens at an arbitrary moment either during a reference or tracking frame. To reliably remove the pen in the tracking frame, we need to ensure that the pulsed light from the pen is visible when creating the mask. This cannot be ensured by taking only a single reference frame into account. For example, the pen's pulse

5. Interactive Meeting Room Redesign

could coincide with the tracking frame so that the pen is visible in the touch tracking image but not in the reference frame. In this case, our approach would fail. To ensure a reliable masking calculation, the cases depicted in Figure 5.12 have to be considered. Within the duration of a single captured frame, the pen's light can be visible in four different variations (case 1 - case 4). However, only if the pen is visible in the used tracking frame, masking is necessary to exclude this blob (case 2 - case 4). In these cases, the pen has to appear in at least one of the three reference frames. Considering these three frames, this requirement is always fulfilled, thus ensuring a stable masking of the pen's light in the camera image.

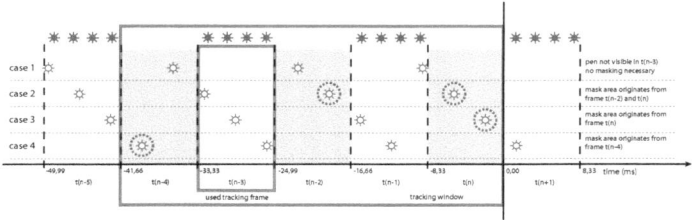

Figure 5.12: Using a capture rate of 120Hz, a total of 3 reference frames are necessary in order to successfully mask a blob created by the pen. Considering 3 reference frames ensures that even though the pen's and the LED frame's flashing IR-LEDs are not synchronized, the pen's IR light appears in at least one of the three reference frames. *Image courtesy of Jakob Leitner.*

Hence, we extend the concept of using a combination of a tracking and a reference frame and consider three reference frames instead of only a single one (cf. Figure 3). In the extended algorithm the current frame $t(n)$ uses a mask which combines three reference frames with $t(n-4) + t(n-2) + t(n)$. Only active light sources like pens are visible in these frames (in Figure 5.13 in frame $t(n-2)$ and $t(n)$). This mask is applied on the tracking frame $t(n-3)$ that shows both touch and pen inputs. Through the masking, the result includes the touch input only. With this approach, the pen can reliably be detected at a capture rate of 120Hz (= 60Hz touch tracking rate). However,

5. Interactive Meeting Room Redesign

the algorithm introduces a lag of 34ms caused by the image processing.

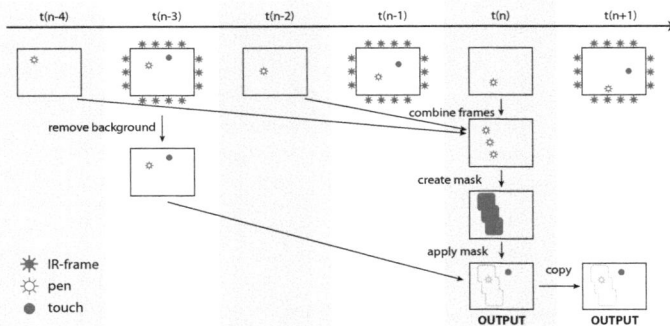

Figure 5.13: The updated software filter pipeline for masking pen input in the touch tracking algorithm for a capture frame rate of 120Hz. *Image courtesy of Jakob Leitner.*

Hardware filter approach

The first approach described above used inexpensive Lee[7] filter foils to block visible light from the camera. The filter-characteristic shown in Figure 5.14 shows that using this filter the camera is able to capture light from the pen as well as light from the LED frame. Notice that the different IR light intensities of pen and touch are not considered in the graph (both are normalized).

The second approach attempts to hide the IR light emitted by the pen by using narrow bandpass and longpass filters. All filters and IR-light sources were measured using a spectrometer and also tested with a prototype touchtable setup. The IR-LEDs (SFH 485P) used for the FTIR-tracking have a spectrum from 780nm to 960nm with a peak wavelength emission at 870nm. These LEDs where specifically chosen to match the sensitivity of the camera chip[8]. The IR-light emitted by the Anoto pen has a wavelength between

---
[7] http://www.leefilters.com
[8] http://www.ptgrey.com/products/fireflymv/fireflymv.pdf

5. Interactive Meeting Room Redesign

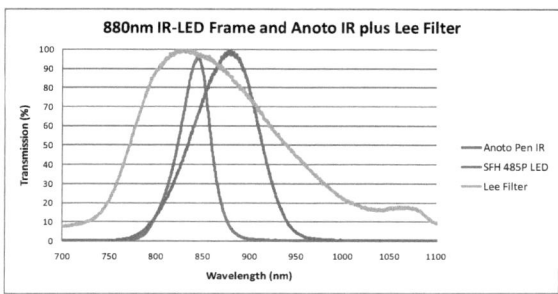

Figure 5.14: Both IR lights from the Anoto pen and the LED frame pass the Lee filter.

780nm and 880nm with a peak at 840nm. In a first attempt, we used a narrow bandpass filter[9] (peak 880 ± 10nm) to exclude the IR-light emitted by the Anoto pen. Figure 5.15 shows the corresponding measurements.

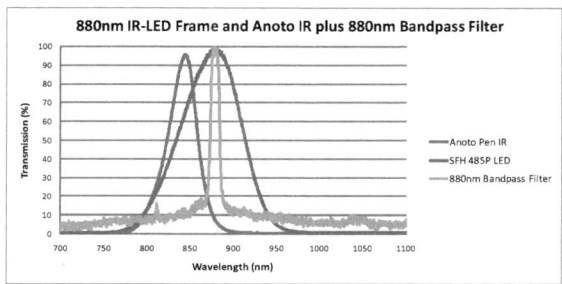

Figure 5.15: The bandpass filter cuts most of the pen's IR light. The LED frame's light passes the filter.

However, the experimental setup showed that the amount of light from the pen that passed the filter was considerably more than expected. The LED in the pen is directly facing the camera while the light of a touch point is

---
[9] http://www.interferenzoptik.de

5. Interactive Meeting Room Redesign

only a small fraction of the light in the acrylic that gets reflected back to the camera. Although the filtering reduces the amount of light picked up from the pen significantly, the pen still appears in the camera image as bright as a touch point. In a second attempt, we exchanged the bandpass filter with a XIL0930 longpass filter in combination with SFH 415 LEDs for the frame. These LEDs have a peak light emission at 950nm, the filter provides 95% transmission at this wavelength (cf. Figure 5.16). Through shifting the LED frame's wavelength to 950nm and selecting the according longpass filter, the pen's light can be reliably filtered with this combination.

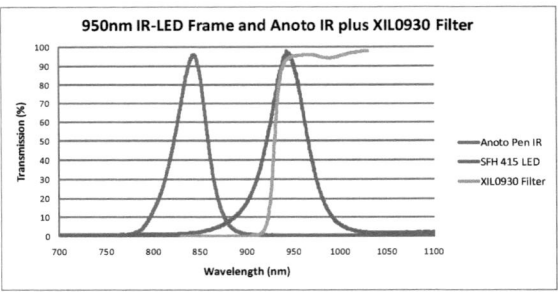

Figure 5.16: With the XIL0930 longpass filter, the Anoto IR-light is reliably cut while the light of the 950nm IR-LEDs passes.

Comparing both approaches

Both approaches have several advantages and disadvantages and whatever option to choose will greatly depend on already available setups, lighting environments and usage scenarios. The following comparison should help to upgrade an existing system or to build a system from scratch.

The main advantages of the computer vision approach using a flashing LED-frame is that several different problems can be addressed with the same setup. In addition to removing unwanted external light sources like the Anoto pen, the setup also allows for removal of ambient light. Moreover, the setup could be used to detect and track simple IR-light pens that do not use

5. Interactive Meeting Room Redesign

blinking IR-LEDs (in the case that Anoto technology is not needed or not available). On the other hand, the filter approach provides faster frame rates, less delay and does not require changing the tracking software.

The computer vision approach on the one hand allows reusing any existing LED-frame setup. Changes to the hardware setup need to be made in form of a small electronic circuit that synchronizes the LED-frame with the camera. This circuit consists of less than a dozen components, which can be purchased for less than 5 dollars. Also a camera with an external trigger to generate the pulse signal is required. This functionality is widely available with industry standard cameras, consumer cameras usually do not provide this functionality [38]. The filter approach on the other hand does not require any additional hardware. However, a significant difference between the wavelength of the pen and the frame is crucial. Thus, existing frames and filters might not be usable in a pen and touch setup.

While the hardware filter approach does not need any modifications of existing tracking software, the image processing approach requires two software changes. Firstly, the external trigger of the camera must be activated in software to synchronize LEDs with camera capture. Secondly, the different filters for tracking touch points need to be adjusted to process reference frames and tracking frames (cf. Figure 5.13). Moreover, this allows implementing continuous background updating which improves system reliability in changing lighting conditions significantly.

The additional processing needed in the software approach introduces a lag of 34ms. Moreover, touches are only tracked with half the camera capture rate. The filter approach, however, does not add additional lag to the image processing but uses full capture frame rate, resulting in a much more responsive system. For direct touch systems, this is definitely preferable. Especially when comparing the two approaches, the lack of responsiveness of the first approach is obvious. However, in combination with Anoto pens, a similar delay of the pen tracking (caused by the Anoto Bluetooth connection) decreases the effect of the short delay.

5.3 Interaction with the Room

Considering the interaction techniques from the first prototype (see Section 4.3), we present our refinements for the redesign of the interactive room. The development is based on the evaluation results of the first implementation as described in Section 4.6 and according to the previously stated redesign goals. In particular, we addressed the requirement for multi-modal input by exploring the design space of combined pen and touch interaction. Furthermore, we accounted for the heterogeneity of documents that are used in meetings by developing techniques for integrating real paper documents with our digital environment.

5.3.1 Pen and Touch Interaction

The results of our first interactive room's evaluation clearly suggested that multi-modal input is a user request for large interactive surfaces. It turned out that pen interaction is not optimal for activities such as workspace organization or document arrangement, for example. For users in our setup, some actions would be more naturally performed with the hand instead of a pen tool. For this reason, this type of direct, "under-the-finger" input device is often called "natural" and "intuitive" when compared to an input device like a pen. On the other hand, occlusion and finger size hamper accurate touch input in a graphical interface. In contrast, a digital pen provides a higher-level of input accuracy, but typically only a single point of input. While choosing any *one* particular input device requires weighing these types of tradeoffs, bimanual input allows us to design input commands using different input devices with the dominant and non-dominant hands. Previous work in this area, along with our observations and experimentation, has convinced us that by combining dominant-hand pen input with non-dominant hand touch input, we can effectively harness the benefits of both pen and touch input while avoiding many of their pitfalls.

In collaboration with MERL we investigated the domain of bimanual pen and touch interaction [18]. The background of this work is based on

5. Interactive Meeting Room Redesign

Guiard's Kinematic Chain model [51], which hypothesizes that the actions of the dominant hand (DH) and the non-dominant hand (NDH) make up a functional kinematic chain. The models suggests that the DH moves within the frame of reference set by the NDH; the DH performs small and frequent actions while the NDH is used for larger and less frequent motions. This behavior can be observed when writing on a piece of paper, for example. The NDH orients the paper while the DH moves the pen to write. Our project aims at applying this knowledge for a digital pen and direct touch enabled environment.

Design Principles

We sought to establish a set of design principles intended to guide developers of bimanual user interfaces. This set is based on an exploration of the possible combinations of bimanual input when each hand may used for either pen or touch input, aided by previous work in bimanual systems. By investigating the possible pairs of input actions, one performed by the DH and one by the NDH, as well as the type of and order in which these commands are performed, we have developed a set of principles that we believe combine the best qualities of pen input and touch input into a single system.

Input Choices for Both Hands

The general structure we propose for the categorization of input variations is shown in Figure 5.17. Both, the DH and the NDH have the same set of input possibilities - pen input, touch input, or no input. When using a pen for input (Figure 5.17, left branch of tree), researchers and system designers typically distinguish between inking and command stroking modes: referring to the usage of a pen for writing or drawing, and for making commands in the second. A barrel-button can be used to delimit these two modes, as can gestural delimiters [61]. Command strokes are interpreted as either point-based interaction (i.e. mouse-like, point-and-click commands) or gestural strokes (e.g. handwriting input).

5. Interactive Meeting Room Redesign

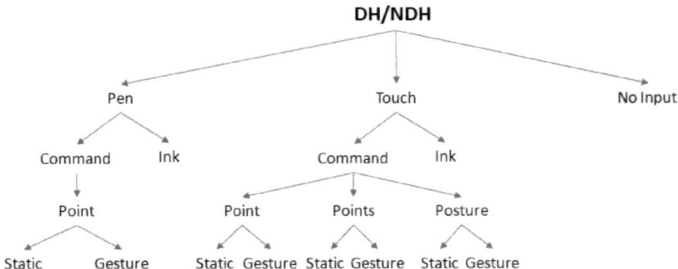

Figure 5.17: Input categorization. Both the DH and NDH can perform one type of input in a bimanual action.

When using touch input (Figure 5.17, center branch), single-finger commands are often interpreted as point-based interaction (i.e. mouse-like interaction). A benefit of touch input with multi-touch devices is the ability to sense and handle multiple points of input, or even different hand postures. Postures can be recognized as commands themselves or moved over time creating high-bandwidth gestures.

For designing bimanual commands, two different inputs are combined to infer a task or operation. Input possibilities are stated in the tree as leaves. One input comes from the dominant and one from the non-dominant hand.

Pros and Cons of Pen and Touch Input

We considered the pros and cons of each technique to motivate the assignment of different input combinations for different tasks (cf. Figure 5.18). We wished to combine the positive qualities of both input mechanisms, while avoiding their pitfalls. According to previous studies on the role of the dominant and non-dominant hands [30] [71], we propose using a pen for precise input with the DH and direct touch for intuitive, high-bandwidth touch commands with the NDH. For example, inking is a typical pen task, as touch input suffers from larger occlusions and lower touch precision. Cutler showed that this use of pen and touch performed better than two-handed touch [30].

5. Interactive Meeting Room Redesign

They found that, especially for asymmetric tasks, the benefit of a distinguished pen point for fine grain gestures and the intuitive use of coarse hand gestures exactly mirrored the asymmetric distribution of labor described by Guiard.

PEN		TOUCH	
PRO	**CONTRA**	**PRO**	**CONTRA**
High sensing resolution	Only one input point	Multiple points of input	Occlusion
Precise touch point	Separate device	Use with low attention	Low touch point preciseness
Leverage existing tool uses		No additional devices	
Less accidental input than touch		„Natural"	

Figure 5.18: Advantages and disadvantages of pen and touch as input devices for tabletops.

Sequencing of Commands

We have already discussed how each hand can issue one of several input commands and that the combination of direct touch and pen input offers the tantalizing opportunity to take advantage of the strengths of each device. Additionally, we explored the sequencing of the DH and NDH actions. A bimanual task can be started by either hand, and the sequence of the start of the paired input streams can set the context for the further action. Wu et al. [180] refer to this concept as the gesture registration phase that defines the beginning of every gesture operation and therefore sets the context for subsequent interactions. They describe a system in which a stylus can be either treated as a writing device or a pointer depending on the mode set in the gesture registration phase. When the sequence of bimanual actions is relevant, a pen's input preceding a touch gesture is different to a touch gesture performed prior to a pen point. According to their temporal occurrence, we distinguish three different types of sequences: sequential, overlapping and

5. Interactive Meeting Room Redesign

simultaneous (cf. Figure 5.19).

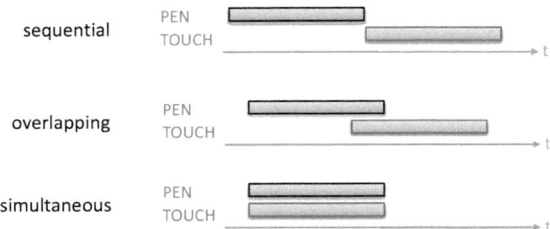

Figure 5.19: Three causal sequencing of commands.

Coupling and Decoupling of Interactions

In terms of sequencing, we dynamically and systematically couple and decouple the input of the two hands. For example, a task that can be performed with the NDH could be supported by the DH to extend the functionality or increase the accuracy. The NDH therefore sets the modal reference frame in which the DH will be acting. We add the input of the DH if necessary (couple) and proceed with single NDH input if this is sufficient (decouple). Coarse positioning of an object, for example, can be achieved with the NDH; for a final accurate placement, the DH can be coupled to add high precision information.

Laboratory Experiment

Previous work has argued for the advantages and disadvantages of pen and touch combinations; however, they have not been investigated in a laboratory experiment. To address this issue, we conducted an experiment that explores the possible assignments of input devices to each of the hands and their effects on efficiency, fluidity, and user preference. Our goal was to understand the differences among the possible input device pairings for a representative task. The experimental task was carefully chosen to tease out the differences between the input device-to-hand pairings, while maintaining ecological validity.

Participants

Twelve subjects were recruited for our study through an on-line community bulletin board, and paid $20 (USD) for participating. Seven were male and five were female, and their ages ranged from 20 to 50 years old. Eleven of the 12 subjects were right-handed.

Apparatus and Task

Our experimental task consisted of solving and navigating through mazes by drawing a path from a green start marker to a red finish marker (Figure 5.20). These mazes were designed so that participants had to magnify the maze in order to successfully follow its paths without colliding with the maze walls as well as zoom out in order to plan a path through the maze that would reach the goal. We believe that the maze solving experimental task has a high-level of ecological validity because it matches many graphical editing operations in which a user repeatedly switches back and forth between detailed editing at a high-zoom level and contextual verification of the changes at a low-zoom level (such as when masking a region of a high-resolution image for clipping). In essence, this is a traditional path following/tunneling task with the added element of route planning.

An error was recorded whenever the participant's stroke intersected with the black walls of the maze. When this collision occurred, a buzzing sound was played, the subject's stroke changed color from blue to red and was stopped. To continue, the participant had to pick a 10 by 10 pixel continue target that was displayed at the last valid position before hitting the wall. Upon returning to the white path of the maze, the stroke returned to blue. To complete the maze, the participants had to draw one continuous stroke; each time they lifted the pen or drawing finger, the continue target at the end of the stroke had to be picked to proceed. Each participant controlled the testing application using three different input techniques. Each of the three techniques was a bimanual input technique in which the dominant

5. Interactive Meeting Room Redesign

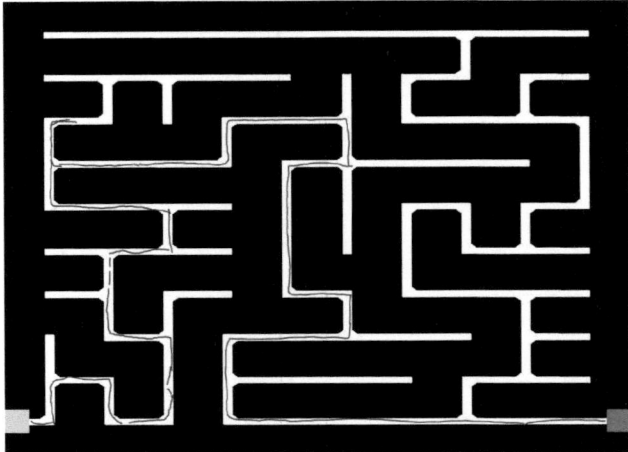

Figure 5.20: A maze from our experiment with the participant's path stroked through the tunnels.

hand created strokes through the maze and the non-dominant hand zoomed and panned the maze itself. The techniques differed in terms of what input device the dominant and non-dominant hands controlled (Figure 5.21).

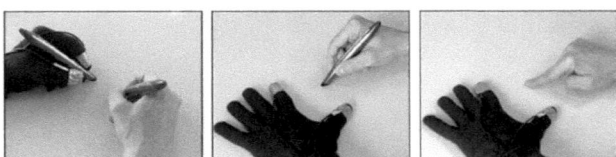

Figure 5.21: The three input techniques used in our experiment - Touch/Touch, Pen/Pen and Pen/Touch.

In the first technique, a participant held two pens, one in each hand. While their dominant hand's pen created strokes through the maze, their non-dominant hand controlled a simple marking menu from which they could

5. Interactive Meeting Room Redesign

zoom in/out and pan the maze..The zoom option was selected with a stroke over the right 90 degree region in front of the pen, the pan selection was performed in the left 90 degree region. In the zooming case, a forward motion would zoom into the scene, whereas a backwards motion zoomed out. After learning the left/right assignment for pan/zoom, this marking menu could be used without paying visual attention. We refer to this technique as Pen/Pen.

In the second technique, the participants held a pen in their dominant hand, which they used to create strokes in the maze, while they performed two simple gestures for zooming and panning with their non-dominant hand. Two fingers spreading apart or pulling together would zoom in or out respectively, one finger panned the maze. We refer to this technique as Pen/Touch. The C/D gain for zooming was the same for the pen's marking menu option and the direct touch stretching gesture. The mapping coefficient was multiplied by a fixed value to achieve a larger zooming effect with less motion. Our third and final input technique, Touch/Touch, combined the non-dominant hand gestures for pan and zoom from the Pen/Touch condition with index-finger stroking performed with the participant's dominant hand.

Hypotheses

Our hypotheses, the confirmation of which will validate our hand / input device pairings, were as follows:

H1: *Participants will complete the mazes in less time while using the Pen/-Touch technique than when use the Pen/Pen or Touch/Touch techniques.*

H2: *Participants will commit fewer errors while using the Pen/Touch technique than when use the Pen/Pen or Touch/Touch techniques.*

H3: *Participants will prefer the Pen/Touch condition over the other conditions.*

Design

We used a within-participant, repeated measures design for our study,

5. Interactive Meeting Room Redesign

with each subject completing 10 mazes using each of the 3 input techniques. The order of the three techniques was balanced between participants. All participants completed the same 30 unique mazes, and maze / technique pairings were balanced. Participants were given instructions before using each technique, and were asked to practice the technique on two practice mazes before starting the experimental trials. In short, our design was:

12 participants × 3 Input Techniques × 10 mazes = 360 trials

Results

Time Analysis. The time of a trial was recorded as the time between the participant's click of the start button that was shown before each maze and their successful crossing through the "finish" rectangle at the end of the maze. A repeated-measures ANOVA shows that there was a significant difference among the three input techniques ($F_{1,11} = 10.70$, $p < 0.01$), thus confirming hypothesis H1. On average, our participants successfully completed each maze in 42.6s, 36.5s, and 52.7s for the Pen/Pen, Pen/Touch, and Touch/Touch conditions respectively. Figure 5.22 shows the mean trial times for each of the three input techniques.

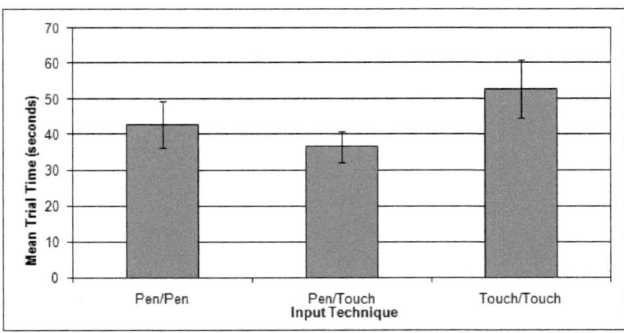

Figure 5.22: The average trial times for each of the three input techniques. Error bars represent 95% confidence interval.

Error Rate Analysis. In our study, an error was recorded whenever the

5. Interactive Meeting Room Redesign

participant's stroke collided with one of the walls of the maze. When this occurred, an error sound was played, the color of the participant's stroke changed from blue to red and could not be continued until the small recover rectangle at the last valid stroke position was picked. Upon reentering the white path of the maze, the sound would stop and the stroke color would return to blue.

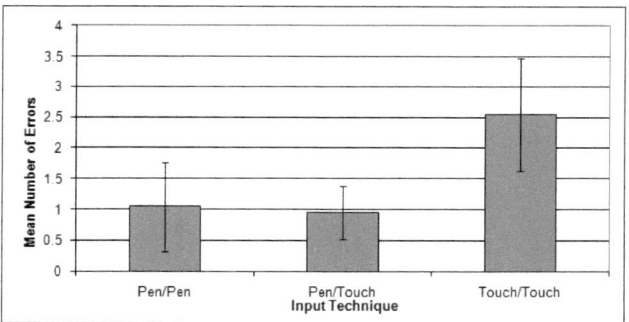

Figure 5.23: The mean number of errors committed during each maze for each of the three input techniques. Error bars represent 95% confidence interval.

A repeated-measures ANOVA suggests that there is a significant difference among the average number of errors committed by our participants while using each of the three input techniques ($F_{1,11} = 11.6$, $p < 0.01$). On average, participants committed 1.05, 0.95, and 2.55 errors per maze for the Pen/Pen, Pen/Touch, and Touch/Touch conditions respectively. A post-hoc comparison of means shows a significant difference between the Touch/Touch and both of the other two input conditions in respect to error rate. Figure 15 shows the average number of errors per maze for each input technique.

Preferential Results. At the end of each session, we asked our participants to rank the three techniques in terms of ease of use, accuracy, and overall preference. Table 5.1 shows the mean rank and standard deviations for each of the three techniques for each of the three measurements (lower numbers

5. Interactive Meeting Room Redesign

	Touch/Touch	Pen/Pen	Pen/Touch
Overall Preference	2.50 (0.67)	2.33 (0.65)	1.17 (0.39)
Ease of Use	2.50 (0.67)	2.25 (0.75)	1.25 (0.45)
Accuracy	2.83 (0.39)	1.92 (0.67)	1.25 (0.45)

Table 5.1: Mean (SD) rankings for each input techniques.

indicate a higher level of preference). These results support hypothesis H3, in that our participants seemed to indicate a strong preference for Pen/Touch input over the other two techniques, with 10 of our 12 participants ranking Pen/Touch as highest in terms of overall preference.

Discussion

In need of investigation is an accounting of the observed differences in task time between our three input techniques. While the number of errors committed certainly accounts for some of the difference in trial times, they do not fully explain it. In addition to recording the trial time and number of errors committed during each trial, our testing application also recorded the number of zoom and pan operations as well as the number of times that a participant lifted the pen (in Pen conditions) or index finger of their drawing hand (Touch/Touch) from the table. These numbers provide details allowing us to provide additional insights from the observed differences in completion time.

An examination of the number of zoom operations provides further insights. An ANOVA shows that each of the input techniques had a significantly different number of zooms ($F_{2,22} = 23.0$, $p < 0.001$). On average, participants zoomed 1.62, 1.89, and 7.91 times per maze for Pen/Pen, Pen/Touch, and Touch/Touch respectively (Figure 5.24). The much larger number of zooms in the Touch/Touch condition is explained by the lack of precision of the finger for drawing input: participants zoomed in to draw, then back out to gain context in navigation. At the other extreme, participants zoomed significantly less often in the Pen/Pen than in the Pen/Touch condition, despite the identical drawing device. We attribute this difference to the increased

5. Interactive Meeting Room Redesign

awkwardness of using the pen-based menu versus gestures.

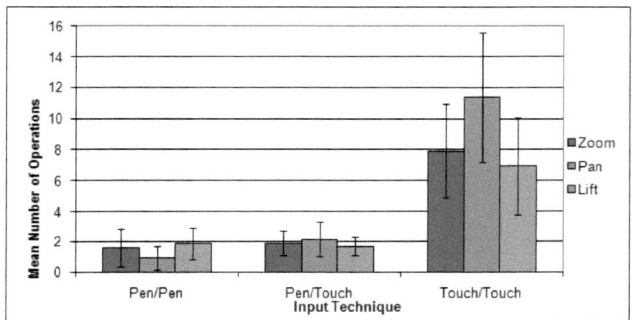

Figure 5.24: Mean pan, lift, and zoom actions per trial.

Additional timing information can be deduced by examining the number of panning operations during each trial (Figure 5.24). The mean number of pans was significantly different in each of the input conditions: 0.93, 2.14, and 11.37 for Pen/Pen, Pen/Touch, and Touch/Touch ($F_{2,22} = 23.8$, $p < 0.001$). Panning is positively correlated with zooming, since zoomed-in mazes require more pans to traverse the space, while requiring frequent zooms in and out to gain context and to draw strokes. As with the mean number of zooms, we see a reduction in the number of pans in the Pen/Pen condition as compared with the Pen/Touch condition. The reason for this result lies in the behavior of the participants, who tried to avoid using the marking menu in the Pen/Pen condition, while hesitating less to perform gestures for zooming in the Pen/Touch condition. Although the marking menu offered only two options to select from and the selection gesture could be learnt after the first usage, we observed a constant focus shift when the participants used the menu. This behavior was not found in the case when they used touch gestures to zoom and pan.

The final measurement that helps to explain the observed differences in

5. Interactive Meeting Room Redesign

task time among the input techniques is the number of times that a participant lifted their dominant hand from the tabletop. Again, we see a significant difference among the input techniques ($F_{2,22} = 15.38$, $p < 0.001$), with a large difference between the Touch/Touch input technique (6.93 lifts/maze), and both the Pen/Pen (1.86 lifts/maze) and Pen/Touch (1.68 lifts/maze) techniques (Figure 5.24). The fact that a significant higher number of lifts occurred with the Touch/Touch technique seems to be caused by two reasons. First, during the zoom and pan operation, most participants lifted the pen or drawing finger. They could have left the finger or pen on the last drawing position while zooming without causing an error. During panning, this would have resulted in a similar effect of dragging a sheet of paper under a pen. Nevertheless, they felt more comfortable to lift the finger or pen during these actions. Second, due to larger occlusion areas in the Touch/Touch scenario, the stroke was frequently interrupted for hand positioning reasons. Taken together, the clear evidence in support of our hypotheses and these additional details provide strong validation for our assignment of input devices to the hands.

5.3.2 Interaction with Digital and Real Documents

Sketching ideas and taking notes is a common activity during meetings or presentations. For this reason, we facilitated these actions through the design of personal workspaces in our first interactive room. Users could sketch with their digital pen in their workspace or on the digital whiteboard. One of the advantages of this approach was the immediate digitizing of all content; this allowed for easy sharing and filing. However, relying on a completely digital environment does not realistically reflect current work practices in meetings. Despite the predictions of the paperless office, we still see paper as an integral part of many activities in office environments. Hence we argue for the combination of digital documents and traditional paper, since certain activities are simply better supported by paper whereas others lend themselves to digital processing. A closer examination of paper characteristics helps to gain an understanding of the design space where paper can complement activities

5. Interactive Meeting Room Redesign

with documents in an interactive room.

Sellen and Harper have explored the reason why paper has not been replaced by digital systems until today in their book *The Myth of the Paperless Office* [141]. They report about the concept of *affordances*, which describes the activities that an object allows or affords. Using this concept, they compare the affordances of paper to the digital world. Paper is tangible; it is easy to pick up and flip through the pages while getting a sense of the length of a document. While navigating in a paper document, the reader gets feedback about his location from the amount of pages already seen and the ones still to be read. Paper can be tailored; it is easy to annotate a paper document, which can be done simultaneously to reading it. It is a common practice to use a notebook for taking notes while reading in another paper document [139]. Furthermore, paper is spatially flexible; it can be spread out and organized in a structure that suits our needs for a specific task. We are able to read across multiple pages at the same time and can further structure them to define a new order. Finally, paper has its own affordances in collaborating groups. Because paper is a tangible object, the actions performed with the paper are visible to the other group members. The exact content of a user's note on the paper may not be recognizable by the others, but the action of taking a note is clearly visible. Referring to the proximities and orientations that people used to establish personal and group spaces on tables [162] [82], paper provides an ideal device through its affordances. Previous research on tabletop setups has shown that users are frequently transitioning between their private space and the group space [39] [95]. The transition from personal to group space, for example, can be easily accomplished by putting a paper document on the table's surface. The action with the paper document already informs the group about the intention and the social context. Another advantage of paper is the immediate feedback of written content without latency or resolution problems. Digital systems that capture handwriting are commonly facing the problem of input latency, which hampers the experience of fluid interaction. At the time of this writing, state-of-the-art graphic tablets like the WACOM Cintiq[10] offered the best available quality for pen input. However, it is still

---

[10] http://www.wacom.com

5. Interactive Meeting Room Redesign

not comparable to the feeling of writing on paper.

Paper and Digital Documents in the Interactive Room

To harness the advantages of traditional paper in our interactive meeting room, we based the development on our initial digital environment but additionally allowed to interact with real paper. In the following, we present a new paper-based interaction device which enables a seamless usage of a digital pen for manipulating real printouts and for controlling a digital whiteboard [19]. Users can simply pick up printed items (e.g. images, text elements) from the real printout and drop them on the digital whiteboard, as proposed by Rekimoto [126]. We suggest a solution where the same pen device can be used for making notes on the real printout as well as for interacting on a digital surface. This is according to our redesign goal from Section 5.1 to minimize input device switching. Using only one device for all interactions guarantees a seamless transition between real paper and digital environment.

Figure 5.25: Users can go to the meeting and present their ideas to the audience either by transferring the real ink data to the digital whiteboard or by transferring printed information of the printout to the digital whiteboard.

5. Interactive Meeting Room Redesign

Our approach is influenced by two different research works: firstly, by Guimbretière's work, who presented a system where real notes are seamlessly transformed to the digital world, and vice versa [54]. In his system, users create digital documents and manipulate them either on a computer or on the paper using Anoto's technology. Users have to make their comments on the real printouts - once finished they can transfer the data to the computer via a USB-based docking station. Secondly, we got influenced by Rekimoto's Pick-and-Drop metaphor, where users seamlessly transferred digital data from one device to the other [126]. In contrast to his work, we postulate not to use tablet PCs or PDAs, but to use real printouts and real notebooks.

Our work is influenced by the previous work, but it is different in a number of important ways. Our system benefits from the following features:

- Seamless combination of both real and virtual data combined with augmented content; in contrast to related work, we allow a seamless switch between the digital and real data. Users can start with a sketch on a real paper, another person can add further annotations on the digital whiteboard, and in parallel the first person can continue the sketch on the real printout. Thus, we support a simultaneous, multi-user interaction in both the real and digital world,

- Users can simply drag-and-drop data from the real printout and move it to the digital environment (e.g. digital whiteboard); thus, we also use the same pen-based interface for interacting with the digital whiteboard,

- For both worlds, users can use the same input Anoto pen input device,

- Our system allows a high degree of accuracy with approximately 600 dpi on the paper and on the whiteboard,

- And finally the setup is relatively inexpensive to be manufactured. One pen costs around 200 USD and the documents can be printed on traditional paper.

5. Interactive Meeting Room Redesign

Paper-Based Interaction

We combine traditional input devices, such as pen & paper, with a digital environment. Designers can create imagery and notes on their real notebooks, make printouts with legacy software (e.g. Powerpoint, Excel, Firefox, etc.), and move them to the interactive wall for further discussion. The pen can be either used as inking or pointing device that allows selections on the paper document and data manipulations on the digital whiteboard. To change the mode for the pen, we integrated special control elements at the bottom of each page (see Figure 5.26). By clicking on them, the pen can change its mode or selected data can be sent to the whiteboard. In addition, we offer some options for defining the ink style including colors and stroke widths. Notice that by changing the color or stroke width, only the digital ink will be changed accordingly, but the real ink still has the same color or width.

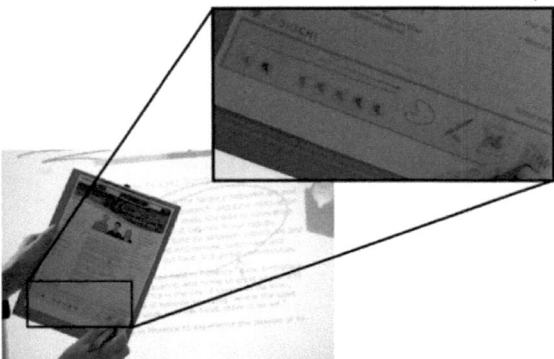

Figure 5.26: Special control elements printed at the bottom of the page can be used for further interaction.

The control elements at the bottom of the page are customizable by our software and allow the integration of further interaction possibilities. Combining the real paper with control elements and the connection to the digital

5. Interactive Meeting Room Redesign

whiteboard offers a variety of interesting options. Our approach is characterized by the following interaction techniques:

- Pick-and-Drop,
- Sketch-and-Send, and
- Present-and-Interact.

Pick-and-Drop

Similar to Rekimoto's Pick-and-Drop metaphor with mobile devices [126], users can pick up data from a printed document and drop it on the interactive surface, the digital whiteboard. Once in selection mode, each item of the printout becomes a selectable content and can be transferred without losing quality, since we transfer the raw data. In our scenario, users have to click with the pen on the corresponding data of the real printout. By using the digital pen, we can calculate the exact position and we can identify the according item. The data gets transferred when clicking again on the digital whiteboard (see Figure 5.27).

(a)   (b)

Figure 5.27: Users can pick up content from the real printout (a) and drop it on the digital surface (b).

Alternatively, selections on the real paper document can be sent to the digital whiteboard by clicking on the send button which is located at the bottom control panel on the paper (see Figure 5.26). In this case, users do

5. Interactive Meeting Room Redesign

not have to stand up and walk to the whiteboard to drop the selected data, but can accomplish this from their remote location.

Summarizing, users can select objects by changing the pen's mode from inking to selecting, define the corresponding part of the page, and finally move it to the digital whiteboard by directly dropping the selection with the pen or sending through the "send control" printed at the bottom of each page.

Sketch-and-Send

Our system supports additional annotations on the real printout that can be performed with the real ink of the pen. The digital version of the ink can be either visualized in real-time on the digital whiteboard or stored on the pen's integrated memory. In both variations, all data that is entered with the pen while in inking mode is processed in one or the other way.

Real-time streaming is mainly used in scenarios where the paper printout and the digital whiteboard are in the same location. Annotations on the paper are also immediately visible on the digital whiteboard. The data transfer is accomplished through Bluetooth streaming from the Anoto pen to the whiteboard PC. Figure 5.28 shows an example where a user is annotating with real ink on the paper document. The results are simultaneously visible as digital ink on the whiteboard.

In this case, the audience can immediately see all changes done on the paper by the writing person. While all manipulations on the real paper are also immediately visible on the digital whiteboard, the system does not support a visual feedback on the real printout in the case of changes on the digital whiteboard. The only possibility is to create a new printout from the sketches done on the whiteboard.

Offering remote sketching in our system allows the participants of a meeting to keep seated around a table and share their ideas by sketching with real ink directly on a paper while the digital whiteboard acts as presentation area. This means that the users have two possibilities: they can either sit at the table and work on the digital whiteboard from their place; or they can stand up, go to the flipchart but still make their comments on the paper, which

5. Interactive Meeting Room Redesign

Figure 5.28: Annotations on the real printout are immediately visible on the digital whiteboard.

also automatically get transferred to the digital whiteboard. In both cases, all sketched information is sent to the whiteboard in real-time, regardless of the user's location. In our system, multiple people (we tested the scenario with 7 participants) can interact simultaneously - independently if they are sitting or standing.

Working in offline mode, the sketched notes can be stored in the pen's integrated memory in advance and moved seamlessly to the whiteboard during a presentation. People can sketch offline on the real paper (e.g. during a flight), come to the meeting and send all sketched data to the digital whiteboard. In this case, the pen allows to store up to 70 full-written pages. In Figure 5.29, we demonstrate a case where a user is preparing a sketch offline (embedded figure) and later in a meeting sends the stored data to the digital whiteboard. This whole functionality can of course also be used during a meeting to prepare sketches on the paper without displaying them in real-time on the whiteboard; presenting it to the audience can be done at any time later during the meeting.

5. Interactive Meeting Room Redesign

Figure 5.29: Users can create new sketches on the paper and send the ideas to the whiteboard for the audience for further presentation.

Figure 5.30: The sent data (e.g. image) can be moved / rotated / scaled on the digital whiteboard.

Present-and-Interact

Finally, notes that are sent to the whiteboard can further be modified with digital ink. In addition, transferred images can be arranged and transformed

5. Interactive Meeting Room Redesign

on the digital surface (see Figure 5.30). In this scenario, we use the same pens for the interactive whiteboard as for the interaction with the real paper, so users do not have to switch to another device. Another advantage is the quality of digital data: sent data still has the same high quality as the item from the printout (e.g. the image from a website printed on the paper and sent to the digital whiteboard still has the same quality as the original image).

The Interactive Paper

Since we used Anoto digital pens as input devices, interaction with the digital surfaces and with real paper are supported simultaneously in our room. In this section, we explain the underlying hardware requirements and the production process of an interactive paper document.

To capture the ink on the real printout, we are using one of the two Anoto data management options: Sketched notes can either be stored on the pen and transferred over BT using the OBEX File Transfer Protocol or directly be streamed via BT in real-time to the digital environment. Users simply have to click special checkboxes, printed on the real paper. Each page has its own paper ID. In combination with the pen ID and the position, we can easily track each ink stroke and send them to the digital whiteboard.

Figure 5.31 depicts a close-up of the printout with the background Anoto pattern and the overlaid graphics. For the page's composition, we use a layer with two different kinds of pattern. The upper part of the layer contains the pattern for the "interaction" region. This pattern has to be different for each page and contains a continuous number (ID). The lower part, a unique page pattern (which is equal for all pages), is used for the special checkboxes, which are printed at the bottom of each page as depicted in Figure 5.32.

Figure 5.33 illustrates the workflow of creating an interactive printout including a registration and an interaction phase. If users want to interact with their printout, they simply have to generate an XPS file, which is supported by all Windows applications, once the .NET Framework 3.0 is installed. This file usually contains multiple pages, which again include further content (the file can be seen as a container with different elements, such as text, images,

5. Interactive Meeting Room Redesign

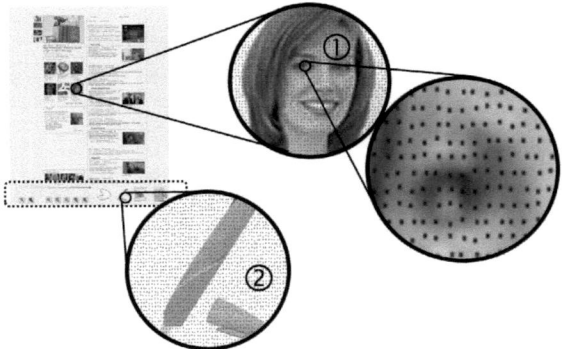

Figure 5.31: After exporting to an XPS file, we add an additional layer with two patterns on top of each printout for tracking the strokes with the digital pen. While the upper part of the layer (1) is used for tracking the ink strokes on the page, the lower one (2) contains a unique ID for the control elements. This pattern is equal for all pages.

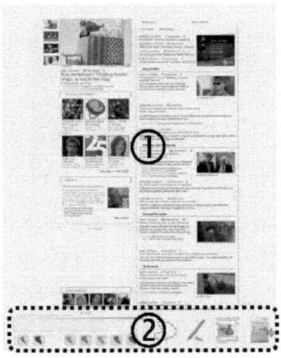

Figure 5.32: Each printout consists of the original content (top of the page, e.g. website) and a control panel (bottom of each page) for additional interaction possibilities and commands.

5. Interactive Meeting Room Redesign

strokes or containers again). In the next step, this file has to be printed on a color printer with our application.

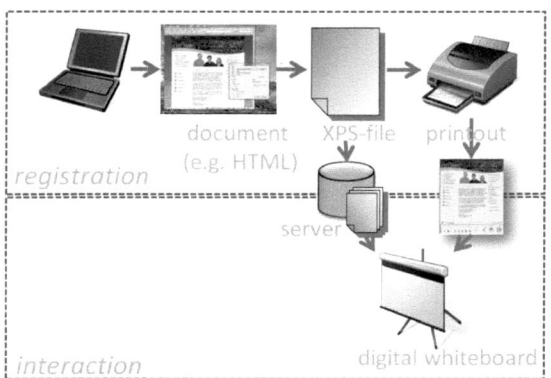

Figure 5.33: The workflow for creating and using an interactive paper document. In the registration phase, the paper document is linked to its digital copy. During interaction, the paper printout serves as a proxy for the digital document.

In our system, we used an HP6940. As described by Guimbretière in [54], the printing process can be very complicated and time-consuming, because of the special requirements of the Anoto-based pattern. While the pattern should be printed with the black ink cartridge (which is not IR transparent and therefore visible for the IR camera), the content should be printed only with Cyan, Magenta, and Yellow (without K); the colors C, M, Y (even composed) are invisible for the IR camera. Usually, printouts contain black content and we need to find a way to make this content invisible for the IR camera. Several solutions have been discussed in [54].

Instead of removing the ink cartridge and printing the document pages twice (once with the pattern using the black ink and again with the content with C, M, Y), we propose to modify dark colors within the page, e.g. RGB (255, 255, 255) to a brighter RGB grey value, such as (169,169,169). The

5. Interactive Meeting Room Redesign

pages still look good and can be printed easily without any complicated hardware changes on the printer. However, the automated color management of the printer has to be switched off. Unfortunately, it is not possible to change the CMYK values directly within the XPS document.

We also store the XPS document on the server with the according ID. The server handles all documents and the corresponding pages including the page IDs used for further operation with the digital whiteboard. After the registration of the paper, users can click on the check boxes for further interaction. There are two ways of interaction: XPS content (e.g. images, paragraphs) can be easily transferred to the digital whiteboard. The objects of the corresponding XPS file are extracted and transferred accordingly. By using the XPS API, we identify digital content in the document and allow the pick-and-drop metaphor to transfer the content from the real paper to the digital world. Users can also select parts of a printed document and drop them on the digital whiteboard. Alternatively, users can make additional notes on the printout with different colors, change the stroke width, select a user-defined region, and transfer the data again to the whiteboard. For both devices, the real printout and the digital wall, we are using the pattern, which allows an easy integration of the real notebook interface. Thus, users do not have to switch the device while working with the printout or with the digital whiteboard.

Early User Feedback

In an initial pilot study we tested 6 employees from our University, who were not affiliated with this project. The overall participants' reaction was very positive. Users really liked the idea of grabbing content from the real printout and using it on a digital whiteboard. It is more convenient since people don't have to use a heavy Tablet PC. Participants also had the impression to work within *one* world.

Giving feedback on the real paper is really challenging and still a problem. The pen that we used in our system, gave a vibration feedback only on errors and whenever the information has been sent successfully to the digital

5. Interactive Meeting Room Redesign

whiteboard. However, people asked for a better visual feedback. Especially when they selected different ink colors, they were not sure if the system accepted their selection or not. Although the system always worked fine during the test, they expected to get a feedback. Giving feedback in the meeting room (in combination with the digital whiteboard) would be easy; in this case, we can provide audio and visual feedback on the digital whiteboard or on an interactive table. We don't have a solution yet for users working offline. However, we also have to ask how often users would change the digital color if they can't do it with the real ink of the pen.

Participants often felt lost while working with the different modes (e.g. users did not recognize immediately that they were in the mode of annotating the paper or that they were in the grabbing mode). One of the participants proposed to have an audio feedback or a visual feedback on the digital whiteboard since the system is mainly used in combination with the digital presentation tool. Another idea proposed by a participant was to modify the pen with corresponding LEDs.

We used two types of pens: In a first scenario, participants worked with a digital pen that had a stylus tip, which did not leave a real ink on the paper. Consequently, participants could also use the same pen while working with the printout and while interacting with the digital whiteboard. In the second scenario, participants worked with a ballpoint tip based digital pen, which did leave real ink traces on the paper. However, using a ballpoint tip would leave ink on the whiteboard. On the other side switching pens would be really cumbersome. Therefore, we propose to modify the pen where users can switch between the two modes (ballpoint tip and stylus tip). Another solution would be to use an ink repellent surface on the digital whiteboard.

Finally, participants also would appreciate it to get a feedback on the real printout once they change the digital content. One solution would be to track the paper and to augment the changes accordingly on the paper. However, Anoto tracking is not able to accomplish this without additional information about the position and orientation of the paper document on the table. We only retrieve relative coordinates on each page, but no absolute values that would allow us to align the digital overlay with the real document. Therefore,

5. Interactive Meeting Room Redesign

feedback directly on the pages would require additional tracking of the pages themselves.

An interesting observation we made was that participants discussed in a different way once they had to work together (e.g. in a brainstorming session). In a classical presentation with a whiteboard where the audience is sitting around a table, the presenter is automatically the leader of the session. Usually he/she moderates the session and the audience is almost acting in the background. In our setup, however, everybody has the chance to interact immediately (see Figure 5.34). Everybody can send sketches, notes and data to the digital whiteboard without standing up and walking to the whiteboard. This raises the question about rights and control management, which we addressed through a social protocol in our first prototype.

Figure 5.34: Users can also sit around the interactive table and interact with the digital whiteboard either through the real printout or the digital table.

The integration of real notes in a digital environment seems to be a good solution for improving the performance of current digital walls and interactive tables. It combines the affordances of paper and electronic data. Related researchers found already that we will still use real printouts in the future - the myth of paperless office environment will still be true a myth in the next couple of years - in contrast, we are currently producing more paper compared to several years ago. In some domains, paper is still necessary (e.g. medical reports etc.). Moreover, digital systems require switching between tools to support different activities such as writing, sketching or manipulating digital object, whereas studies that focused on traditional tabletop work sessions showed that people are frequently transitioning between writing and drawing without making a distinction of their activities [17] [162]. Sketching and writing on paper is naturally supporting this work practice, as there is no difference in the type of input. A sketch or a note is treated equally on a sheet of paper. With paper as the input surface, interaction is not effected by additional technology imposed overhead.

Our proposed interface provides an intuitive and easy-to-use manipulation of digital information while working together on large vertical/horizontal electronic displays. Our approach is easy and inexpensive to construct and allows a scalable and multi-user environment, where simultaneous work is supported. In contrast to most related work, we use a system that allows working with the same digital pen in different situations. This is supporting the rule to avoid frequent switching of input devices. Moreover, it allows for a very fluid work process even with the integration of such different input sources as paper and digital surfaces.

5.4 Workspace and Menu Design

According to the results of the first interactive room's evaluation, we redesigned the digital workspace to better fit the user requirements of a collaborative space (Section 5.4.1). We modified the workspace concept from providing separate personal workspaces for each user towards the design of a single shared workspace. Along with this development, we adapted the menu design to maintain multi-user functionality while generalizing the overall workspace concept (Section 5.4.2).

5. Interactive Meeting Room Redesign

5.4.1 Shared Workspace Concept

For the tabletop's digital workspace, we developed a common shared space layout called ISIS. Without the visible boundaries of personal workspaces, each user has the same rights to work on the surface, to create, manipulate and share data. Without the need to actively grant access to objects for other users, we expected the workflows to be more fluid compared to the separated workspace version. Figure 5.35 shows a comparison of the personal workspace layout (*left*) and the redesigned shared public space layout (*right*). Compared to the first generation approach where each user had a personal workspace with interface elements, each user now has a separate menu and can use the entire surface as a workspace.

Figure 5.35: Two different layouts for the tabletop's workspace. For the first prototype, we designed window-style personal workspaces for each user (*left*). The redesign is based on a single large shared workspace where all users work simultaneously (*right*).

Since the users equally share the tabletop, the interaction is influenced by the *social protocol* of the group. But previous studies showed that the *social protocol* among users is not always sufficient on multi-user tabletops [102]. Actions that affect the whole workspace, like changing the view or clearing it for example, are critical if controls are replicated and each user has the right to perform them. In this context, we experimented with tangible palettes that can physically restrict controls to a single user, if there is only one palette available for a certain task. With this one copy it is assured that only one person takes over the control. Moreover it is visible for the group who is in

5. Interactive Meeting Room Redesign

charge of it and when it is used. Similar to the first generation application, different colors and stroke widths are available to customize the input. But in contrast to the first implementation of these tools in form of hardware palettes, the new version features additional selections through the digital menu. The palettes are still available as a shortcut (as there is no navigation in a menu necessary), but the same parameters can also be set through the digital menu.

The space management of our first prototype was based on a page concept within the personal workspaces. If additional space was required, pages could be added to the workspace similar to a new tab window in a browser. In addition, the whole workspace could be resized in order to create a larger work area. In contrast to this first approach, the new implementation features one large workspace that is organized in pages across a session. A page represents the current work area that is accessible for all users. Each page is treated as an infinite large workspace which can be controlled through moving and zooming the current view on the page (see Figure 5.36).

Figure 5.36: Controlling the view on the session. Original view (left), and zoomed in view (right).

Since the control of the current view changes the whole workspace, it affects all users in a collaborative session. Therefore, the control over the view locks the current workspace and can only be used by a single person exclusively. The same exclusive control is used for skipping pages or changing to the page overview. As already mentioned, the pages in the redesigned version

5. Interactive Meeting Room Redesign

span over the entire surface. In order to navigate through these full-screen pages in a session, the page overview as depicted in Figure 5.37 provides a compact view on all pages with fast access to a specific page.

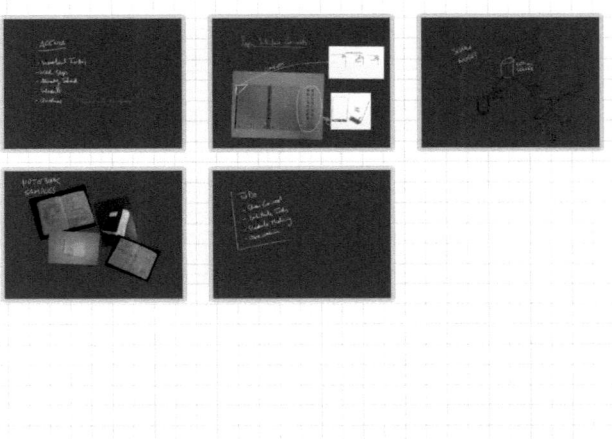

Figure 5.37: The page overview provides access to all pages of a session.

5.4.2 Menu Design for Large Shared Workspaces

As described in the previous section, we exchanged the concept of user specific personal workspaces with a single large shared workspace as part of the meeting room's redesign. As Figure 5.38 (a) illustrates, the first prototype featured delimited workspaces for each user that provided all interface elements. However, the single workspace design depicted in Figure 5.38 (b) does not feature user specific areas anymore; instead the whole surface is one large page that is available for all users. This of course requires alternative ways of accessing personal information. Our solution is based on individual menus for each user that are assigned by the Anoto pens' IDs.

5. Interactive Meeting Room Redesign

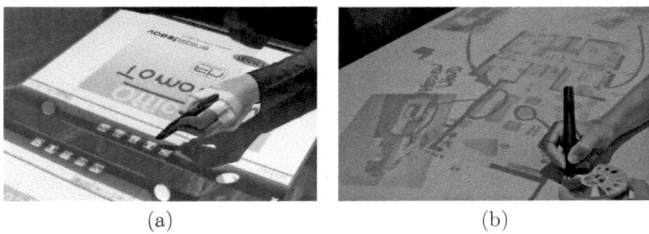

(a) (b)

Figure 5.38: The personal workspace in the first prototype exposed all interface elements in the digital layout (a). The redesigned large workspace required alternative user specific menus for interaction (b).

We noticed that traditional graphical user interfaces, which are mainly designed for desktop PCs, are often used for large surfaces. However, such menus are not appropriate for tabletops or digital whiteboards. For example, the larger dimensions of interactive surfaces introduce reachability problems, menus on tabletops must be orientation independent or multi-user input must be handled. Consequently, we developed a novel menu for digital tabletops that addresses these issues. Within the large shared space, each user has a unique menu that allows accessing tools for interacting with the meeting room application.

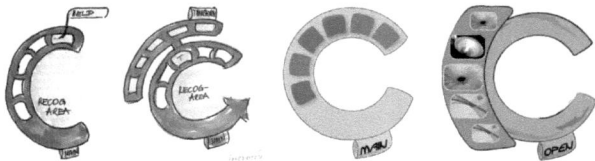

Figure 5.39: Different design stages for menu, ranging from a rough draft showing the semi circle sector shape to a more detailed submenu layout. *Image courtesy of Verena Lugmayr.*

The menu was designed around the ergonomic range of motion allowed by the user's wrist. We ran through several design iterations, starting with a

5. Interactive Meeting Room Redesign

half circle shape as illustrated in Figure 5.39. We noticed that a circle sector design was generally liked, but the predefined orientation of the items was not comfortable for every user. We also noticed that the distance of the items from the menu's center was a crucial factor for their ease-of-use, especially for direct input surfaces where the hand's reach is a limiting factor. Some people had problems to reach items, because the radius from the center of the pie menu to the border was too large. Moreover, occlusions caused by the users hand affected the usability. The open side of the pie menu was not in the optimal position for many users, even though our system could be configured for left or right handed users. These observations led us to the decision to explore the ergonomic factors of pie menus in detail and to apply the findings to a novel menu design [20].

The problem of occlusions on direct input surfaces has been previously investigated on small mobile devices like PDAs and on tabletops. Bieber et al. [11], for example, explored screen coverage for pen interaction and touch screens. They presented an analytic approach to measure the covering of touch screen areas and interaction elements. They mentioned that the differences between left and right-handed users have an effect on screen coverage, but for their analysis, they assume that the average user is right-handed. Leithinger et al. [86] investigated six different menu layouts for interactive tables under various cluttering conditions. In their study, they found out that menu types suffering from occlusion (pie menus for example) showed significant disadvantages compared to their proposed user-drawn context menus. Our approach contributes to these works by describing an occlusion avoiding menu design. We furthermore show a possibility to use partly occluded areas for gesture input.

The second issue that we address with our redesign is the adaption of the menu placement to the user's handedness. There have been previous research projects dealing with the automatic detection of the user's handedness. They are based on different input devices and assumptions about the user behavior. Kurtenbach et al. [84] present a method of automatically determining handedness of users for a bimanual drawing application that utilizes a stylus in one hand and a puck in the other. Hancock et al. [57] suggest three different

5. Interactive Meeting Room Redesign

approaches to detect the user's handedness and according menu placements for one-handed pen interaction. They discuss a simple heuristic approach, a neural network and a Bayesian network model. Harrison et al. [59] explored annotation of digital documents on a handheld computer where they determined the handedness via pressure sensitive pads placed on the back of the device. Our approach for adapting to the user's handedness is suitable for one-handed pen input and does not require any predefined settings. In contrast to Hancock's network models, our method does not need a learning phase of the system.

Our approach concentrates on the occlusions and handedness problems on tabletops. Based on that, we propose a new design for a tabletop menu that avoids occlusions created by the user's hand. By using partly occluded areas for gesture input, we extend the functionality of a traditional point-and-click menu. To account for the handedness of users we apply an adaptive menu placement method based on direct touch and pen tracking. In addition, we show that our flexible system also works for multi-user tabletop setups.

In order to identify the factors that are related to occlusions on tabletops, we conducted two experiments. The first study investigated the users' hand postures on the tabletop. In the second setup, we explored the problem of occlusion of a menu by the hand.

Posture Experiment

For this study, we invited 18 participants, twelve male and six female between 18 and 45 years. Three of the 18 subjects were left handed. All participants were frequent computer users and had experience with Windows. All participants performed both tests.

The participants had to interact using digital pens by clicking at any position on an empty surface. Whenever participants clicked once, a circle appeared. By clicking again, the circle disappeared. We chose this task, because it reflects the simplest interaction with a pie menu, a simple click for activating the menu and click-again for choosing an item or for hiding the pie menu. Each participant had to perform this task 10 times on the tabletop. During

5. Interactive Meeting Room Redesign

the test, we observed their hand postures and the way they interact with the surface. We distinguished between three different hand postures: touching only with the pen (*pen*), touching with the wrist and the pen (*wrist+pen*) and contact with the elbow while clicking with the pen (*elbow+pen*).

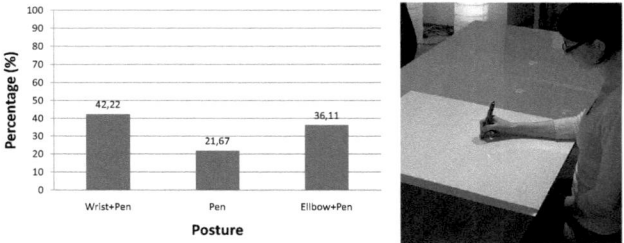

Figure 5.40: In the postures experiment, 21.67% of the users touched the surface only with the pen, the others stabilized with the wrist or elbow.

The results showed that 21.7% of the participants touched the table only with the pen, without resting with the wrist and/or elbow. 42.2% performed the click task while resting their wrist on the table (*wrist+pen*) and 36.1% put their elbow on the table for this test (*elbow+pen*). These results support the suggestion that users tend to rest their arm on the surface to stabilize during interaction.

Occlusion Experiment

In order to be able to design a menu that avoids occlusions, we observed differences of occlusions for left and right-handed users on horizontal surfaces. We printed a circle with a radius of 30 mm which was divided into 16 segments (named from A to P) onto a sheet of paper for our test (Figure 5.41). The radius of 30 mm was chosen according to our experience with digital tabletops. With a menu of this size, items are large enough to be recognizable but still reachable with the pen. We decided to use 16 subdivision segments of the circle because it allowed us to determine the occluded area with enough precision for our further design considerations. The circle was

5. Interactive Meeting Room Redesign

placed at a distance of 25 cm from the table edge and exactly in front of the user's chair.

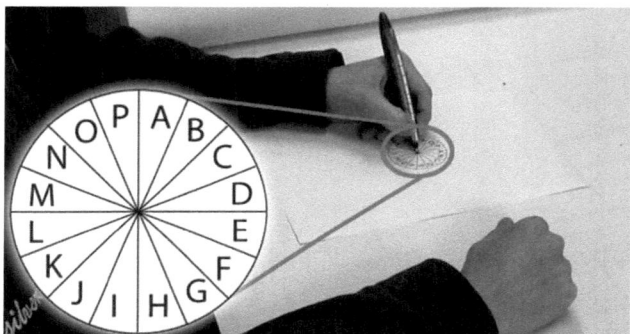

Figure 5.41: The occlusion of the hand was tested with a circle divided in 16 segments. Each participant reported the visible segments.

Each of the 18 participants had to touch the center of the circle with the tip of the pen. Then, while keeping the same posture, the participant had to tell which characters were completely visible and which characters were partly occluded but still recognizable. We also recorded the posture and the position where the user held the pen. Figure 5.42 shows the results of our observation. The mirror effect of occlusions for left and right-handed participants is clearly visible. The average number of visible segments was 11.70 (SD=0.99) out of 16 segments for right-handed users and 11.17 (SD=0.56) for left-handed users. This mirrored pattern for left and right-handed users was also noticed by Hancock et al. [57].

These results led us to the design of a menu with two specific features: First, we avoid placing items in occluded areas, thus improving the interaction with the menu. Second, we propose a method for adaptive menu placement on tabletops that addresses the problem of left and right handedness.

5. Interactive Meeting Room Redesign

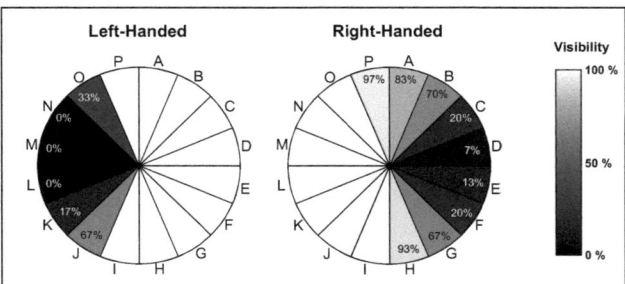

Figure 5.42: The visibility of each segment for left-handed and right-handed users shows a mirror effect.

Prototype

Based on our observations of occlusions we developed a menu for tabletops with direct pen input that is always visible to the user. The visibility of the menu is mainly influenced by the occlusion caused by the user's hand. Referring to a full 360° circle of possible item placements around an invocation point, we found that 92° of the circle are occluded on average.

Menu Design. According to this result, we designed a menu with items placed only in areas that are not occluded by the hand. Our design is inspired by the layout of circular menus [63]. The position of the menu is centered at the point of activation (cf. Figure 5.43).

Frequently used items are placed in the menu according to Hancock's results [57]. He reports that the movement along the "top-left to bottom-right axis is fastest for left-handed users" and the mirrored movement along the "top-right to bottom-left axis for right-handed users". Therefore we placed the undo buttons in those fast access positions in our design.

Adaptive Menu Placement. The proposed design as shown in Figure 5.43 would only work for right-handed users and it would require a distinct orientation of the hand to ensure full visibility of all items. There are generally two different ways to overcome these restrictions: The first method

5. Interactive Meeting Room Redesign

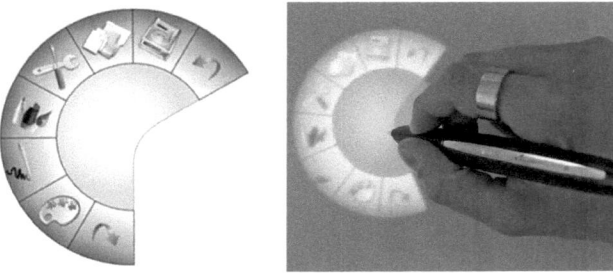

Figure 5.43: Design of a menu that avoids occlusions caused by the user's hand.

is to adapt the placement to the user's preferences which he/she defines in advance. This method is not suitable for direct tabletop interaction, because we have to deal with different user positions around the surface. The other option is an adaptive menu placement which automatically adjusts to the user's current position. There are different methods for an adaptive solution [84] [57] [59]. We use a combination of FTIR multi-touch tracking [56] and Anoto pen tracking to determine the user's hand position and the current pen position.

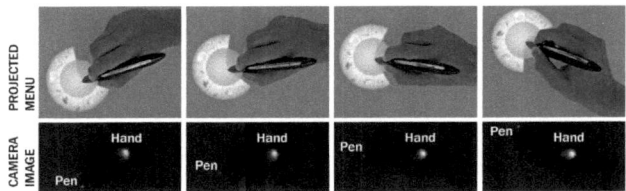

Figure 5.44: Adaptive menu placement through a combination of FTIR multi-touch and Anoto pen tracking. The direction vector from the hand to the pen is used to determine the correct orientation.

We observed that users tend to rest their hand on the surface when using direct pen input on tabletops due to fatigue effects. This behavior has also

5. Interactive Meeting Room Redesign

been noticed in previous research projects [57]. If we know the position where the users rest their hand and the position where they want to activate the menu, we can easily determine the correct placement for the menu.

In our current setup, we assume that the hand is in contact with the surface when the user activates the menu. To obtain the correct orientation of the menu, we simply use the direction vector from the hand to the pen tip. The menu is centered on the pen's position and rotated with the information of the direction vector. Figure 5.44 shows four different examples for a right-handed user. This procedure provides two advantages: First, we have an automatic adaption for left and right-handed users, as the menu rotates according to the direction vector from hand to pen. Second, the orientation is correct from any perspective on the tabletop and occlusions are avoided.

We demonstrate only one possible solution that shows how adaptive menu placement in combination with our occlusion avoiding menu design works. Other methods like shadow tracking would provide a more general solution that also works if the users do not rest their hand on the surface.

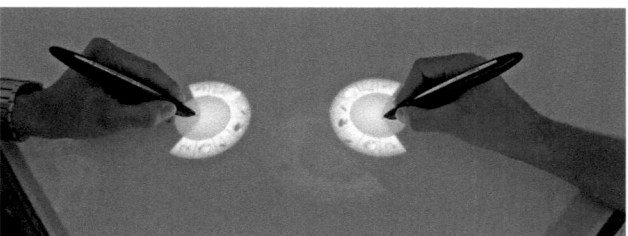

Figure 5.45: The system supports multiple menus adapting to each user's position and handedness.

Multi-User Scenario. Our system identifies the user through the ID that every Anoto pen delivers and assigns one menu to each of them. Hence we can support interaction of multiple users simultaneously. Due to the adaptive placement, the menu will be oriented towards the user independent of its position (cf. Figure 5.45).

5. Interactive Meeting Room Redesign

Point-and-Click Area vs. Gesture Area. We propose to use the occluded area as part of an interactive area for gesture input inside the menu (cf. Figure 5.46). Our observations showed that occlusions are not a problem in this case if the area can be recognized and the user knows where he can start a gesture and which gestures he can use. The outer region of the menu should be used for the items which can be accessed with a simple point-and-click.

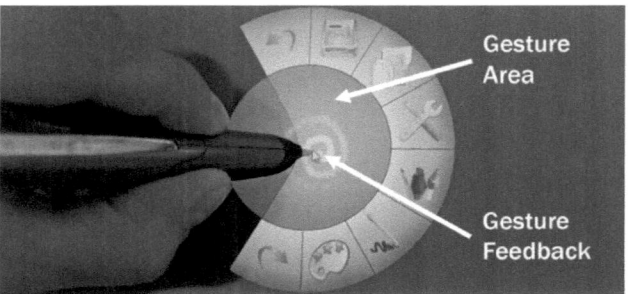

Figure 5.46: Users can perform gestures on the circular gesture area inside the menu.

5.5 Meeting Activities in the Interactive Room

For the redesigned meeting room, we consider the same meeting activities that should be supported as in the first version. A key activity during meetings is to share different kinds of data. This activity involves more than the exchange of artifacts between members of a group. It starts with the import of data into a session or sometimes its creation during the session. The existing data can be further modified or presented to the group. At the end of a meeting, produced data has to be stored or exported from the session. In order to support these typical activities that occur during meetings, we implemented different ways to handle data within ISIS. Since ISIS features

5. Interactive Meeting Room Redesign

a single large workspace layout in contrast to the personal workspaces of the first prototype, the data handling is based on different concepts that are adapted to this new design. For example, sharing of data in the first version was based on a workflow between two personal spaces via the public space. In the redesigned approach, this workflow is obsolete since the single shared space enables simultaneous access to the entire data for all users. In the following sections, further advancements for presentation and data handling support that were realized in the second version are described.

5.5.1 Presentations

For the redesigned application, we implemented two different possibilities for giving presentation. The first is similar to the previously used traditional presentation; the presenter's computer screen is replicated on the presentation wall. The second is especially aiming at PowerPoint presentations. Through a new import interface, PowerPoint presentations can be directly integrated in the current session.

However, there are generally two possibilities to treat the import of a presentation that consists of several slides. First, the presentation could be embedded inside the current page of the application. With additional control functions, it can be navigated without changing the current page of the session. Second, the slides of the presentation can be assigned to one page in the application each. This would require to navigate through the application pages in order to show the pages of the PowerPoint presentation. For the first kind of presentation import, PowerPoint presentations are embedded as slide-decks into the current page of a session. On top of the presentation, control elements including *previous slide*, *next slide* and *slideshow* can be used for navigating the presentation. A *full screen* option shows the maximized presentation. Figure 5.47 (*left*) shows an example of such an embedded PowerPoint presentation. However, with this way of including PowerPoint, we noticed that presentations are never performed in the small embedded view but always in the full screen mode. Moreover, the embedded view does not allow to show the slides in an overview and directly jump to a selected page.

5. Interactive Meeting Room Redesign

As a consequence, the navigation is sequentially restricted which influences the user experience.

This led us to the decision to directly integrate the slides in a maximized view into our ISIS application. The current ISIS application imports PowerPoint slides in a way that each slide is assigned to separate a page of the session. An example of this kind of integration is shown in Figure 5.47 (*right*) where a four page PowerPoint presentation has been imported to four separate ISIS pages. Considering the feedback we collected from our partners who tested the application, this approach seems to better support presentation practices than the embedded version. For example, fast navigation is supported through the page overview that allows to directly access a specific page of the whole presentation. In addition, the solution to use one page for each PowerPoint slide allows to directly export the whole session to PowerPoint again. One usage scenario would be to import a presentation, collaboratively work directly on the slides and export the modified presentation in PowerPoint format again.

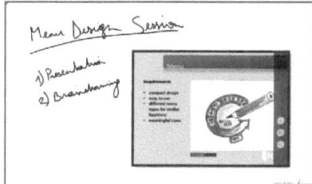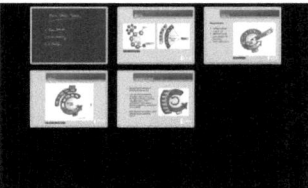

Figure 5.47: The first approach uses embedded PowerPoint presentations on page (*left*). For the second approach, each PowerPoint slide is assigned to a new page in ISIS, here shown in the page overview (*right*).

5.5.2 Data Import

The import functions include an interface that allows to load image material, PowerPoint presentations and sketched content containing vector strokes. Since the data that should be imported can be stored in different locations on the computer or on mobile storage devices like USB sticks, the standard Windows file dialog allows to search for the files. To enable the interaction with the window, the input of the invoking device is redirected to control the Windows cursor as soon as the focus on the ISIS application is lost. The events from the input device (the digital pen, for example) are interpreted as mouse events in that case. This allows to control any window that is started on top of the ISIS application through the traditional cursor. However, this approach restricts the multi-user functionality of the system to a single user for that kind of interaction since Windows can only interpret a single cursor input on a window. But after closing the file dialog, the ISIS application allows multi-user input again.

In addition to the support of importing image material and PowerPoint presentations in a session, we facilitate the integration of data from real paper documents. Motivated by the opportunities that paper could offer together with a digital environment, we investigated the potential of this combination. Section 5.3.2 gives a detailed description of our approach. For the data import to the ISIS session, two solutions are relevant. First, information can be imported through *Pick-And-Drop* (see Section 5.3.2). Selected images or whole areas of a paper document can be integrated into the digital session. Since the Anoto pen tracking is working on paper documents and on our digital surfaces as well, no device switching is necessary. However, the paper document must be printed on Anoto pattern and it must be registered within the system to enable the extraction of content. Both requirements are met through the customized production process.

Second, the *Sketch-And-Send* technique allows to contribute sketches to the ISIS session (see Section 5.3.2). To support the transfer of sketched information between the application and real paper, we implemented two different versions. The first method allows to send a group of strokes on demand. The strokes are transferred to the system in a single step and appear on the digital surface. In this mode, the user has the control over the moment when the sketches should be sent. The alternative way to send sketches to the system is via a real-time streaming paper. In this case, the strokes appear on the digital surface immediately. For example, this mode is useful for explanations

5. Interactive Meeting Room Redesign

that require to develop a sketch in front of the group step by step. The group can watch the digital representation of the sketches that the presenter draws on his paper.

Finally, data can be imported to a session through our screen capture interface[11]. This additional input enables users to easily integrate data from external applications into their meeting activities. In contrast to the snapshot application in the first interactive room, it facilitates capturing snapshots from their personal content and applications without the need for additional software on the connected device. This would, for example, allow a customer in a meeting to present and share information from his own computer within the interactive room by simply connecting to the VGA signal grabber. Snapshots are included in the session as images that can be further manipulated as described in the following section.

5.5.3 Data Manipulation

Once data has been imported into the ISIS session, different manipulation functions allow for collaborative editing. For example, this can involve such different activities like annotating presentation slides or using selection and transformation tools for structuring content. Since the large shared workspace superseded the need to share data between workspaces, it is more likely that data is partitioned and organized in user defined areas across the large workspace.

To support these activities, ISIS offers a set of tools that enable easy and intuitive manipulation of images and sketched content. With the selection tool, for example, single objects or groups of objects can be selected. A simple click on an object selects it, whereas a lasso selection is started on the empty page background and draws the path of the selection. Figure 5.49 shows this two different ways of selecting objects.

Selected objects can be manipulated through the handles that appear after a selection has been finished. We implemented two kinds of handles: one for rotating and scaling and another one for translating objects. Figure 5.48

---
[11]http://www.epiphan.com/products/frame-grabbers/vga2usb/

5. Interactive Meeting Room Redesign

  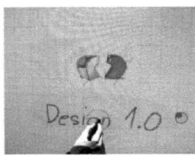

Figure 5.48: Different options for manipulating selections in ISIS. Selections can be rotated and scaled (*middle*) or translated (*right*).

(*middle*) depicts a scale operation performed on a selection. For the translation, two different techniques are integrated in ISIS: a simple translation and the rotate and translate approach. For the first method, the translate handle in the center of the selection is dragged which causes the selection to move. In this case, only a translation is applied to the selection. The second version allows to rotate and translate a selection in one step. The rotate and translate (RNT) technique has been introduced by Kruger et al. [83]. Their work shows that the combined rotation and translation of objects are more efficient than the separate mechanism on a tabletop. Moreover, they argue that the RNT technique provides a better support for collaborative tasks. They identified that rotation and orientation of objects on tabletops influences three major roles during collaboration: comprehension, coordination and communication [82]. With the RNT technique, these roles are better supported than with sequential rotate and translate actions.

As already mentioned, PowerPoint slides are imported in a way that each slide is placed on a separate ISIS page. The slides are set as a page background and the manipulation is performed on a layer on top of the slide. A typical action is to annotate on a slide or highlight parts during a presentation. However, the content of a slide cannot be modified within ISIS, but it is possible to export slides that are enhanced with annotations back to PowerPoint.

5. Interactive Meeting Room Redesign

Figure 5.49: Imported image with annotation in ISIS (*left*). A single click selects the image object and offers handles for manipulation (*middle*). The lasso can select groups of objects (*right*).

5.5.4 Data Export

A session in ISIS can be exported to PowerPoint or saved as a collection of *eXtensible Application Markup Language* (XAML) pages. For the PowerPoint export, each page is converted into a slide. The slides finally include all images and annotations that have been created in ISIS. With the interface to PowerPoint, we support one of the most common presentation tool. We tried to avoid exporting the ISIS slides as images to PowerPoint since this would prevent further modification of the content in PowerPoint itself. For our approach, we use Microsoft's primary interop assembly for PowerPoint. The primary interop assembly acts as a bridge between ISIS and the COM object model in PowerPoint. Images and annotations are exported in the appropriate format for PowerPoint. Therefore, exported annotations and images remain separated objects in PowerPoint that still can be selected and modified.

5.6 Implementation

With the redesign of the interactive room, we were aiming at building a flexible and extendable framework that allows for fast development, testing and modification of prototypes. The presentation layer of Windows Vista called *Windows Presentation Foundation* (WPF) offers a rich functionality that seemed well suited for our approach. For example, stroke rendering can be accomplished through Microsoft Ink support, object loader for images and videos are already integrated and the graphical user interface can be

5. Interactive Meeting Room Redesign

simply scripted. WPF uses vector based graphics, another important feature especially for the digital representation of notes. The interopability with other applications is handled through assemblies that provide an interface to access their features.

Combining graphical layout that is described in the XAML with additional code offers rich possibilities for fast GUI prototyping and redesigns. However, WPF was designed to be used for standard desktop applications that are based on the WIMP paradigm. In order to use WPF for a multiuser application, we developed a modified event handling that allows to map events from multiple input devices to WPF user interface elements. In the following two sections, we present this input device framework and a short description how applications can be build on the framework.

5.6.1 Input Device Framework

The function of the input framework is to provide a unified interface for connecting new input devices to the ISIS application. Basically, the architecture can be divided into two main parts: the device dependent and the application related processing. The input from the registered devices is interpreted by the device processing unit. This data is then passed to the application in form of events. Figure 5.50 shows the UML diagram of the input framework.

The central part of the architecture is the `DeviceManager` that connects the device dependent and the application specific part. The `DeviceManager` therefore hosts a list of input devices (`mPointDevices`) and the functions to add or remove devices from that list (`AddPointDeviceDriver`, `RemovePointDeviceDriver`). For each device a specific device driver has to be implemented that is derived from `PointDeviceDriver`. The device drivers are responsible to listen to events from the specific device and fire unified events that can be interpreted by the application. For that purpose, the `PointDeviceDriver` provides the function to fire `PointEvents`. The structure of the `PointEvents` is defined in the `PointEventArgs` and includes the following data:

- `DeviceUID` (unique id of the device)

5. Interactive Meeting Room Redesign

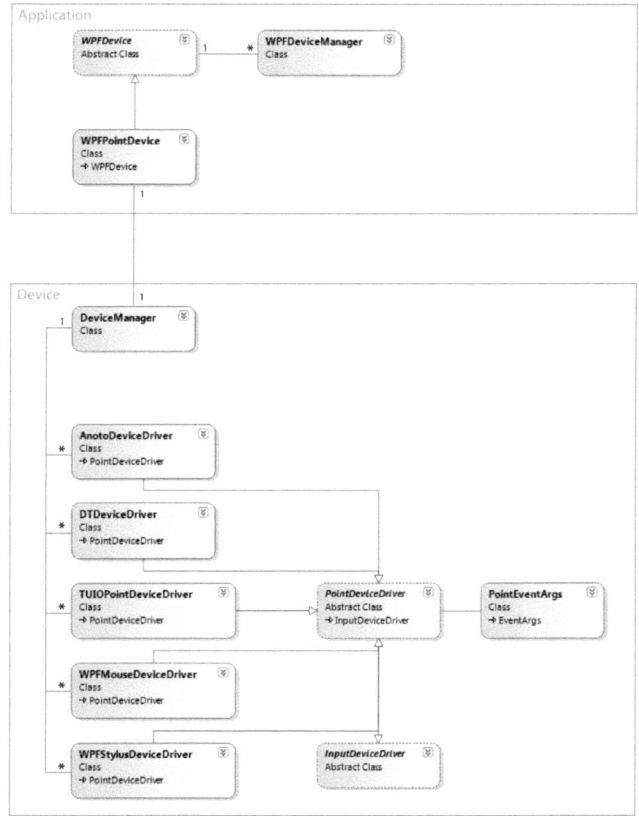

Figure 5.50: Input framework UML diagram.

- `DeviceType` (device type)
- `PointEventType` (up, down, move, ...)
- `PointScreen` (screen coordinates of point)

5. Interactive Meeting Room Redesign

- **Args** (additional device specific data)

At the time of this writing, drivers for the **DeviceTypes** Mouse, Stylus, Anoto Pen, DiamondTouch, WiiMote[12] and TUIO[13] were already developed. To integrate a new input device in the interactive room, the according **PointDeviceDriver** has to implemented.

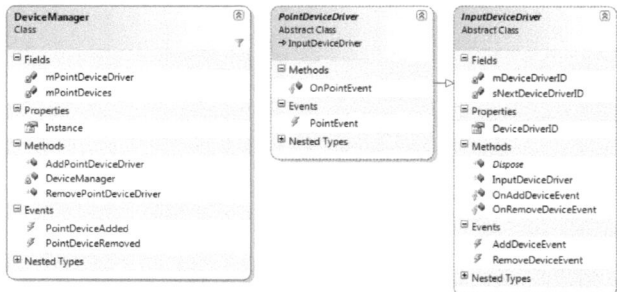

Figure 5.51: The **DeviceManager** provides the functions for handling the input devices that are implemented as drivers that are derived from **PointDeviceDriver**.

As an example for a **PointDeviceDriver**, the following code snippets show how the essential parts of the Anoto pen device driver were implemented.

1. Initialize the Anoto device and the Bluetooth streaming server and register the anotoServer_OnStroke event

    ```
    AnotoPen.Initialize();
    mAnotoStreamingServer = new AnotoStreamingServer();
    mAnotoStreamingServer.OnStroke += new
    AnotoStreamingServer.AnotoEventHandler(anotoServer_OnStroke);
    mAnotoStreamingServer.Start();
    ```

---
[12] http://www.nintendo.com/wii
[13] http://www.tuio.org/

5. Interactive Meeting Room Redesign

2. Handle events from the Anoto device in anotoServer_OnStroke() and create the according `PointEventArgs` that are used as paramter for the `OnPointEvent()` method

```
switch (args.Type)
{
  case AnotoPenEventType.StrokeStart:
    pointEventArgs.PointEventType = PointEventType.LeftDown;
  break;

  case AnotoPenEventType.StrokeDrag:
    pointEventArgs.PointEventType = PointEventType.Drag;
  break;

  case AnotoPenEventType.StrokeEnd:
    pointEventArgs.PointEventType = PointEventType.LeftUp;
  break;
}

OnPointEvent(pointEventArgs);
```

Devices that are already implemented in WPF have to be re-routed through our device handling in order to communicate with the ISIS application. Events from the mouse and the stylus are intercepted by the according device driver and assembled to `PointEvents`. For example, the implementation of the mouse driver handles the mouse down events and creates the according `PointEvents` as shown in the following example:

1. Register the WPF mouse events *PreviewMouseDown*, *PreviewMouseUp*

5. Interactive Meeting Room Redesign

and *PreviewMouseMove*

```
mWindow.PreviewMouseDown += new
MouseButtonEventHandler(window_PreviewMouseDown);

mWindow.PreviewMouseUp += new
MouseButtonEventHandler(window_PreviewMouseUp);

mWindow.PreviewMouseMove += new
MouseEventHandler(window_PreviewMouseMove);
```

2. Handle *PreviewMouseDown* events in window_PreviewMouseDown() and create the according `PointEventArgs` that are used as paramter for the `OnPointEvent()` method

```
switch (mouseButtonEventArgs.ChangedButton)
{
  case MouseButton.Left:
    pointEventArgs.PointEventType = PointEventType.LeftDown;
  break;

  case MouseButton.Middle:
    pointEventArgs.PointEventType = PointEventType.MiddleDown;
  break;

  case MouseButton.Right:
    pointEventArgs.PointEventType = PointEventType.RightDown;
  break;

  default:
    pointEventArgs.PointEventType = PointEventType.Unknown;
  break;
}

OnPointEvent(pointEventArgs);
```

5. Interactive Meeting Room Redesign

In the application's part of the input framework, the `WPFDeviceManager` is responsible for communicating events that are invoked by input devices to the ISIS application. Therefore, the class has an instance of the `DeviceManager` (`mDeviceManager`) and a list of `WPFPointDevices` (`mWPFPointDevices`). If a new device is registered at the `DeviceManager`, the list in the `WPFDeviceManager` is updated accordingly.

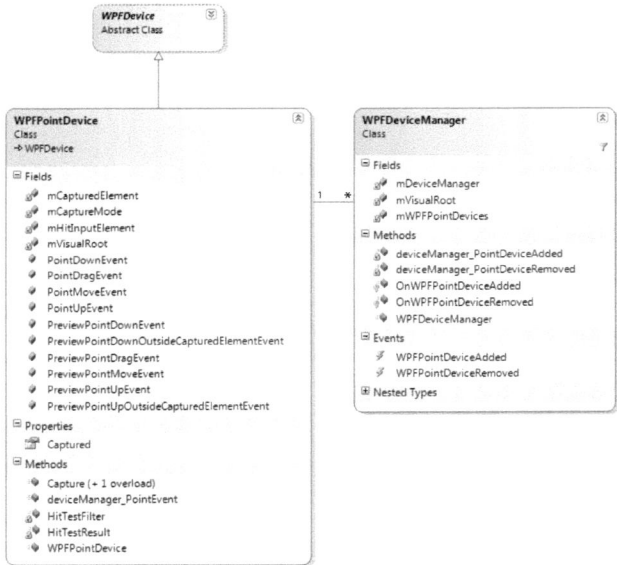

Figure 5.52: The `WPFDeviceManager` handles the events from connected devices on the application side. The devices are stored as `WPFPointDevices`.

The `WPFPointDevices` provide the `RoutedEvents` to access WPF control elements in the application. In order to understand the `RoutedEvents`, it is necessary to know that WPF user interfaces are constructed in a layered approach that is represented through the *Visual Tree*. The *Visual Tree* describes

5. Interactive Meeting Room Redesign

the hierarchy of visible layers in a user interface, where one visual element can have zero or more child elements. The `RoutedEvents` that have been introduced with WPF are events that can *tunnel* down the *Visual Tree* to the target element, or *bubble* up to the root element. Therefore, `RoutedEvents` often come in pairs, with one being the bubbling event and the other being the tunneling event. If the input event is a pair of tunneling and bubbling event, a single action from the input element, such as a mouse down, raises both routed events in sequence. First, the tunneling event traverses down the *Visual Tree*. Then the bubbling event is raised and traverses the *Visual Tree* in reverse direction. The naming convention for tunneling events uses the prefix "Preview" with the bubbling event name. For instance, *PreviewMouseLeftButtonDown* is the tunneling event for the *MouseLeftButtonDown* bubbling event.

The following example from MSDN's routed event documentation[14] clearly illustrates the event handling process. In this example, **leaf element #2** is the source of both a *PreviewMouseDown* and then a *MouseDown* event.

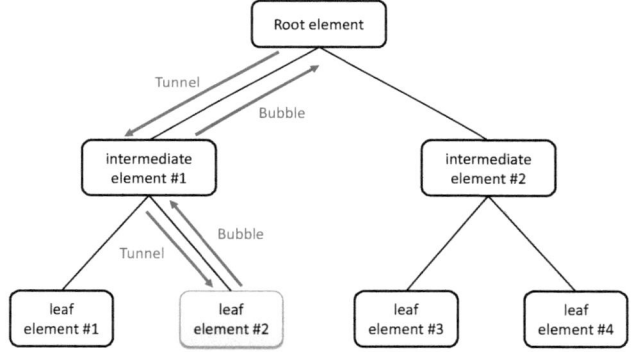

Figure 5.53: WPF routed events in the visual tree.

The order of event processing for this example is as follows:

---
[14] http://msdn.microsoft.com/en-us/library/ms742806.aspx

5. Interactive Meeting Room Redesign

   1. *PreviewMouseDown* (tunnel) on root element.
   2. *PreviewMouseDown* (tunnel) on intermediate element #1.
   3. *PreviewMouseDown* (tunnel) on source element #2.
   4. *MouseDown* (bubble) on source element #2.
   5. *MouseDown* (bubble) on intermediate element #1.
   6. *MouseDown* (bubble) on root element.

For the `WPFPointDevices`, we use this concept of routed event handling to convert our `PointEvents` to `RoutedEvents` that can be handled by WPF. Therefore, the following steps are necessary:

1. Find `mHitInputElement` through a hit-test

2. Process the `PointEventArgs` of the `mHitInputElement` and set tunneling / bubbling event types

   ```
   switch (pointEventArgs.PointEventType)
   {
     case PointEventType.LeftDown:
       tunnelingEventType = WPFPointDevice.PreviewPointDownEvent;
       bubbelingEventType = WPFPointDevice.PointDownEvent;
     break;
   }
   ```

3. Create the tunneling `RoutedEvent`

   ```
   RoutedPointEventArgs tunnelingEventArgs = new
   RoutedPointEventArgs(tunnelingEventType, pointEventArgs, this);
   ```

4. Raise the tunneling `RoutedEvent`

   ```
   mHitInputElement.RaiseEvent(tunnelingEventArgs);
   ```

5. Interactive Meeting Room Redesign

5. Check if tunneling event was handled, if not, create the according bubbling `RoutedEvent`

   ```
   if (!tunnelingEventArgs.Handled)
     RoutedPointEventArgs bubblingEventArgs = new
     RoutedPointEventArgs(bubbelingEventType, pointEventArgs, this);
   ```

6. Raise the bubbling `RoutedEvent`

   ```
   mHitInputElement.RaiseEvent(bubblingEventArgs);
   ```

Since it may be necessary to exclusively send events to a specific control, WPF provides the capture concept that allows to define a receiver element for events. Through the `Capture` method of the `WPFPointDevice`, a target control can be specified that will receive all events from the device. Control elements are registered for the capture property with the function

```
Capture(UIElement element, CaptureMode captureMode)
```

that requires the receiver element and an optional `CaptureMode`. The `CaptureMode` defines the scope of the event processing. Either the events are received by the specified element only or its whole Visual-Sub-Tree. If the capture function is used with an input device, control elements that are not registered will not receive events from that device.

However, it is often necessary to interrupt this mechanism for certain elements. For that purpose, the WPF preview events can be used. Preview events are received before the actual event and therefore allow to react independently of the actual event. To interrupt the capture event, the `PreviewPointDownOutsideCapturedElementEvent` and the `PreviewPointUpOutsideCapturedElementEvent` can be used to catch the events before the `PointDownEvent` and `PointUpEvent`. The not-registered element could then set the captured element to `null` or register itself as capture element.

5. Interactive Meeting Room Redesign

5.6.2 Application Development

As described in the previous section, the conversion of device depended events to unified events is handled by the input device framework. The interactive meeting room application uses this input framework as a layer between the low-level hardware device events and the higher-level interaction logic and visualization as shown in Figure 5.54.

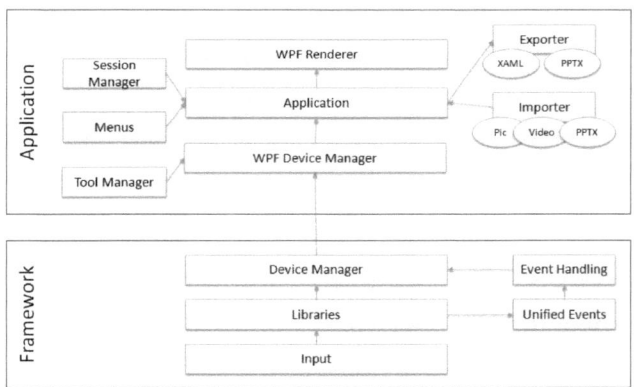

Figure 5.54: The ISIS system architecture for applications that are based on the input device framework.

On the application layer, the `WPFDeviceManager` receives the events from the input framework and forwards them to the tools. Tools in this context are the basic interaction elements that allow the users to work with the shared workspace environment. Tools are associated with the devices by a tool manager. According to the current tool, the events from the device layer are either handled by a user interface element or processed as a command for the application. The application that creates the shared workspace for the meeting room is controlled by a session manager that is responsible for defining the correct view on the scene. In the course of this thesis, main parts of the application layer (`SessionManager`, `Menus`, `ToolManager`, `WPF`

5. Interactive Meeting Room Redesign

`Renderer`) were developed as an example implementation that is based on the input device framework. The design of the input framework was defined in collaboration with the colleagues from the research team.

Discussion

In the previous two chapters, we described our development of a first interactive meeting room (Chapter 4) and the refinement of particular parts with its redesign (Chapter 5). Summarizing the results, this chapter reflects the actual implementation of the design parameters that were postulated in Chapter 3 in form of the two prototypes.

With the development from the first prototype setup to the second generation version, we integrated multi-user functionality for both the digital tabletop and the whiteboard. This enhancement aimed at the aspect of providing a sufficient surface size for group activities on the tabletop and the whiteboard. The dimension of the table (175cm × 90cm) offers enough space for groups of four to six people, although we recognized that six people are the maximum reasonable group size that can be accommodated. The digital whiteboard (120cm × 85cm) offers enough space for up to two persons simultaneously. However, in reality we observed that the whiteboard was always used by a single person only. Through the integration of multi-user functionality into both digital surfaces, we technically offered the possibility to use both surfaces collaboratively. For future developments, a larger sized digital whiteboard and the effect on the group activities would be an interesting modification.

The enhanced space that our digital tabletop and whiteboard offer accounts for the design parameter of visible and transparent actions. In contrast to traditional meeting situations where laptops often hinder visibility

6. Discussion

and transparency of actions in a group, the shared view on a large coincident input and display surface provides a new dimension of group awareness. In both implementations of the interactive room, actions performed by a person on the digital surface are visible and transparent for the rest of the group. Moreover, these actions are enriched with peripheral information. For example, it is clearly visible for the group if a participant is aiming at accessing a document on the tabletop, because the physical action of approaching the document on the surface already informs about the intended action.

Two further key design criteria for the collaborative room are to support heterogeneous tasks and to assist the creation of shared documents. The room should be adaptable according to the changing needs of the collaborative behavior during meetings and foster the joint creation of documents with a shared view for all participants. With both prototype setups, we showed different possibilities for developing a collaborative digital workspace that fulfills these requirements. In our first approach, we designed the tabletop with separated individual workspaces and explored the suitability for collaborative tasks. However, the workflows were not satisfyingly improved due to the influence of the interaction design we chose. That is why we changed the concept for the second generation prototype to simplify the integration and exchange of media and to better support the seamless control of the space. With only a single large shared space that allows to create, modify and share data, we expect optimized workflows for these activities. A formal comparison of both approaches has not been carried out at the time of this writing.

The presented concepts of separated workspaces versus a large shared workspace show two possibilities for the design of individual and shared spaces in the collaborative room context. Both overcome the limitations of traditional meeting spaces that are often physically separating a shared view for all participants from the personal interaction spaces. While the large digital tabletop provides sufficient space for supporting a shared view for all participants, it has to additionally account for different orientations. In both implementations we showed methods of dealing with orientation on horizontal surfaces. For the first prototype, we experimented with transformable

6. Discussion

private workspaces and shared documents in the public space. Although the concept behind the free modifiable content targeted the orientation issue, the interaction between private and public space was too cumbersome. Hence we modified the concept for the reimplementation and provide a more consistent interface for working with digital objects that are all equally transformable in size, position and rotation.

In the course of redesigning the interface from separated individual workspaces to a large shared workspace, we investigated novel menu designs for large digital surfaces (Section 5.4.2). This part of our development contributes to the area of user interface research for direct input on horizontal and vertical screens. We showed a menu design that is suitable for multiple users and that accounts for different orientations as well as occlusions on digital tabletops. Moreover, our approach fulfills the design requirement of arranging content within reach of the user, since the personal menu is always at hand.

For ensuring the consistency of input devices, we investigated new hardware solutions that allow the integration of the Anoto digital pen technology for different digital surfaces (see Section 4.2.3). While the first prototype was using a combination of Mimio and Anoto pens, we managed to enhance the setup for the second generation prototype that uses Anoto technology only. As a consequence, device switching is avoided and the same high input accuracy can be ensured throughout the whole room. Moreover, the integration of real paper is enabled through this consistent use of Anoto technology. In order to simplify the integration of additional input devices such as direct touch, we implemented an input framework that provides a unified interface for connecting new devices to the interactive room application.

Moreover, we demonstrated different possibilities of combining pen and touch interaction. We noticed from the evaluation of the first room prototype that users automatically tried to perform certain activities rather through touch than with a pen. Since our first version of the room only allowed to interact with digital pens, we conducted a study to explore the usability of a combined pen and touch solution as described in Section 5.3.1. We found clear evidence that combining pen and touch has the potential to excel each of the separate input technologies. Consequently, we presented three different

6. Discussion

solutions for combining pen and touch input on large interactive surfaces in Section 5.2.2.

In both prototypes, we demonstrated different possibilities to support multiple and interrelated documents digital within the room environment. The first version relied on a screen capture application that allowed to access arbitrary content in form of screenshots. For the reimplementation, we integrated a hardware solution for capturing external input sources through a VGA to USB converter. Through this solution, we advanced the first version that required the installation of additional software to a solution that works by simply connecting an external laptop to the capturing device. Moreover, we additionally examined variations of importing the PowerPoint presentation format into our application.

Since paper documents are still frequently used for preparing or during a meeting or presentation, we finally investigated possibilities to connect this traditional document source to the digital environment of our room. With the development from the first interactive room to the second generation, we noticed that a purely digital work environment does not sufficiently support real work practices in meetings. Many activities are related to paper documents and the translation to the digital is best accomplished by using these documents as an interface to the digital world. In Section 5.3.2, we detailed the underlying production process of interactive paper documents and applied this technology to demonstrate novel interaction techniques.

Conclusions

This dissertation has explored the design space of interactive meeting rooms. The motivation for this work is based on the shortcomings of current meeting rooms that result in a suboptimal support of typical workflows. One focus of this dissertation was to explore the design parameters that influence the development of a novel interactive room in order to address these deficits. This involved the discussion about the effect of the activities and different types of media that are used during meetings. Based on these design parameters, we showed how emerging technologies can be used for a practical implementation of an interactive meeting room. In particular, we presented a possible room setup and, as a second step, its redesign to better fit the requirements of real meetings. Our argumentation for the development from the first to the second room basically followed three lines. First, we developed hardware solutions that support the meeting room concept and showed advancements form the first to the second prototype. Second, we explored interaction techniques that illustrate how the components of the meeting room can facilitate typical workflows. Finally, we investigated the design of applications for this collaborative workspace. While our first approach focused on supporting common activities during meetings, the redesign concentrated on a unified input framework that was developed to simplify the combination of multiple input devices.

Since paper traditionally plays an important role in workspaces, we explored possibilities to bridge the gap between real paper and digital systems.

7. Conclusions

The solution we propose benefits from the natural affordances of paper while providing the advantages of digital documents. This results in a system that supports intuitive interaction through paper interfaces. The discussed solutions can also be used for the development of future paper-based systems.

In this dissertation, we furthermore presented our results of applying the Anoto pen tracking technologies for the development of large interactive surfaces. We discussed the enabling base technology that enables versatile possibilities to extend existing surfaces with interactivity. In order to show the potential of this approach, we demonstrated several prototypes that are using large Anoto surfaces. In addition, we explored possible combinations of this technology with direct touch interaction.

This chapter concludes the dissertation by summarizing the research contributions and a perspective of potential future work. First, the research hypothesis and the five research objectives set in Chapter 1 are revisited and the accomplishment of these goals is discussed. Second, possible extensions of this work are described as future research directions that could lead to follow-up projects based on the presented solutions.

7.1 Research Contributions

The hypothesis of this dissertation is that the appropriate design principles for multi-user multi-surface systems can help to enhance the workflows in meetings and enable the exploration of new communication paradigms. This hypothesis was investigated through the accomplishment of our five initial research objectives. In the following, we are going to revise these objectives and discuss how they have been reached.

7.1.1 Identifying design parameters for a collaborative interactive space

First, we observed current meeting practices in order to understand the activities, types of media and related tools that are used. The main focus of this exploratory field study investigated the collaborative interactions between

7. Conclusions

the participants of meetings and their handling of documents. Moreover, we explored the influence of the physical setup of the meeting room itself on the meeting process. In Chapter 3, we formulated the results of this exploratory field study as design parameters that should inform the development of an collaborative interactive meeting space. We identified parameters such as the management of shared documents or the importance of individual and shared spaces that are essential for the broader context of an interactive room. In addition, we noticed particular differences that effect the design of horizontal and vertical surfaces. Considerations about the size of the displays are for example directly related to the group size that can be accommodated and the reachability of content. The results of our investigation are drawing from the insights we could gain in real world meetings. This is an important contribution, since the derived design parameters reflect the needs of real meetings instead of experimental simulations. Thus, the discussion of the design parameters not only motivated the design decisions for our two prototype implementations but can be used as guidelines for similar projects.

7.1.2 Developing an interactive room prototype

Based on the design parameters that we identified in Chapter 3, we developed a prototype interactive room for collaboration as described in Chapter 4. The setup included a tabletop, a digital whiteboard and additional presentation displays. As main devices for interacting with the surfaces, we used digital pens from Anoto. A detailed description about the necessary steps to apply this technology to large surfaces can be found in Section 4.2. We scheduled meetings in our prototype room in order to evaluate its performance. Through the feedback that we gathered from these meetings, we advanced our understanding about the effects of the hardware and software solutions on the meeting activities. Consequently, we redesigned parts of the interactive room (the whiteboard and the application for collaborative work) and integrated new solutions to bridge the gap between analogue and digital media. The redesign aimed at better reflecting the design parameters that we discussed in Chapter 3. For the interaction with the interactive room,

7. Conclusions

we developed a novel user interface design that is tailored for the use on large digital surfaces. The proposed menu design addresses occlusion issues and the automatic adjustment to the user's handedness. Our implementation demonstrates the applicability of this design for digital tabletops and multi-user setups.

7.1.3 Evaluating in a real world environment

The research objective to evaluate the developed prototypes in real meetings was accomplished in two ways. Firstly, we improved our understanding of processes during meetings through the initial exploratory field study. As described in Chapter 3, we derived the design parameters for the interactive room from these observations. Although this step did not evaluate a prototype implementation, it was important to gather these insights from real meetings in order to identify the real requirements for the later implementation. Secondly, we evaluated the applicability of our first interactive room prototype through meetings that were arranged in this room. The results from this observation showed that the overall concept supported the meetings processes, but particular improvements were necessary. For example, the design of personal workspaces was generally well accepted, but led to distractions during data exchange and occupied too much screen estate. Moreover, we realized that physical objects such as paper notebooks or documents were soon removed since they occluded the workspaces. However, these artifacts are important resources that have to be at hand during a meeting. The details about these observations were discussed in Chapter 4.

7.1.4 Refining the first prototype and development of particular interaction solutions

With the development of the first interactive room prototype and the evaluation of the applied design parameters, we gained in experience about the benefits and shortcomings of our approach. Consequently, we built on this

7. Conclusions

first prototype and identified areas of improvement. In particular, we decided to further explore four areas that should significantly enhance our solution. These four advancements were developed into a second interactive room prototype as described in Chapter 5. The first improvement concerns the digital whiteboard which we modified from a Mimio based version to our first Anoto-based rear-projected surface. Through this modification, we achieved the coherent interaction with digital pens on all surfaces in the interactive room. Along with that development, we accomplished to build rear-projected Anoto surfaces, an enhancement of the technology from our first room prototype. The second achievement was the investigation of direct touch interaction in combination with pen input. We motivated the benefit of bimanual pen and touch interaction and presented design principles that were intended to guide developers of bimanual user interfaces. Our third enhancement concerned the digital workspace layout. We generalized the workspace to a single large shared space instead of multiple separate delimited workspaces. Simultaneously, we investigated a novel menu design for multi-user tabletop workspaces. Finally, we explored the possibilities to integrate real paper into the digital environment of the interactive room. We presented a new paper-based interaction device which allowed the seamless usage of the digital pens for manipulating real printouts and for interacting with the interactive meeting room.

7.1.5 Combining and developing emerging technologies

Finally, we demonstrated how different emerging technologies can be applied to build a collaborative interactive space for meetings. One of the main contributions that we presented is the applicability of the Anoto pen and paper technology for large interactive surfaces. Based on this development, we showed how front and rear-projected digital surfaces can be realized. In Chapter 4, we discussed the enabling base technology to provide the understanding about the requirements to apply it on different surface materials. We explored the combination of the Anoto technology with direct touch that

7. Conclusions

showed several variations to satisfy different needs for digital surfaces. As described in Chapter 4 and 5, we finally used these results to build the surfaces in our interactive room prototype. Firstly, we modified a traditional table to build a front-projected digital tabletop based on Anoto tracking technology. Secondly, we used the achievement of rear-projected Anoto surfaces for our digital whiteboard in combination with shadow hand tracking. To seamlessly manage the interaction with these surfaces and the transition to traditional paper documents, we finally used the Anoto technology for tangible palettes and showed how the connection between real documents and the digital system can be realized.

7.2 Future Work

The thesis raised a variety of issues for potential future research directions that are logical follow-ups to the presented work. These directions relate to the areas of hardware, application and evaluation methods of interactive room setups. We will investigate some of these issues by outlining future research activities.

7.2.1 Extended use of paper for overarching activities

In this work, we have demonstrated several possibilities how paper can be used in an interactive room context (see Section 5.3.2). For example, we used paper as an interface for transferring data to digital surfaces. From the discussion about the natural affordances of paper, we can draw some further conclusions about its usability for a broader range of meeting activities. Paper allows to simply, fast and easily create notes, a feature that is especially useful in on-the-way situations. The information that is kept as notes should be accessible for activities such as presenting, sharing or collaborative editing in a meeting. Thus, it would be a potential area of future research to investigate the capabilities of paper for managing information in and around meetings.

7. Conclusions

7.2.2 Remote connection of multiple meeting rooms

The setup that has been developed in the course of this thesis was based on a co-located working approach. However, meetings often involve remote collaboration via telephone or video conferences. Hence a remote connection between multiple interactive rooms would be an extension for future developments. The implementation of such a distributed system is a complex task since issues like additional feedback channels, altered social protocols and technical restrictions due to network latencies must be considered.

7.2.3 Alternative room setups

The proposed setup in Chapter 4 is only one possibility for creating an interactive meeting room. We argued for using a tabletop, a digital whiteboard and an additional presentation screen based on the requirements that we defined in Section 4.1. The realized setup is specific in a way that it fulfills the surveyed requirements from our company partner. On the other hand, the setup demonstrates a prototypical solution that can be applied for similar interactive meeting room projects, since the general design parameter described in Chapter 3 and the developed hardware solutions are generally applicable in this area. Nevertheless, it would be interesting to experiment with extensions of the environment through additional digital surfaces or modifications of the surfaces' dimensions and according investigations of the effects on the workflows in the room.

7.2.4 Pen and touch combinations

In Section 5.3.1, we presented a combination of pen and touch input that was specifically aiming at bimanual interaction with digital surfaces. The discussion revealed that this combination has a great potential for a variety of tasks. Hence, additional technical advancements in this area (bringing this technology from tabletop to whiteboards, for example) would help to enlarge potential application areas. At the time of this writing, there was already a trend towards commercial pen and touch solutions visible. However, most

7. Conclusions

of these developments are tailored for the tablet PC market and cannot be directly applied for large-scale interactive surfaces. Our future research interests therefore concentrate on a more flexible combination of pen and touch input that should enable developers of natural user interfaces to benefit from its powerful capabilities.

7.2.5 Evaluation methods

For the evaluation of the prototypes in this work, we used a combination of experimental and observational studies. The results from these studies not only influenced the solutions that are described in this thesis, but also guided our continuing research in this area. For example, main parts of the hardware and software implementations have been further developed. A follow-up interactive room has been designed and realized that uses the same interactive table (although with a different projection setup using only a single HD projector), a large-scale Anoto digital whiteboard, tangible menus and paper for note taking. As a few other research groups are exploring the design space of interactive meeting rooms, it would be worth comparing different setups. Along with that, appropriate evaluation methods must be found that allow to collect meaningful data from such comparisons. One outcome of these studies could be room setup recommendations for different meeting scenarios.

7.2.6 Meeting supporting applications

The applications that we presented were designed to support the collaborative activities in the interactive meeting room. From the feedback we got when we presented and tested our prototypes, there is high interest in further developing the applications towards more intelligent behavior. For example, this could include the implementation of guided meetings that facilitate more effective meeting procedures. Another possible extension would be to provide established creativity tools for brainstorming within the application. While these developments directly affect the work during a meeting, a careful investigation of overarching activities could improve the phases of preparation and protocol creation.

7. Conclusions

7.3 Closing Remarks

This dissertation explored the design and development of an interactive meeting room that addresses some of the shortcomings of traditional meeting rooms. We have shown how the combination of emerging technologies can support the activities and workflows during meetings. The advancement of traditional workspaces through digital surfaces as described in this thesis belongs to an active area of research, and standardized solutions are still not available. Thus, the presented considerations and findings are intended to help other developers designing and implementing natural user interfaces and large-scale interactive surfaces. There still remain many open questions in this context, but with the further development of hardware solutions that are increasingly transformed into products, a growing community has the chance to work on the answers through exploring appropriate concepts. This work represents a step towards practically supporting real world meeting activities and, more generally, towards understanding the design parameters for interactive meeting rooms.

7. Conclusions

Bibliography

[1] Marc Alexa, Björn Bollensdorff, Ingo Bressler, Stefan Elstner, Uwe Hahne, Nino Kettlitz, Norbert Lindow, Robert Lubkoll, Ronald Richter, Claudia Stripf, Sebastian Szczepanski, Karl Wessel, and Carsten Zander. Continuous reference images for ftir touch sensing. In *SIGGRAPH '08: ACM SIGGRAPH 2008 posters*, pages 1–1, New York, NY, USA, 2008. ACM.

[2] Dzmitry Aliakseyeu and Jean bernard Martens. Physical paper as the user interface for an architectural design tool. In *Proceedings of Interact 2001*, pages 680–681, 2001.

[3] Dzmitry Aliakseyeu, Jean bernard Martens, Sriram Subramanian, and Vroubel Wieger Wesselink. Visual interaction platform. In *Proceedings of Interact 2001*, pages 232–239, 2001.

[4] Toshifumi Arai, Dietmar Aust, and Scott E. Hudson. Paperlink: a technique for hyperlinking from real paper to electronic content. In *CHI '97: Proceedings of the SIGCHI conference on Human factors in computing systems*, pages 327–334, New York, NY, USA, 1997. ACM Press.

[5] Toshifumi Arai, Kimiyoshi Machii, and Soshiro Kuzunuki. Retrieving electronic documents with real-world objects on interactivedesk. In *UIST '95: Proceedings of the 8th annual ACM symposium on User interface and software technology*, pages 37–38, New York, NY, USA, 1995. ACM Press.

[6] Mark Ashdown. Personal projected displays. Technical Report UCAM-CL-TR-585, University of Cambridge, Computer Laboratory, March 2004.

[7] Mark Ashdown and Peter Robinson. Escritoire: a personal projected display. *Multimedia, IEEE*, 12(1):34–42, Jan.-March 2005.

Bibliography

[8] Ravin Balakrishnan and Ken Hinckley. Symmetric bimanual interaction. In *CHI '00: Proceedings of the SIGCHI conference on Human factors in computing systems*, pages 33–40, New York, NY, USA, 2000. ACM.

[9] Ravin Balakrishnan and Pranay Patel. The padmouse: facilitating selection and spatial positioning for the non-dominant hand. In *CHI '98: Proceedings of the SIGCHI conference on Human factors in computing systems*, pages 9–16, New York, NY, USA, 1998. ACM Press/Addison-Wesley Publishing Co.

[10] Hrvoje Benko, Andrew D. Wilson, and Patrick Baudisch. Precise selection techniques for multi-touch screens. In *CHI '06: Proceedings of the SIGCHI conference on Human Factors in computing systems*, pages 1263–1272, New York, NY, USA, 2006. ACM.

[11] Gerald Bieber, Emad Abd Al Rahman, and Bodo Urban. Screen coverage: A pen-interaction problem for pda's and touch screen computers. In *ICWMC '07: Proceedings of the Third International Conference on Wireless and Mobile Communications*, page 87, Washington, DC, USA, 2007. IEEE Computer Society.

[12] Jacob T. Biehl and Brian P. Bailey. Aris: an interface for application relocation in an interactive space. In *GI '04: Proceedings of Graphics Interface 2004*, pages 107–116, School of Computer Science, University of Waterloo, Waterloo, Ontario, Canada, 2004. Canadian Human-Computer Communications Society.

[13] Eric A. Bier and Steven Freeman. Mmm: a user interface architecture for shared editors on a single screen. In *UIST '91: Proceedings of the 4th annual ACM symposium on User interface software and technology*, pages 79–86, New York, NY, USA, 1991. ACM.

[14] Eric A. Bier, Maureen C. Stone, Ken Pier, William Buxton, and Tony D. DeRose. Toolglass and magic lenses: the see-through interface. In *SIGGRAPH '93: Proceedings of the 20th annual conference on*

Bibliography

Computer graphics and interactive techniques, pages 73–80, New York, NY, USA, 1993. ACM.

[15] Mark Billinghurst, Hirkazu Kato, and Ivan Poupyrev. The magicbook - moving seamlessly between reality and virtuality. *IEEE Comput. Graph. Appl.*, 21(3):6–8, 2001.

[16] Renaud Blanch, Yves Guiard, and Michel Beaudouin-Lafon. Semantic pointing: improving target acquisition with control-display ratio adaptation. In *CHI '04: Proceedings of the SIGCHI conference on Human factors in computing systems*, pages 519–526, New York, NY, USA, 2004. ACM Press.

[17] Sara A. Bly. A use of drawing surfaces in different collaborative settings. In *CSCW '88: Proceedings of the 1988 ACM conference on Computer-supported cooperative work*, pages 250–256, New York, NY, USA, 1988. ACM.

[18] Peter Brandl, Clifton Forlines, Daniel Wigdor, Michael Haller, and Chia Shen. Combining and measuring the benefits of bimanual pen and direct-touch interaction on horizontal interfaces. In *AVI '08: Proceedings of the working conference on Advanced Visual Interfaces*, pages 154–161, New York, NY, USA, 2008. ACM.

[19] Peter Brandl, Michael Haller, Juergen Oberngruber, and Christian Schafleitner. Bridging the gap between real printouts and digital whiteboard. In *AVI '08: Proceedings of the working conference on Advanced Visual Interfaces*, pages 31–38, New York, NY, USA, 2008. ACM.

[20] Peter Brandl, Jakob Leitner, Thomas Seifried, Michael Haller, Bernard Doray, and Paul To. Occlusion-aware menu design for digital tabletops. In *CHI EA '09: Proceedings of the 27th international conference extended abstracts on Human factors in computing systems*, pages 3223–3228, New York, NY, USA, 2009. ACM.

[21] Harry Brignull, Shahram Izadi, Geraldine Fitzpatrick, Yvonne Rogers, and Tom Rodden. The introduction of a shared interactive surface

Bibliography

into a communal space. In *CSCW '04: Proceedings of the 2004 ACM conference on Computer supported cooperative work*, pages 49–58, New York, NY, USA, 2004. ACM.

[22] Colin G. Butler and Robert St. Amant. Habilisdraw dt: a bimanual tool-based direct manipulation drawing environment. In *CHI '04: CHI '04 extended abstracts on Human factors in computing systems*, pages 1301–1304, New York, NY, USA, 2004. ACM.

[23] William Buxton and Brad Myers. A study in two-handed input. volume 17, pages 321–326, New York, NY, USA, 1986. ACM.

[24] Didier Casalta, Yves Guiard, and Michel Beaudouin Lafon. Evaluating two-handed input techniques: rectangle editing and navigation. In *CHI '99: CHI '99 extended abstracts on Human factors in computing systems*, pages 236–237, New York, NY, USA, 1999. ACM.

[25] Stéphane Chatty. Extending a graphical toolkit for two-handed interaction. In *UIST '94: Proceedings of the 7th annual ACM symposium on User interface software and technology*, pages 195–204, New York, NY, USA, 1994. ACM.

[26] Stephané Chatty. Issues and experience in designing two-handed interaction. In *CHI '94: Conference companion on Human factors in computing systems*, pages 253–254, New York, NY, USA, 1994. ACM.

[27] Xinlei Chen, Hideki Koike, Yasuto Nakanishi, Kenji Oka, and Yoichi Sato. Two-handed drawing on augmented desk system. In *International Conference on Advanced Visual Interfaces*, 2002.

[28] Elizabeth F. Churchill, Les Nelson, Laurent Denoue, Jonathan Helfman, and Paul Murphy. Sharing multimedia content with interactive public displays: a case study. In *DIS '04: Proceedings of the 5th conference on Designing interactive systems*, pages 7–16, New York, NY, USA, 2004. ACM.

Bibliography

[29] Damon J. Cook and Brian P. Bailey. Designers' use of paper and the implications for informal tools. In *OZCHI '05: Proceedings of the 19th conference of the computer-human interaction special interest group (CHISIG) of Australia on Computer-human interaction*, pages 1–10, Narrabundah, Australia, Australia, 2005. Computer-Human Interaction Special Interest Group (CHISIG) of Australia.

[30] Lawrence D. Cutler, Bernd Fröhlich, and Pat Hanrahan. Two-handed direct manipulation on the responsive workbench. In *SI3D '97: Proceedings of the 1997 symposium on Interactive 3D graphics*, pages 107–114, New York, NY, USA, 1997. ACM.

[31] Kelly L. Dempski and Brandon L. Harvey. Multi-user affordances for rooms with very large, interactive, high resolution screens. In *CHI 2005*, 2005.

[32] Kelly L. Dempski and Brandon L. Harvey. Touchable interactive walls: Opportunities and challenges. In *ICEC*, pages 192–202, 2005.

[33] Paul Dietz and Darren Leigh. Diamondtouch: a multi-user touch technology. In *UIST '01: Proceedings of the 14th annual ACM symposium on User interface software and technology*, pages 219–226, New York, NY, USA, 2001. ACM.

[34] Joan Morris DiMicco, Anna Pandolfo, and Walter Bender. Influencing group participation with a shared display. In *CSCW '04: Proceedings of the 2004 ACM conference on Computer supported cooperative work*, pages 614–623, New York, NY, USA, 2004. ACM.

[35] Klaus Dorfmüller and Hanno Wirth. Real-time hand and head tracking for virtual environments using infrared beacons. In *CAPTECH '98: Proceedings of the International Workshop on Modelling and Motion Capture Techniques for Virtual Environments*, pages 113–127, London, UK, 1998. Springer-Verlag.

[36] Klaus Dorfmüller-Ulhaas and Dieter Schmalstieg. Finger tracking for interaction in augmented environments, 2001.

Bibliography

[37] Marc Dymetman and Max Copperman. Intelligent paper. In *EP '98/RIDT '98: Proceedings of the 7th International Conference on Electronic Publishing, Held Jointly with the 4th International Conference on Raster Imaging and Digital Typography*, pages 392–406, London, UK, 1998. Springer-Verlag.

[38] Florian Echtler, Tobias Sielhorst, Manuel Huber, and Gudrun Klinker. A short guide to modulated light. In *TEI '09: Proceedings of the 3rd International Conference on Tangible and Embedded Interaction*, pages 393–396, New York, NY, USA, 2009. ACM.

[39] Mary Elwart-Keys, David Halonen, Marjorie Horton, Robert Kass, and Paul Scott. User interface requirements for face to face groupware. In *CHI '90: Proceedings of the SIGCHI conference on Human factors in computing systems*, pages 295–301, New York, NY, USA, 1990. ACM.

[40] Alan Esenther and Kathy Ryall. Fluid dtmouse: better mouse support for touch-based interactions. In *AVI '06: Proceedings of the working conference on Advanced visual interfaces*, pages 112–115, New York, NY, USA, 2006. ACM.

[41] Matthias Finke, Anthony Tang, Rock Leung, and Michael Blackstock. Lessons learned: game design for large public displays. In *DIMEA '08: Proceedings of the 3rd international conference on Digital Interactive Media in Entertainment and Arts*, pages 26–33, New York, NY, USA, 2008. ACM.

[42] Martin Fischer, Maureen Stone, Kathleen Liston, John Kunz, and Vibha Singhal. Multi-stakeholder collaboration: The cife iroom. In *Proceedings of CIB W78 conference 2002, Distributing Knowledge in Building.*, 2002.

[43] Mark J. Flider and Brian P. Bailey. An evaluation of techniques for controlling focus+context screens. In *GI '04: Proceedings of Graphics*

Bibliography

Interface 2004, pages 135–144, School of Computer Science, University of Waterloo, Waterloo, Ontario, Canada, 2004. Canadian Human-Computer Communications Society.

[44] Clifton Forlines and Ryan Lilien. Adapting a single-user, single-display molecular visualization application for use in a multi-user, multi-display environment. In *AVI '08: Proceedings of the working conference on Advanced visual interfaces*, pages 367–371, New York, NY, USA, 2008. ACM.

[45] Clifton Forlines and Chia Shen. Dtlens: multi-user tabletop spatial data exploration. In *UIST '05: Proceedings of the 18th annual ACM symposium on User interface software and technology*, pages 119–122, New York, NY, USA, 2005. ACM.

[46] Clifton Forlines, Chia Shen, Daniel Wigdor, and Ravin Balakrishnan. Exploring the effects of group size and display configuration on visual search. In *CSCW '06: Proceedings of the 2006 20th anniversary conference on Computer supported cooperative work*, pages 11–20, New York, NY, USA, 2006. ACM.

[47] Clifton Forlines, Daniel Wigdor, Chia Shen, and Ravin Balakrishnan. Direct-touch vs. mouse input for tabletop displays. In *CHI '07: Proceedings of the SIGCHI conference on Human factors in computing systems*, pages 647–656, New York, NY, USA, 2007. ACM.

[48] Malcom Gladwell. The social life of paper. March 2002.

[49] Saul Greenberg, Michael Boyle, and Jason Laberge. Pdas and shared public displays: Making personal information public, and public information personal. Technical report, Personal Technologies, 1999.

[50] Saul Greenberg and Michael Rounding. The notification collage: posting information to public and personal displays. In *CHI '01: Proceedings of the SIGCHI conference on Human factors in computing systems*, pages 514–521, New York, NY, USA, 2001. ACM.

Bibliography

[51] Yves Guiard. Asymmetric division of labor in human skilled bimanual action: The kinematic chain as a model. *Journal of Motor Behavior*, 19:486–517, 1987.

[52] Yves Guiard, Renaud Blanch, and Michel Beaudouin-Lafon. Object pointing: a complement to bitmap pointing in guis. In *GI '04: Proceedings of the 2004 conference on Graphics interface*, pages 9–16, School of Computer Science, University of Waterloo, Waterloo, Ontario, Canada, 2004. Canadian Human-Computer Communications Society.

[53] Francois Guimbretière. *Fluid interaction for high resolution wall-size displays*. PhD thesis, Stanford, CA, USA, 2002. Adviser-Terry Winograd.

[54] François Guimbretière. Paper augmented digital documents. In *UIST '03: Proceedings of the 16th annual ACM symposium on User interface software and technology*, pages 51–60, New York, NY, USA, 2003. ACM.

[55] François Guimbretière, Maureen Stone, and Terry Winograd. Fluid interaction with high-resolution wall-size displays. In *In Proceedings of UIST 2001*, pages 21–30. ACM Press, 2001.

[56] Jefferson Y. Han. Low-cost multi-touch sensing through frustrated total internal reflection. In *UIST '05: Proceedings of the 18th annual ACM symposium on User interface software and technology*, pages 115–118, New York, NY, USA, 2005. ACM.

[57] Mark S. Hancock and Kellogg S. Booth. Improving menu placement strategies for pen input. In *GI '04: Proceedings of Graphics Interface 2004*, pages 221–230, School of Computer Science, University of Waterloo, Waterloo, Ontario, Canada, 2004. Canadian Human-Computer Communications Society.

[58] Mark S. Hancock, Sheelagh Carpendale, Frederic D. Vernier, Daniel Wigdor, and Chia Shen. Rotation and translation mechanisms for tabletop interaction. In *TABLETOP '06: Proceedings of the First IEEE*

Bibliography

International Workshop on Horizontal Interactive Human-Computer Systems, pages 79–88, Washington, DC, USA, 2006. IEEE Computer Society.

[59] Beverly L. Harrison, Kenneth P. Fishkin, Anuj Gujar, Carlos Mochon, and Roy Want. Squeeze me, hold me, tilt me! an exploration of manipulative user interfaces. In *CHI '98: Proceedings of the SIGCHI conference on Human factors in computing systems*, pages 17–24, New York, NY, USA, 1998. ACM Press/Addison-Wesley Publishing Co.

[60] David L. Hecht. Printed embedded data graphical user interfaces. *Computer*, 34(3):47–55, 2001.

[61] Ken Hinckley, Patrick Baudisch, Gonzalo Ramos, and Francois Guimbretiere. Design and analysis of delimiters for selection-action pen gesture phrases in scriboli. In *CHI '05: Proceedings of the SIGCHI conference on Human factors in computing systems*, pages 451–460, New York, NY, USA, 2005. ACM.

[62] Ken Hinckley, Randy Pausch, Dennis Proffitt, James Patten, and Neal Kassell. Cooperative bimanual action. In *CHI '97: Proceedings of the SIGCHI conference on Human factors in computing systems*, pages 27–34, New York, NY, USA, 1997. ACM.

[63] Don Hopkins. The design and implementation of pie menus. *Dr. Dobb's J.*, 16(12):16–26, 1991.

[64] Shahram Izadi, Harry Brignull, Tom Rodden, Yvonne Rogers, and Mia Underwood. Dynamo: a public interactive surface supporting the cooperative sharing and exchange of media. In *UIST '03: Proceedings of the 16th annual ACM symposium on User interface software and technology*, pages 159–168, New York, NY, USA, 2003. ACM.

[65] Brad Johanson, Armando Fox, and Terry Winograd. The interactive workspaces project: Experiences with ubiquitous computing rooms. *IEEE Pervasive Computing*, 1(2):67–74, 2002.

Bibliography

[66] Brad Johanson, Greg Hutchins, Terry Winograd, and Maureen Stone. Pointright: experience with flexible input redirection in interactive workspaces. In *UIST '02: Proceedings of the 15th annual ACM symposium on User interface software and technology*, pages 227–234, New York, NY, USA, 2002. ACM.

[67] Brad Johanson, Shankar Ponnekanti, Caesar Sengupta, and Armando Fox. Multibrowsing: Moving web content across multiple displays. In *UbiComp '01: Proceedings of the 3rd international conference on Ubiquitous Computing*, pages 346–353, London, UK, 2001. Springer-Verlag.

[68] Walter Johnson, Herbert Jellinek, Jr. Leigh Klotz, Ramana Rao, and Stuart K. Card. Bridging the paper and electronic worlds: the paper user interface. In *CHI '93: Proceedings of the SIGCHI conference on Human factors in computing systems*, pages 507–512, New York, NY, USA, 1993. ACM Press.

[69] Sergi Jordà, Günter Geiger, Marcos Alonso, and Martin Kaltenbrunner. The reactable: exploring the synergy between live music performance and tabletop tangible interfaces. In *TEI '07: Proceedings of the 1st international conference on Tangible and embedded interaction*, pages 139–146, New York, NY, USA, 2007. ACM.

[70] Paul Kabbash and William Buxton. The "prince" technique: Fitts' law and selection using area cursors. In *CHI '95: Proceedings of the SIGCHI conference on Human factors in computing systems*, pages 273–279, New York, NY, USA, 1995. ACM Press/Addison-Wesley Publishing Co.

[71] Paul Kabbash, I. Scott MacKenzie, and William Buxton. Human performance using computer input devices in the preferred and nonpreferred hands. In *CHI '93: Proceedings of the INTERACT '93 and CHI '93 conference on Human factors in computing systems*, pages 474–481, New York, NY, USA, 1993. ACM.

Bibliography

[72] Martin Kaltenbrunner and Ross Bencina. reactivision: a computer-vision framework for table-based tangible interaction. In *TEI '07: Proceedings of the 1st international conference on Tangible and embedded interaction*, pages 69–74, New York, NY, USA, 2007. ACM.

[73] Martin Kaltenbrunner, Till Bovermann, Ross Bencina, and Enrico Costanza. Tuio: A protocol for table-top tangible user interfaces. In *Proc. of the The 6th International Workshop on Gesture in Human-Computer Interaction and Simulation*, 5/1/2006 2005.

[74] Thomas Kienzl, Ulf Marsche, Nadja Kapeller, and Adam Gokcezade. tangible workbench "tw": with changeable markers. In *SIGGRAPH '08: ACM SIGGRAPH 2008 new tech demos*, pages 1–1, New York, NY, USA, 2008. ACM.

[75] Hyosun Kim and Dieter W. Fellner. Interaction with hand gesture for a back-projection wall. In *Computer Graphics International*, pages 395–402, 2004.

[76] Tim Kindberg, John Barton, Jeff Morgan, Gene Becker, Debbie Caswell, Philippe Debaty, Gita Gopal, Marcos Frid, Venky Krishnan, Howard Morris, John Schettino, Bill Serra, and Mirjana Spasojevic. People, places, things: web presence for the real world. *Mob. Netw. Appl.*, 7(5):365–376, 2002.

[77] Scott R. Klemmer, Jamey Graham, Gregory J. Wolff, and James A. Landay. Books with voices: paper transcripts as a physical interface to oral histories. In *CHI '03: Proceedings of the SIGCHI conference on Human factors in computing systems*, pages 89–96, New York, NY, USA, 2003. ACM Press.

[78] Scott R. Klemmer, Mark W. Newman, Ryan Farrell, Mark Bilezikjian, and James A. Landay. The designers' outpost: a tangible interface for collaborative web site. In *UIST*, pages 1–10, 2001.

Bibliography

[79] Hideki Koike, Shinichiro Nagashima, Yasuto Nakanishi, and Yoichi Sato. *EnhancedTable: An Augmented Table System for Supporting Face-to-Face Meeting in Ubiquitous Environment*. 2005.

[80] Hideki Koike, Yoichi Sato, Yoshinori Kobayashi, Hiroaki Tobita, and Motoki Kobayashi. Interactive textbook and interactive venn diagram: natural and intuitive interfaces on augmented desk system. In *CHI '00: Proceedings of the SIGCHI conference on Human factors in computing systems*, pages 121–128, New York, NY, USA, 2000. ACM Press.

[81] Myron Krueger. *VIDEOPLACE and the Interface of the Future*. Addison-Wesley Professional, January 1990.

[82] Russell Kruger, Sheelagh Carpendale, Stacey D. Scott, and Saul Greenberg. How people use orientation on tables: comprehension, coordination and communication. In *GROUP '03: Proceedings of the 2003 international ACM SIGGROUP conference on Supporting group work*, pages 369–378, New York, NY, USA, 2003. ACM.

[83] Russell Kruger, Sheelagh Carpendale, Stacey D. Scott, and Anthony Tang. Fluid integration of rotation and translation. In *CHI '05: Proceedings of the SIGCHI conference on Human factors in computing systems*, pages 601–610, New York, NY, USA, 2005. ACM.

[84] Gordon Kurtenbach, George Fitzmaurice, Thomas Baudel, and Bill Buxton. The design of a gui paradigm based on tablets, two-hands, and transparency. In *CHI '97: Proceedings of the SIGCHI conference on Human factors in computing systems*, pages 35–42, New York, NY, USA, 1997. ACM.

[85] Celine Latulipe, Stephen Mann, Craig S. Kaplan, and Charlie L. A. Clarke. symspline: symmetric two-handed spline manipulation. In *CHI '06: Proceedings of the SIGCHI conference on Human Factors in computing systems*, pages 349–358, New York, NY, USA, 2006. ACM.

[86] Daniel Leithinger and Michael Haller. Improving menu interaction for cluttered tabletop setups with user-drawn path menus. *Horizontal*

Bibliography

Interactive Human-Computer Systems, 2007. TABLETOP '07. Second Annual IEEE International Workshop on, pages 121–128, Oct. 2007.

[87] Christian Leubner, Christian Brockmann, and Heinrich Müller. Computer-vision-based human-computer interaction with a back-projection wall using arm gestures. In *Proceedings of 27th Euromicro Conference, Warsaw, IEEE Press, 2001.*, 2001.

[88] Chunyuan Liao, François Guimbretière, and Ken Hinckley. Papiercraft: a command system for interactive paper. In *UIST '05: Proceedings of the 18th annual ACM symposium on User interface software and technology*, pages 241–244, New York, NY, USA, 2005. ACM.

[89] Peter Ljungstrand, Johan Redström, and Lars Erik Holmquist. Web-stickers: using physical tokens to access, manage and share bookmarks to the web. In *DARE '00: Proceedings of DARE 2000 on Designing augmented reality environments*, pages 23–31, New York, NY, USA, 2000. ACM Press.

[90] John MacCormick and Michael Isard. Partitioned sampling, articulated objects, and interface-quality hand tracking. In *ECCV '00: Proceedings of the 6th European Conference on Computer Vision-Part II*, pages 3–19, London, UK, 2000. Springer-Verlag.

[91] Wendy E. Mackay. Is paper safer? the role of paper flight strips in air traffic control. *ACM Trans. Comput.-Hum. Interact.*, 6(4):311–340, 1999.

[92] Wendy E. Mackay, Guillaume Pothier, Catherine Letondal, Kaare Boegh, and Hans Erik Sorensen. The missing link: augmenting biology laboratory notebooks. In *UIST '02: Proceedings of the 15th annual ACM symposium on User interface software and technology*, pages 41–50, New York, NY, USA, 2002. ACM Press.

[93] I. Scott MacKenzie and Yves Guiard. The two-handed desktop interface: are we there yet? In *CHI '01: CHI '01 extended abstracts on*

Bibliography

Human factors in computing systems, pages 351–352, New York, NY, USA, 2001. ACM.

[94] I. Scott MacKenzie and Shaidah Jusoh. An evaluation of two input devices for remote pointing. In *EHCI '01: Proceedings of the 8th IFIP International Conference on Engineering for Human-Computer Interaction*, pages 235–250, London, UK, 2001. Springer-Verlag.

[95] Munir Mandviwalla and Lorne Olfman. What do groups need? a proposed set of generic groupware requirements. *ACM Trans. Comput.-Hum. Interact.*, 1(3):245–268, 1994.

[96] Mitsunori Matsushita, Makoto Iida, Takeshi Ohguro, Yoshinari Shirai, Yasuaki Kakehi, and Takeshi Naemura. Lumisight table: a face-to-face collaboration support system that optimizes direction of projected information to each stakeholder. In *CSCW '04: Proceedings of the 2004 ACM conference on Computer supported cooperative work*, pages 274–283, New York, NY, USA, 2004. ACM.

[97] Nobuyuki Matsushita, Yuji Ayatsuka, and Jun Rekimoto. Dual touch: a two-handed interface for pen-based pdas. In *UIST '00: Proceedings of the 13th annual ACM symposium on User interface software and technology*, pages 211–212, New York, NY, USA, 2000. ACM.

[98] Nobuyuki Matsushita and Jun Rekimoto. Holowall: designing a finger, hand, body, and object sensitive wall. In *UIST '97: Proceedings of the 10th annual ACM symposium on User interface software and technology*, pages 209–210, New York, NY, USA, 1997. ACM Press.

[99] Michael McGuffin and Ravin Balakrishnan. Acquisition of expanding targets. In *CHI '02: Proceedings of the SIGCHI conference on Human factors in computing systems*, pages 57–64, New York, NY, USA, 2002. ACM Press.

[100] Zhenyao Mo, J. P. Lewis, and Ulrich Neumann. Smartcanvas: a gesture-driven intelligent drawing desk system. In *IUI '05: Proceedings of the*

Bibliography

10th international conference on Intelligent user interfaces, pages 239–243, New York, NY, USA, 2005. ACM Press.

[101] Meredith Ringel Morris. *Supporting effective interaction with tabletop groupware*. PhD thesis, Stanford, CA, USA, 2006. Adviser-Terry Winograd.

[102] Meredith Ringel Morris, Kathy Ryall, Chia Shen, Clifton Forlines, and Frederic Vernier. Beyond "social protocols": multi-user coordination policies for co-located groupware. In *CSCW '04: Proceedings of the 2004 ACM conference on Computer supported cooperative work*, pages 262–265, New York, NY, USA, 2004. ACM.

[103] Brad A. Myers, Rishi Bhatnagar, Jeffrey Nichols, Choon Hong Peck, Dave Kong, Robert Miller, and A. Chris Long. Interacting at a distance: measuring the performance of laser pointers and other devices. In *CHI '02: Proceedings of the SIGCHI conference on Human factors in computing systems*, pages 33–40, New York, NY, USA, 2002. ACM Press.

[104] Brad A. Myers, Kin Pou Lie, and Bo-Chieh Yang. Two-handed input using a pda and a mouse. In *CHI '00: Proceedings of the SIGCHI conference on Human factors in computing systems*, pages 41–48, New York, NY, USA, 2000. ACM.

[105] Brad A. Myers, Herb Stiel, and Robert Gargiulo. Collaboration using multiple pdas connected to a pc. In *CSCW '98: Proceedings of the 1998 ACM conference on Computer supported cooperative work*, pages 285–294, New York, NY, USA, 1998. ACM.

[106] Elizabeth D. Mynatt, Takeo Igarashi, W. Keith Edwards, and Anthony Lamarca. Flatland: New dimensions in office whiteboards. pages 346–353. ACM Press, 1999.

[107] Miguel A. Nacenta, Dzmitry Aliakseyeu, Sriram Subramanian, and Carl Gutwin. A comparison of techniques for multi-display reaching. In

Bibliography

CHI '05: Proceedings of the SIGCHI conference on Human factors in computing systems, pages 371–380, New York, NY, USA, 2005. ACM Press.

[108] Yasuto Nakanishi, Yoichi Sato, and Hideki Koike. Enhanceddesk and enhancedwall: Augmented desk and wall interfaces with real-time tracking of using's motion. In *Ubicomp2002 Workshop on Collaborations with Interactive Walls and Tables*, pages 27–30, 2002.

[109] Les Nelson, Satoshi Ichimura, and Elin Rønby Pedersen. Palette: a paper interface for giving presentations. In *CHI '99: Proceedings of the SIGCHI conference on Human factors in computing systems*, pages 354–361, New York, NY, USA, 1999. ACM Press.

[110] William Newman and Pierre Wellner. A desk supporting computer-based interaction with paper documents. In *CHI '92: Proceedings of the SIGCHI conference on Human factors in computing systems*, pages 587–592, New York, NY, USA, 1992. ACM.

[111] Moira C. Norrie. General framework for the rapid development of interactive paper applications. In *In Proceedings of CoPADD 2006, 1st International Workshop on Collaborating over Paper and Digital Documents*, pages 9–12, 2006.

[112] Ji-Young Oh and Wolfgang Stuerzlinger. Laser pointers as collaborative pointing devices, 2002.

[113] Russell Owen, Gordon Kurtenbach, George Fitzmaurice, Thomas Baudel, and Bill Buxton. When it gets more difficult, use both hands: exploring bimanual curve manipulation. In *GI '05: Proceedings of Graphics Interface 2005*, pages 17–24, School of Computer Science, University of Waterloo, Waterloo, Ontario, Canada, 2005. Canadian Human-Computer Communications Society.

[114] Gian Pangaro, Dan Maynes-aminzade, and Hiroshi Ishii. The actuated workbench: computer-controlled actuation in tabletop tangible

Bibliography

interfaces. In *Interfaces, Proceedings of Symposium on User Interface Software and Technology (UIST '02*, pages 181–190. Press, 2002.

[115] Joseph Paradiso, Che King Leo, Nisha Checka, and Kaijen Hsiao. Passive acoustic sensing for tracking knocks atop large interactive displays, 2002.

[116] James Patten, Hiroshi Ishii, Jim Hines, and Gian Pangaro. Sensetable: a wireless object tracking platform for tangible user interfaces. In *CHI '01: Proceedings of the SIGCHI conference on Human factors in computing systems*, pages 253–260, New York, NY, USA, 2001. ACM.

[117] Elin R. Pedersen, Kim McCall, Thomas P. Moran, and Frank G. Halasz. Tivoli: an electronic whiteboard for informal workgroup meetings. In *INTERCHI '93: Proceedings of the INTERCHI '93 conference on Human factors in computing systems*, pages 391–398, Amsterdam, The Netherlands, The Netherlands, 1993. IOS Press.

[118] Elin R. Pedersen, Tomas Sokoler, and Les Nelson. Paperbuttons: expanding a tangible user interface. In *DIS '00: Proceedings of the conference on Designing interactive systems*, pages 216–223, New York, NY, USA, 2000. ACM Press.

[119] Peter Peltonen, Esko Kurvinen, Antti Salovaara, Giulio Jacucci, Tommi Ilmonen, John Evans, Antti Oulasvirta, and Petri Saarikko. It's mine, don't touch!: interactions at a large multi-touch display in a city centre. In *CHI '08: Proceeding of the twenty-sixth annual SIGCHI conference on Human factors in computing systems*, pages 1285–1294, New York, NY, USA, 2008. ACM.

[120] Richard Watts Robert Harding Peter Robinson, Dan Sheppard and Steve Lay. A framework for interacting with paper. In *Proceedings of Eurographics '97*, pages 378–385, 1997.

[121] Richard Watts Robert Harding Peter Robinson, Dan Sheppard and Steve Lay. Paper interfaces to the world-wide web. In *Proceedings of*

Bibliography

WebNet '97, World Conference on the WWW, Internet and Intranet, 1997.

[122] Jeffrey S. Pierce, Matthew Conway, Maarten van Dantzich, and George Robertson. Toolspaces and glances: storing, accessing, and retrieving objects in 3d desktop applications. In *I3D '99: Proceedings of the 1999 symposium on Interactive 3D graphics*, pages 163–168, New York, NY, USA, 1999. ACM Press.

[123] Salil Pradhan, Cyril Brignone, Jun-Hong Cui, Alan McReynolds, and Mark T. Smith. Websigns: Hyperlinking physical locations to the web. *Computer*, 34(8):42–48, 2001.

[124] Walter Johnson Leigh Klotz Ramana Rao, Stuart K. Card and Randy Trigg. Protofoil: Storing and finding the information worker's paper documents in an electronic file cabinet. In *Proceedings of CHI '94, ACM Conference on Human Factors in Computing Systems*, pages 180–185, 1994.

[125] James M. Rehg and Takeo Kanade. Digiteyes: Vision-based human hand tracking. Technical report, Pittsburgh, PA, USA, 1993.

[126] Jun Rekimoto. Pick-and-drop: a direct manipulation technique for multiple computer environments. In *UIST '97: Proceedings of the 10th annual ACM symposium on User interface software and technology*, pages 31–39, New York, NY, USA, 1997. ACM Press.

[127] Jun Rekimoto. Smartskin: an infrastructure for freehand manipulation on interactive surfaces. In *CHI '02: Proceedings of the SIGCHI conference on Human factors in computing systems*, pages 113–120, New York, NY, USA, 2002. ACM.

[128] Jun Rekimoto and Masanori Saitoh. Augmented surfaces: a spatially continuous work space for hybrid computing environments. In *CHI '99: Proceedings of the SIGCHI conference on Human factors in computing systems*, pages 378–385, New York, NY, USA, 1999. ACM.

Bibliography

[129] Jun Rekimoto, Brygg Ullmer, and Haruo Oba. Datatiles: A modular platform for mixed physical and graphical interactions. In *CHI '01: Proceedings of the SIGCHI conference on Human factors in computing systems*, pages 269–276, New York, NY, USA, 2001. ACM Press.

[130] Miguel Ribo, Axel Pinz, and Anton Fuhrmann. A new optical tracking system for virtual and augmented reality applications. In *IEEE Instrumentation and Measurement Technology Conference, IMTC*, 2001.

[131] Meredith Ringel, Kathy Ryall, Chia Shen, Clifton Forlines, and Frederic Vernier. Release, relocate, reorient, resize: fluid techniques for document sharing on multi-user interactive tables. In *CHI '04: CHI '04 extended abstracts on Human factors in computing systems*, pages 1441–1444, New York, NY, USA, 2004. ACM.

[132] Yvonne Rogers, William Hazlewood, Eli Blevis, and Youn-Kyung Lim. Finger talk: collaborative decision-making using talk and fingertip interaction around a tabletop display. In *CHI '04: CHI '04 extended abstracts on Human factors in computing systems*, pages 1271–1274, New York, NY, USA, 2004. ACM.

[133] Yvonne Rogers, Youn-Kyung Lim, and William R. Hazlewood. Extending tabletops to support flexible collaborative interactions. In *TABLETOP '06: Proceedings of the First IEEE International Workshop on Horizontal Interactive Human-Computer Systems*, pages 71–78, Washington, DC, USA, 2006. IEEE Computer Society.

[134] Yvonne Rogers and Siân E. Lindley. Collaborating around vertical and horizontal large interactive displays: which way is best? volume 16, pages 1133–1152, 2004.

[135] Daniel M. Russell, Clemens Drews, and Alison Sue. Social aspects of using large public interactive displays for collaboration. In *UbiComp '02: Proceedings of the 4th international conference on Ubiquitous Computing*, pages 229–236, London, UK, 2002. Springer-Verlag.

Bibliography

[136] Daniel M. Russell, Jay P. Trimble, and Andreas Dieberger. The use patterns of large, interactive display surfaces: Case studies of media design and use for blueboard and merboard. In *HICSS*, 2004.

[137] Kathy Ryall, Clifton Forlines, Chia Shen, and Meredith Ringel Morris. Exploring the effects of group size and table size on interactions with tabletop shared-display groupware. In *CSCW '04: Proceedings of the 2004 ACM conference on Computer supported cooperative work*, pages 284–293, New York, NY, USA, 2004. ACM.

[138] Yoichi Sato, Yoshinori Kobayashi, and Hideki Koike. Fast tracking of hands and fingertips in infrared images for augmented desk interface. In *FG '00: Proceedings of the Fourth IEEE International Conference on Automatic Face and Gesture Recognition 2000*, page 462, Washington, DC, USA, 2000. IEEE Computer Society.

[139] Bill N. Schilit, Gene Golovchinsky, and Morgan N. Price. Beyond paper: supporting active reading with free form digital ink annotations. In *CHI '98: Proceedings of the SIGCHI conference on Human factors in computing systems*, pages 249–256, New York, NY, USA, 1998. ACM Press/Addison-Wesley Publishing Co.

[140] Stacey D. Scott. *Territoriality in collaborative tabletop workspaces*. PhD thesis, Calgary, Alta., Canada, Canada, 2005.

[141] Abigail J. Sellen and Richard H. R. Harper. *The Myth of the Paperless Office*. MIT Press, Cambridge, MA, USA, 2001.

[142] Chia Shen, Katherine Everitt, and Kathleen Ryall. Ubitable: Impromptu face-to-face collaboration on horizontal interactive surfaces. In *In Proc. UbiComp 2003*, pages 281–288, 2003.

[143] Chia Shen, Neal Lesh, Baback Moghaddam, Paul Beardsley, and Ryan Scott Bardsley. Personal digital historian: user interface design. In *CHI '01: CHI '01 extended abstracts on Human factors in computing systems*, pages 29–30, New York, NY, USA, 2001. ACM.

Bibliography

[144] Chia Shen, Neal B. Lesh, Frederic Vernier, Clifton Forlines, and Jeana Frost. Sharing and building digital group histories. In *CSCW '02: Proceedings of the 2002 ACM conference on Computer supported cooperative work*, pages 324–333, New York, NY, USA, 2002. ACM.

[145] Chia Shen, Frédéric D. Vernier, Clifton Forlines, and Meredith Ringel. Diamondspin: an extensible toolkit for around-the-table interaction. In *CHI '04: Proceedings of the SIGCHI conference on Human factors in computing systems*, pages 167–174, New York, NY, USA, 2004. ACM.

[146] Garth Shoemaker and Carl Gutwin. Supporting multi-point interaction in visual workspaces. In *CHI '07: Proceedings of the SIGCHI conference on Human factors in computing systems*, pages 999–1008, New York, NY, USA, 2007. ACM.

[147] Beat Signer. *Fundamental Concepts for Interactive Paper and Cross-Media Information Spaces,*. PhD thesis, SWISS FEDERAL INSTITUTE OF TECHNOLOGY, Zurich, 2006.

[148] Beat Signer and Moira C. Norrie. Paperpoint: a paper-based presentation and interactive paper prototyping tool. In *TEI '07: Proceedings of the 1st international conference on Tangible and embedded interaction*, pages 57–64, New York, NY, USA, 2007. ACM.

[149] Itiro Siio, Toshiyuki Masui, and Kentaro Fukuchi. Real-world interaction using the fieldmouse. In *UIST '99: Proceedings of the 12th annual ACM symposium on User interface software and technology*, pages 113–119, New York, NY, USA, 1999. ACM Press.

[150] Itiro Siio and Yoshiaki Mima. Iconstickers: Converting computer icons into real paper icons. In *Proceedings of HCI International (the 8th International Conference on Human-Computer Interaction) on Human-Computer Interaction: Ergonomics and User Interfaces-Volume I*, pages 271–275, Mahwah, NJ, USA, 1999. Lawrence Erlbaum Associates, Inc.

Bibliography

[151] SMARTTech. Digital vision touch technology. Technical report, http://www.smarttech.com/dvit/, 2003.

[152] Olov Ståhl, Anders Wallberg, Jonas Söderberg, Jan Humble, Lennart E. Fahlén, Adrian Bullock, and Jenny Lundberg. Information exploration using the pond. In *CVE '02: Proceedings of the 4th international conference on Collaborative virtual environments*, pages 72–79, New York, NY, USA, 2002. ACM.

[153] Mark Stefik, Daniel G. Bobrow, Gregg Foster, Stan Lanning, and Deborah Tatar. Wysiwis revised: early experiences with multiuser interfaces. volume 5, pages 147–167, New York, NY, USA, 1987. ACM.

[154] Jason Stewart, Benjamin B. Bederson, and Allison Druin. Single display groupware: a model for co-present collaboration. In *CHI '99: Proceedings of the SIGCHI conference on Human factors in computing systems*, pages 286–293, New York, NY, USA, 1999. ACM.

[155] Norbert A. Streitz, Jörg Geißler, Torsten Holmer, Christian Müller-Tomfelde, Wolfgang Reischl, Petra Rexroth, Peter Seitz, and Ralf Steinmetz. i-land: An interactive landscape for creativity and innovation. pages 120–127. ACM Press, 1999.

[156] Norbert A. Streitz, Thorsten Prante, Christian Müller-Tomfelde, Peter Tandler, and Carsten Magerkurth. Roomware: The second generation. In *CHI '02: CHI '02 extended abstracts on Human factors in computing systems*, pages 506–507, New York, NY, USA, 2002. ACM.

[157] Joshua Strickon and Joseph Paradiso. Tracking hands above large interactive surfaces with a low-cost scanning laser rangefinder. In *CHI '98: CHI 98 conference summary on Human factors in computing systems*, pages 231–232, New York, NY, USA, 1998. ACM Press.

[158] Sriram Subramanian, Dzimitry Aliakseyeu, and Andrés Lucero. Multilayer interaction for digital tables. In *UIST '06: Proceedings of the 19th annual ACM symposium on User interface software and technology*, pages 269–272, New York, NY, USA, 2006. ACM.

Bibliography

[159] Peter Tandler. Architecture of beach: The software infrastructure for roomware environments. In *ACM Conference on ComputerSupported Cooperative Work (CSCW 2000*, pages 2–6, 2000.

[160] Peter Tandler. The beach application model and software framework for synchronous collaboration in ubiquitous computing environments. *J. Syst. Softw.*, 69(3):267–296, 2004.

[161] Peter Tandler, Thorsten Prante, Christian Müller-Tomfelde, Norbert A. Streitz, and Ralf Steinmetz. Connectables: dynamic coupling of displays for the flexible creation of shared workspaces. In *UIST '01: Proceedings of the 14th annual ACM symposium on User interface software and technology*, pages 11–20, New York, NY, USA, 2001. ACM.

[162] J. C. Tang. Findings from observational studies of collaborative work. pages 11–28, 1991.

[163] L.J. Terpstra. A security model for the Workspace groupware architecture. Master's thesis, Royal Military College of Canada, Kingston, Ontario, May 2002.

[164] Irene Tollinger, Michael McCurdy, Alonso H. Vera, and Preston Tollinger. Collaborative knowledge management supporting mars mission scientists. In *CSCW '04: Proceedings of the 2004 ACM conference on Computer supported cooperative work*, pages 29–38, New York, NY, USA, 2004. ACM.

[165] Edward Tse and Saul Greenberg. Rapidly prototyping single display groupware through the sdgtoolkit. In *AUIC '04: Proceedings of the fifth conference on Australasian user interface*, pages 101–110, Darlinghurst, Australia, Australia, 2004. Australian Computer Society, Inc.

[166] Brygg Ullmer and Hiroshi Ishii. The metadesk: Models and prototypes for tangible user interfaces. pages 223–232. ACM Press, 1997.

[167] John Underkoffler and Hiroshi Ishii. Illuminating light: An optical design tool with a luminous-tangible interface. In *CHI '98: Proceedings of*

Bibliography

the SIGCHI conference on Human factors in computing systems, pages 542–549, New York, NY, USA, 1998. ACM Press/Addison-Wesley Publishing Co.

[168] Frederic Vernier, Neal Lesh, and Chia Shen. Visualization techniques for circular tabletop interfaces. pages 257–263, 2002.

[169] Christian von Hardenberg and François Bérard. Bare-hand human-computer interaction. In *PUI '01: Proceedings of the 2001 workshop on Perceptive user interfaces*, pages 1–8, New York, NY, USA, 2001. ACM Press.

[170] Marek Walczak, Michael McAllister, and Jakub Segen. Dialog table. In *DIS '04: Proceedings of the 5th conference on Designing interactive systems*, pages 311–311, New York, NY, USA, 2004. ACM.

[171] Mark Weiser. The computer for the 21st century. *SIGMOBILE Mob. Comput. Commun. Rev.*, 3(3):3–11, 1999.

[172] Pierre Wellner. The digitaldesk calculator: tangible manipulation on a desk top display. In *UIST '91: Proceedings of the 4th annual ACM symposium on User interface software and technology*, pages 27–33, New York, NY, USA, 1991. ACM Press.

[173] Pierre Wellner. Interacting with paper on the digitaldesk. *Commun. ACM*, 36(7):87–96, 1993.

[174] Wayne Westerman. *Hand Tracking, Finger Identification and Chordic Manipulation on a Multi-Touch Surface*. PhD thesis, University of Delaware, 1999.

[175] Daniel Wigdor and Ravin Balakrishnan. Empirical investigation into the effect of orientation on text readability in tabletop displays. In *ECSCW'05: Proceedings of the ninth conference on European Conference on Computer Supported Cooperative Work*, pages 205–224, New York, NY, USA, 2005. Springer-Verlag New York, Inc.

Bibliography

[176] Daniel Wigdor, Chia Shen, Clifton Forlines, and Ravin Balakrishnan. Table-centric interactive spaces for real-time collaboration. In *AVI '06: Proceedings of the working conference on Advanced visual interfaces*, pages 103–107, New York, NY, USA, 2006. ACM.

[177] Andrew D. Wilson. Touchlight: an imaging touch screen and display for gesture-based interaction. In *ICMI '04: Proceedings of the 6th international conference on Multimodal interfaces*, pages 69–76, New York, NY, USA, 2004. ACM Press.

[178] Andrew D. Wilson. Playanywhere: a compact interactive tabletop projection-vision system. In *UIST '05: Proceedings of the 18th annual ACM symposium on User interface software and technology*, pages 83–92, New York, NY, USA, 2005. ACM.

[179] Mike Wu and Ravin Balakrishnan. Multi-finger and whole hand gestural interaction techniques for multi-user tabletop displays. In *UIST '03: Proceedings of the 16th annual ACM symposium on User interface software and technology*, pages 193–202, New York, NY, USA, 2003. ACM.

[180] Mike Wu, Chia Shen, Kathy Ryall, Clifton Forlines, and Ravin Balakrishnan. Gesture registration, relaxation, and reuse for multipoint direct-touch surfaces. In *TABLETOP '06: Proceedings of the First IEEE International Workshop on Horizontal Interactive Human-Computer Systems*, pages 185–192, Washington, DC, USA, 2006. IEEE Computer Society.

[181] Ka-Ping Yee. Two-handed interaction on a tablet display. In *CHI '04: CHI '04 extended abstracts on Human factors in computing systems*, pages 1493–1496, New York, NY, USA, 2004. ACM.

[182] Ron Yeh, Chunyuan Liao, Scott Klemmer, François Guimbretière, Brian Lee, Boyko Kakaradov, Jeannie Stamberger, and Andreas Paepcke. Butterflynet: a mobile capture and access system for field biology research. In *CHI '06: Proceedings of the SIGCHI conference on*

Bibliography

Human Factors in computing systems, pages 571–580, New York, NY, USA, 2006. ACM.

I want morebooks!

Buy your books fast and straightforward online - at one of world's fastest growing online book stores! Environmentally sound due to Print-on-Demand technologies.

Buy your books online at
www.morebooks.shop

Kaufen Sie Ihre Bücher schnell und unkompliziert online – auf einer der am schnellsten wachsenden Buchhandelsplattformen weltweit! Dank Print-On-Demand umwelt- und ressourcenschonend produziert.

Bücher schneller online kaufen
www.morebooks.shop

KS OmniScriptum Publishing
Brivibas gatve 197
LV-1039 Riga, Latvia
Telefax: +371 686 204 55

info@omniscriptum.com
www.omniscriptum.com

Printed by Books on Demand GmbH, Norderstedt / Germany